HOMEGROWN

CRITICAL CULTURAL COMMUNICATION

GENERAL EDITORS: Jonathan Gray, Aswin Punathambekar, Nina Huntemann
FOUNDING EDITORS: Sarah Banet-Weiser and Kent A. Ono

Homegrown

*Identity and Difference in the
American War on Terror*

Piotr M. Szpunar

NEW YORK UNIVERSITY PRESS

New York

NEW YORK UNIVERSITY PRESS
New York
www.nyupress.org
© 2018 by New York University
All rights reserved

Library of Congress Cataloging-in-Publication Data
Names: Szpunar, Piotr M., author.
Title: Homegrown : identity and difference in the American war on terror /
Piotr M. Szpunar.
Description: New York : New York University, [2018] |
Series: Critical cultural communication |
Includes bibliographical references and index.
Identifiers: LCCN 2017044869| ISBN 9781479841905 (cl : alk. paper) |
ISBN 9781479870332 (pb : alk. paper)
Subjects: LCSH: Terrorism—United States—Prevention. | Terrorism—Social aspects—
United States.
Classification: LCC HV6432 .S97 2018 | DDC 363.325/170973—dc23
LC record available at https://lccn.loc.gov/2017044869

Manufactured in the United States of America
10 9 8 7 6 5 4 3 2 1
Also available as an ebook

For Hanna and Roman

CONTENTS

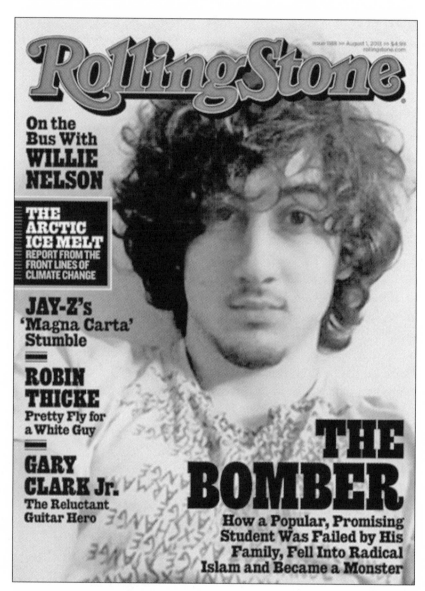

Figure 1. *Rolling Stone*, August 1, 2013.

Entrance

A Theory of the Double

Twarz wroga przeraża mnie wtedy, gdy widzę, jak bardzo jest podobna do mojej.
(The face of the enemy terrifies me when I see how very similar it is to mine.)
—Stanisław Jerzy Lec, *Myśli Nieuczesane*

THE BOMBER. The all-caps bolded declaration juxtaposed against the image of an attractive teenager is a dissonant composition, one that scribbles in a tense interval into the score of the war on terror. For some, the image and its placement, reminiscent of Jim Morrison's posthumous *Rolling Stone* cover (September 17, 1981), not only glamorized a terrorist, but worse still disrespected his victims. Three people were killed and about 260 injured on the final stretch of the 2013 Boston Marathon when Dzhokhar Tsarnaev and his older brother Tamerlan remotely detonated two homemade bombs. Tamerlan was killed during a shootout with police. The younger brother's fate was foreshadowed by the caption accompanying the 1981 Morrison cover to which the 2013 one was widely compared: "He's hot, he's sexy, and he's dead." Tsarnaev was tried, found guilty of all thirty counts with which he was charged, and sentenced to death in 2015.

For others the image marked a cadence, the shifting of the war on terror into a new modality, however unpleasing. This sentiment was most clearly expressed by the *Rolling Stone's* Matt Taibbi who ruminated about the nature of the "modern terrorist": "You can't see him coming. He's not walking down the street with a scary beard and a red X through his face. He looks just like any other kid." In Taibbi's juxtaposition of the Tsarnaev cover to a 2011 *Time* magazine cover that posthumously featured Osama bin Laden (with "a scary beard and a red X"), the image of the enemy-terrorist morphs from a clearly delineated other packed in neat Orientalist binaries into a figure that confuses the boundaries that demarcate us from other. This figure is the Double.

After 9/11 philosopher and cultural critic Slavoj Žižek asked, "Are we in a war? Do we have an enemy?" echoing the French philosopher Jacques Derrida's post–Cold War reflections in which he lamented the violence that the loss of an identifiable enemy might bring. This lost enemy is the spatial-political structuring enemy central to the thought of German jurist Carl Schmitt.[1] Yet, even as Žižek acknowledged the dispersion of the enemy into a shadowy network, he recognized the re-invigoration of the binary logic of the enemy image. Indeed, for the first decade of the twenty-first century, bin Laden (in name and image) acted as a synecdochic figure that stood in for a dispersed global enemy, pro-viding a template for countless popular and political representations of threat, one built atop age-old Orientalist fantasies. The enemy, imagined as other, unifies a collective. By embodying what a collective *is not*—and externalizing blame, aggression, and evil—the other provides a clearly bounded adversary (by race, culture, religion, ideology, etc., however porous the political borders) against which to identify and be identified, against which to mobilize and be mobilized.[2]

In 2010, Attorney General Eric Holder publicly announced that the threat facing the United States had changed. He warned Americans that they had reason to fear their neighbors, those "raised here, born here, and who for whatever reason, have decided that they are going to become radicalized and take up arms against the nation in which they were born."[3] Janet Napolitano, secretary of homeland security, reiterated Holder's assertion in a statement to the Senate Commit-tee on Homeland Security and Governmental Affairs. She testified that the threat of homegrown terrorism—Americans taking up arms against their own country—has no "typical profile."[4] Certainly, the claim that the enemy is "walking among us" is a commonplace war on terror assertion. But it is a claim based on the loosening of state boundaries—the enemy *walks* across borders and within our cities. In the context of the war on terror, analysis of what threat *looks* like, that is, how it is represented, has continued to center on what the Italian political philosopher Carlo Galli calls the "hyper-representation" of others (the racialized enemy images that Žižek sees as reinvigorated).[5]

But the Double figure that I develop in this book, and that Napolitano and Holder invoke, does not fit this mold. Rather, it is a threat explicitly communicated as one not clearly or categorically identifiable. It demarks a foe running loose within the country's borders who might look, talk, and/or act "like us," who might materialize in the people and places one would least expect, even a good-looking, pot-smoking, popular university student.

This book fills this gap and analyzes security discourses that do not depend exclusively on hyper-representations of threat. Instead, it focuses on discourses that also rely on the regular invocation of markers of likeness and similarity. The articulations of likeness in security discourse are not to be taken as self-evident claims. Rather, much like those of difference they are "non-factual" constructs. In other words, I examine the exploitation of the murkiness against which hyper-representations are said to be deployed by the state. Here, the bin Laden image is overlaid (and as I will show neither erased nor discarded) by multiple, shifting others; Tsarnaev's is only one iteration in an ever-expanding series. Contra the other, the Double is a figure that, in failing to externalize the negative of a collective's own self-image, functions to disrupt the collective, marking the group as fractured. It takes the ambivalent and productive splitting of cultural theorist Homi Bhabha's stereotype (simultaneously dangerous/active and obedient/passive) and redirects it onto one's own community.[6] More broadly, I show throughout this book that the Double is a modality of communicating threat that reflects the cultural-political plane on which contemporary security discourses operate. Here, the spectrality of the structuring enemy migrates onto the plane of representation. In this process members of a collective are marked as potentially dangerous, both suspect and susceptible.

Indeed, the breadth of events and actors described as terrorist has expanded in recent years, accompanied by the proliferation of debates concerning who is "the real terrorist" (though the seed of either growth is not to be found in the rubble of the Twin Towers). Referring to groups who participate in arson and other acts of sabotage, the Federal Bureau of Investigation announced in 2008 that "ecoterrorism" was the country's number-one domestic terror threat. In both 2009 and 2015, the Department of Homeland Security stated that the nation's most dangerous terrorists sprang from the political right—racist white supremacists and the Sovereign Citizen movement, respectively. The violence of the former most recently materialized when nine African American churchgoers were massacred in Charleston, South Carolina. The latter consists of loosely affiliated individuals who reject the authority of the federal government, several of whom have targeted and killed police officers. The violence against persons and property in these contexts is carried out by white men. However, in their warnings to the American public, Holder and Napolitano were concerned with neither the activist left nor the racist right. Rather, in both instances they were referring to jihadists.

There have certainly been incidents of jihadist violence in addition to the Boston Marathon bombing that have perplexed commonplace war on terror stereotypes. In 2011, Daniel Patrick Boyd, a former high school football star and small business owner from North Carolina, plead guilty to conspiracy to provide material support to terrorists. As did a New Jersey woman, Colleen LaRose (aka Jihad Jane), that same year in an unrelated case. In 2015, a Protestant-raised Oregon man turned al-Qaeda operative named Adam Gadahn was killed in a drone strike. A federal grand jury indicted him for treason nine years earlier. All three homegrown jihadists are Caucasian. More recently, sympathizers and recruits of the self-proclaimed "Islamic State" (ISIS) have left pundits similarly perplexed (such as the case of a nineteen-year-old white woman, Shannon Maureen Conley, from Colorado who was arrested by federal agents as she was about to board an Istanbul-bound flight, her first and last stop before heading to Syria). But, as this book will show, invocations of likeness in the context of terrorist threat, like those found in the statements of Holder and Napolitano, are not limited to those who are white. In this effort, here I depart from the Tsarnaev case and return to it in the conclusion.

In this book, I am not interested in adjudicating whether or not, or how much, an individual (threat, enemy, or foe) is "like us." This is often the work of rabid nationalists, though hardly exclusive to them. Rather, I approach claims of likeness from a more oblique angle. The original valence of Polish poet Stanisław Lec's aphorism in the epigraph is ethical and unhinging.[7] It draws attention to how a collective can take on the monstrous qualities it projects onto its adversary in times of war. The moment he describes is not one of identification, nor is it simply a matter of role reversal. It is a fundamentally disruptive experience of asymmetrical refraction in which identification itself is put into doubt. Holder and Napolitano's statements, however, are best read as instrumentalizing Lec's aphorism, in what I call the discourse of the Double. What terrifies both Holder and Napolitano is not the simultaneous yet disjointed and disjointing realization of one's own brutality and one's adversary's humanity, but an enemy that blends into the crowd. Certainly, their conjuring of the Double is also disruptive, but is enacted through a governmental modality that services contemporary securitization. When Žižek illustrates that the work of identifying the enemy through markers of difference is never factual, but rather a laborious constructive process sometimes intricate sometimes crude, he risks naturalizing likeness, stating, "[the enemy] cannot be directly recognized because it looks like one of us." Here, without naturalizing the expressions of difference often used in producing images of the enemy, I seek to investigate the work of constructing likeness in the realm of security. This book focuses on the functionalities of making the claim that a terrorist is "like us" in a variety of respects, the historical and media backdrop against which this claim is and can be made, and the political repercussions of doing so.

America's anxieties concerning traitors and turncoats are hardly new. The Oath of Allegiance conscripts new Americans into the service of defending the nation "against all enemies, foreign and domestic." In the same vein, one need only think of the Cold War cries of "Reds under the bed." Thus, this book falls within a well-tread interdisciplinary nexus that grapples with the relationship between identity, media, and citizenship in times of conflict. However, within this tradition, homegrown terrorism in its specificity has received little attention. Terrorism as an idea has had several lives, but only recently has security discourse sprouted the concept of homegrown terrorism, generating a unique context within which the spectral or phantom enemy materializes in the communication of threat.[8] Moreover, while the Double resurfaces in various historical moments, albeit in period-specific articulations, it has not been deployed as a heuristic through which to make sense of identity in and for war. The academic tradition that has examined the ways in which an adversary is imagined as or made identifiable and knowable has largely rested on notions of the other. American

World War II propaganda exemplifies the use of stereotyped images—of the Japanese, for example—to mark threat, as do the many fictional portrayals both pre- and post-9/11 that the face of Osama bin Laden has come to represent. While the histories to which these examples are tied belie assertions that conflict is ever so neatly bounded, the question remains: how does the formulation of a threat as one that explicitly blurs the boundaries of representation in and for security, those thought so crucial for waging a successful campaign, affect the rhythms played on the drums of war?

This book breaks down this question into component parts in order to adequately address the issues of identity, media, belonging, and citizenship it raises. How is difference—racial, ethnic, classed, and religious—communicated within articulations of a threat that is said to be indistinguishable from the citizen (distinct from those in response to a lost enemy)? How is likeness injected into visual and textual representations of the homegrown threat? How do media practices (digital and analog) of terrorist groups, citizens, and counterterrorism efforts inform and structure invocations of the Double? What does the conjuring of the Double reveal about contemporary modalities of enmity and power? How are citizenship and belonging reimagined through the Double? What is the relationship of the Double to the other, to boundaries of inclusion and exclusion? What securitizing practices does the Double accompany and facilitate?

An adequate footing from which to address these questions requires a genealogy of homegrown terrorism, one that addresses the discourses, representations, conceptualizations, practices, and strategies of communicating threat found in both popular culture and official government matters. Too often the concept of terrorism is applied retroactively ignoring the conditions that facilitate its resonance and historical particularity. In contrast, here I situate homegrown terrorism in (and as arising out of) the past forty years or so of security discourse in the context of US politics. While history is surely replete with terror and doubles, the genealogy mapped in this introduction is intended to reveal the historical conditions and theoretical maneuvers that underwrite the concept of homegrown terrorism as it emerged during the Obama administration (a period accompanied by premature and politically motivated assertions of postraciality) and provide a base from which to theorize its accompanying figure, the Double.

The historical ground out of which homegrown terrorism and the Double arise is multilayered. Making sense of it involves retracing the transformation of terrorism from a vilifying term used in piecemeal fashion into a concept around which contemporary conflict is organized. Also required are surveys of the increased racialization of Arabs and Muslims coalescing in the brown-Arab-Muslim-other as well as the depoliticization of particular modes of violence; both are internal to the organization of actionable knowledge on and about terrorism. Together, these three intertwined histories illustrate how the Double takes its shape in the confounded boundaries of conflict, acquires its existentially threatening quality, and is formulated as a figure that inversely mirrors the citizen, respectively. In short, this genealogical triad forms the complex harmony over which the dissonant melody of the Double is played.

Terrorism: From Epithet to Refrain

International-Domestic-Homegrown

The word "terror" was introduced into European languages in the writings of the Benedictine monk Bersuire in the fourteenth century. It was not until another half millennium had passed that, in the wake of the French Revolution, "terrorism" entered popular parlance and, soon after, the *Oxford English Dictionary*: "a government policy intended to strike with terror those against whom it is adopted."[9] Over the following century, terrorism would be divorced from the state and become "associated with anti-state violence under the impact of the Russian terrorists of the 1880s and the anarchists of the 1890s."[10] Out of the transformation from state to non-state violence arose the central conundrum of terrorism: one man's terrorist is another's freedom fighter.

In the United States terrorism has long been a label used to vilify non-state actors. The pages of the *New York Times* provide a glimpse into this practice. The term first appeared in the newspaper in the 1850s, in column inches allocated to stories concerning anti-Abolitionist ("Pro-Slavery Ruffian") violence in Kansas, Iowa, and Tennessee. The actions of racist groups, such as the Ku Klux Klan, have also long been—though certainly not consistently—referred to as terrorism therein. October 19, 1859, marked the first time the term was used in a headline within the *New York Times* (in reference to vigilante violence in Louisiana).[11]

In the early 1970s there was a distinct change in how terrorism was invoked in US politics. From a solitary staccato invective, terrorism gradually became an increasingly sustained (and sustaining) reverbera-tion, namely, a refrain. Much like in its more conventional usage—a re-curring phrase that connects various melodic and harmonic elements and gives a piece of music its identity—a refrain (*ritournelle*) in the work of French philosophers Gilles Deleuze and Félix Guattari marks out a territory by aggregating and holding together various objects, bodies, utterances, movements, and actions. At times referred to in Foucauld-ian terms—as an episteme and/or dispositif—the terrorism refrain, as a constellation of symbols, statements, definitions, presuppositions, and practices through which to make sense of particular violent phenomena, marks what is and can be discussed and dealt with as terrorism.[12]

The turning point at which terrorism coalesced into a guiding lens through which to make sense of the world is contested. Sociologist Lisa Stampnitzky's study on how experts created terrorism marks the 1972 massacre at the Munich Olympics as a decisive event. For others, the Palestinian-Israeli conflict is central.[13] The political context in which discourses of terrorism took hold in the United States was undoubtedly complex: the American war in Vietnam spurned a crisis of legitimacy in US politics; wars of decolonization continued to illustrate how a state's monopoly on violence could be wrestled away; airplane hijackings surged in the 1960s and 1970s; anti-Communist hysteria continued to fuel mis-guided global operations; and political violence within US borders peaked in 1970. Perhaps, the defining act to come out of all of this was not one that involved any direct physical harm. Rather, it was an executive com-mand. In 1974, with the United States on the brink of defeat in Vietnam, President Richard Nixon abolished the Attorney General's List of Subver-sive Organizations, setting in motion a shift in security focus from subver-sion to terrorism (though these anxieties remained overlaid until the end of the Cold War and beyond). Nixon's move was prefigured earlier that year when the House Committee on Internal Security held hearings and published a staff study under the rubric of terrorism.[14]

Around the same time, an academic field began to take shape around the notion of terrorism, a key landmark of which was the 1977 establishment of *Terrorism: An International Journal*. The connection between government agencies and the academy in ushering in an era in which political violence was increasingly made sense of as terrorism cannot be understated. Researchers and agency representatives attended the same conferences and government perspectives were regularly published in academic journals; Stampnitzky vividly outlines the details and nuances of this process. The resulting alignment of interests is unsurprising: one Cold War–era study asserted that 90 percent of terrorist groups either were Marxist or had pro-Marxist sympathies.[15] Similarly predictable is that even in the proliferation of definitions and debates about terrorism that began to emerge at the time, much of the field of terrorism studies adopted an uncritical statist view that precluded or explained away the possibility of "state terrorism."[16] In effect, the delegitimizing valence of terrorism—which was never done away with in the transformation of terrorism from epithet to refrain—was maintained and institutionalized under the guise of objective inquiry in favor of the state. This relationship continues into the present through journals, think tanks, and sanctioned talking heads on network news.

Early on, the purview of terrorism was international in scope, concentrated on foreign policy with a particular emphasis on how left-wing and revolutionary groups affected the interests of the United States. In other words, terrorism was largely a foreign land. For example, an early classification of terrorist organizations mentioned only one US group.[17] More revealing in this respect is terrorism's initial migration into the US Legal Code. First introduced by the Foreign Intelligence Surveillance Act of 1978, the definition in the code currently cited by legislation was introduced by the 1987 Foreign Relations Authorization Act. These acts placed terrorism into Titles 50 (War and National Defense) and 22 (Foreign Relations and Intercourse), respectively; that is, they firmly situated terrorism in the realm of foreign policy.[18] A preoccupation with the foreign or international continued into the 1990s and beyond as domestic groups were mentioned only in passing in many academic studies. The work of one prominent commentator on terrorism, journalist Brigitte L. Nacos, is indicative. Her 1994 *Terrorism and the Media* made no mention of domestic groups. The second edition of the book changed the subtitle to include the Oklahoma City bombing. In a later work, *Mass-Mediated Terrorism*, she asserted that the incident brought about an increased awareness of domestic terrorism in the United States but did not devote any significant attention to domestic terrorism until her 2005 *Terrorism and Counterterrorism*.

Despite the preeminent focus placed on the world outside of the United States, over time domestic spaces incrementally garnered more attention, altering the territory enclosed by the terrorism refrain. While the Attorney General's List of Subversive Organizations has never been replaced by a list of domestic terror groups, the FBI was nonetheless designated as the lead agency on terrorism within the United States in 1982. The agency focused on a variety of groups, such as Puerto Rican separatists and racist right-wing groups under the umbrella of "Aryan Nation Affiliates."[19] It was not until 1992, however, that a distinction between international and domestic varieties of terrorism was entrenched in the US Legal Code. From the mid- to late 1980s and into the 1990s, academics followed suit and a variety of extremisms within America increasingly found their way into the pages of journals and books about terrorism. This included the racist, white supremacist right, abortion-clinic arsons and bombings—which, at the time, were increasing in frequency and exposure—and environmental terrorism or ecoterrorism. While the state and its violence was rarely the subject of inquiry, forms of racist violence endemic to US history were partially absorbed into discourses of terrorism, partially, it suffices to say, because the categorization of racist violence as terrorism remains more inconsistent than other forms.[20]

In 1995 two white supremacists brought down much of the Alfred P. Murrah Federal Building by detonating a forty-eight-hundred-pound truck bomb. The Oklahoma City bombing was certainly a catalyst in annexing domestic spaces into the territory of terrorism. More importantly, it was also in the unsettled dust of the attack that "homegrown terrorism" was first uttered in US political discourse (the reasons and repercussions of which will be discussed in conjunction with the racialization of Arabs and Muslims below). Homegrown terrorism became a permanent fixture in security discourse a decade later in the wake of the 2005 London bombings when it was discovered that the perpetrators had grown up in the United Kingdom. In the United States, the term became widespread around 2009. While homegrown and domestic are often used interchangeably, the Department of Homeland Security offers the following definition:

> A homegrown violent extremist (HVE) is a person of any citizenship who has lived and/or operated primarily in the United States or its territories who advocates, is engaged in, or is preparing to engage in ideologically-motivated terrorist activities (including providing support to terrorism) in furtherance of political or social objectives promoted by a foreign terrorist organization, but is acting independently of direction by a foreign terrorist organization. HVEs are distinct from traditional domestic terrorists who engage in unlawful acts of violence to intimidate civilian populations or attempt to influence domestic policy without direction from or influence from a foreign actor.[21]

Much like the increased focus on domestic terrorism before it, home-grown terrorism also reconfigures the territory of terrorism. It does so not by expanding the space encompassed therein, but by altering the organization of the terrorism refrain in a more fundamental way. At first encompassing largely foreign actors, then an increasing amount of domestic players, with homegrown, a global quality emerges. The once guiding spatial distinction (domestic/foreign) collapses in homegrown: domestic actors (Americans or, at least, American residents) are operating in line with foreign ideologies. The Double begins to take shape in this confounded boundary.

Homegrown terrorism distinctively captures what Carl Schmitt called "absolute hostility," a mode of enmity characterized by global ideologies and a lack of any spatial or temporal limits: adversaries are not confined or locatable in delineated spaces and operations of combat are not constrained to a particular battlefield.[22] But changes in the nature of conflict—a result of technological, tactical, and normative innovations—do not fully account for the emergence of the phenomenon of homegrown terrorism, particularly in how it is conceptualized, debated, and combated. Another key lineage integral to the problematic of homegrown terrorism is hinted at in the DHS definition above. It makes explicit something that the term "homegrown" itself implies: a *foreign* seed (of terror) takes root in American soil (in a manner beyond infiltration), the outgrowth of which can take multiple and shifting forms. Thus, as homegrown collapses the neat binary between foreign and domestic, it does so without fully negating either category—even if, as I will show, they do not exclusively manifest in forms of hyper-representation.

The Brown-Arab-Muslim-Other

The history of the contemporary terrorism refrain is simultaneously that of the foreign actor, the brown-Arab-Muslim-other. The oft-cited passage from French philosopher Alain Badiou's *Infinite Thought* illustrates the intimate link between this figure and terrorism:

> When a predicate is attributed to a *formal* substance (as is the case with any derivation of a substantive from a formal adjective) it has no other consistency than that of giving an ostensible content to that form. In "Islamic terrorism," the predicate "Islamic" has no other function except that of supplying an apparent content to the word "terrorism" which is itself devoid of all content (in this instance, political).[23]

Here, "Islamic" is not only a designation of religiosity, but also a racialized marker of difference. I use this triple-hyphenated term, "brown-Arab-Muslim-other," to indicate that these identity positions are often conflated and used interchangeably in discourses of threat.

Race or racialization in this context is a formation or process that goes beyond phenotype. Building on the work of Hannah Arendt, sociologist Sherene Razack explains that race thinking is a "structure of thought that divides up the world between the deserving and the undeserving according to descent."[24] In the war on terror this division is traced and cut along civilizational lines, naturalized by an emphasis on the incommensurable difference between cultures and informed by the binary structures of Orientalist thinking. Following the work of Palestinian American cultural critic Edward Said, the West/Orient dichotomy depicts the latter as a space of oppression, backwardness, irrationality, danger, and extremism, in contrast to Western freedom, forwardness, rationality, stability, and moderateness. Racial superiority, when not unabashedly explicit, is certainly inflected in such "culture talk" and is no less evident in liberal discourses that distinguish between "good" and "bad" Muslims. The result is often framed as regrettable, yet necessary (or even "respectable") racism.[25]

The history of terrorism by no means began—and perhaps may not end—with the brown-Arab-Muslim-other. Nevertheless, the development of terrorism *qua* refrain and the marking of Arabs, Muslims, and other brown bodies as undeserving share important landmarks. At a time when terrorism was coming to the fore in foreign policy circles, the brown-Arab-Muslim-other figured prominently in the representation and narrativization of key events: the 1967 Arab-Israeli War, the Oil Embargoes of 1967 and 1973, the Munich massacre of 1972, and the Iranian Revolution in 1979. Within the United States, this link fomented suspicion of Arab and Muslim American communities, transforming invisible minorities into a problem population.[26] For example, in 1972 President Nixon's Operation Boulder targeted individuals of "Arabic-speaking descent" for intrusive surveillance and possible detention or deportation under the guise of fears of sabotage. The initiative was largely driven by assumptions regarding the stance of particular communities on the Palestinian-Israeli conflict. A similar anxiety emerged a thousandfold in the wake of 9/11.[27] The intimate cross-stitching of the geographically ever-shifting Middle East and terrorism in US thought is plainly evident in the 1987 Foreign Relations Authorization Act, which introduced a definition of international terrorism into the US Legal Code. The authors of the act made a point of stating, "Middle Eastern terrorism accounted for 60 percent of international terrorism."[28]

Islam did not begin to be dogmatically associated with terrorism until the 1980s, a process that was equally serpentine. At a time when America witnessed anti-Semitic violence perpetrated by racist white supremacists, the killing of a prominent Arab American by the Jewish Defense League, and the first fatality of the Unabomber, an FBI report relegated the "Islamic threat" within the United States to a passing mention as "Other" lumped with Anti-Nuclear Activists and United Freedom Fighters.[29] Moreover, those warring under the banner of Islam in the 1980s, the Mujahideen in Afghanistan, where heavily supported by the United States. Hailed as freedom fighters by President Ronald Reagan, they were positioned as allies of the United States against a godless evil empire. At the same time, in 1984, Benjamin Netanyahu warned the Second International Conference on Terrorism that the threat of terrorism came not only from Communism but also from Islamic extremism.[30] These contradictory narratives are not unconnected. Financing not only weapons but promotional tours seeking volunteers for the Afghan warfront, the United States was an active agent in aiding the internationalization of religious rhetoric in and for war. Representing a policy of supporting groups who opposed Communism in the Middle East that stems back to the Eisenhower Doctrine of the 1950s, the "Islamic" terror Netanyahu warned of was birthed out of Communist hysteria.[31]

The end of the Cold War was accompanied by hawkish declarations of a "clash of civilizations."[32] The resulting shift in bipolar groupings transformed the brown-Arab-Muslim-other from a potential agent of sabotage into an inassimilable presence. The World Trade Center bombing in 1993 was further used to solidify a connection between a civilization/culture and a particular trademark of violence, an association so ingrained that the Oklahoma City bombing was initially reported as being "Middle Eastern" in style, with the suspects described as dark-haired, bearded, and of Mideastern origin.[33] In effect, the concept of homegrown in American popular and political discourse was birthed in a fear of the brown-Arab-Muslim-other. The confusion sparked by the revelation that the perpetrators were white is one replayed over and over again, though with different inflections, in cases of homegrown terrorism.

The inassimilable character of the brown-Arab-Muslim-other was only further entrenched by the advent of "New Terrorism" just before the end of the twentieth century. For Walter Laqueur, an American historian of terrorism, the New Terrorism is the result of a shift over time in the motivations of terrorists, from Marx to Muhammad to Armageddon.[34] These are, however, not exclusive categories. Rather, in security discourse the movement from one to the next signals an upping of the ante in the clash of civilizations—even if it is a tendency relegated to "bad" Muslims, as a clash within civilization. The antipathy and pathology of the "East" intensifies from a premodern condition and morphs into an antimodern fanaticism that is necessarily millenarian, ringing cries of annihilation. A hallmark of Schmitt's absolute hostility, annihilation signals a change in the nature of the enemy (into what he calls a foe). In conventional conflict between nation-states, one's adversary is evil because she is one's adversary (which manifests for a variety of political reasons) and is thus targeted for defeat. In the ideological battles of absolute hostility, one's adversary is an enemy in the first instance *because she is evil*. Such articulations are evident in contemporary government and terrorist communiqués alike. Thus, one's adversary must be annihilated rather than defeated, a logic found in the often uttered (though historically disingenuous) statement, "We don't negotiate with terrorists." Here, the Double acquires its existentially threatening quality.

The existential threat posed by such an adversary exponentially intensifies when it manifests not only within US borders, but within people and places marked as familiar. When clearly bounded notions are confounded, different ways of making sense of the fanaticism of terrorism arise. In the context of homegrown terrorism, radicalization has most evidently resonated in recent years. Therein, this figure is often positioned as an agent of infiltration. But in other instances it is also invoked in more complex ways that cannot be reduced to the hyper-representation of an other and merges with or is shaped by that which is marked as American or familiar (suggestive of Galli's "Global War").[35] In either case, the realities of increased contact and exchange fostered by digital, social, and global media are certainly a key aspect in this regard but do not fully account for the particularity of radicalization discourse in the US context. Enter the third lineage constitutive of a genealogy of homegrown terrorism, clues to which lie in the marking of threat as existential. To speak about threats as existential and necessitating annihilation (whether emanating from all or "bad" Muslims, or a distinct individual/group marked as such via simile) is to depoliticize violence. While undoubtedly deeply tied to the formulation of a civilizational other, the reduction of violence to irrationality and evil is equally tied to the increasing codification and routinization of terrorism in and through the US legal apparatus.

~~Political~~ *Violence*

The idea that the kernel of hostility lies in inherent cultural or civilizational traits uproots acts of violence from their historical-political contexts. As does the framing of particular modes of violence as wrought exclusively for vengeance, bloodlust, and fanaticism rather than in the service of resistance or decolonization. The confluence of these notions has ushered in practices marked by the emergency or suspension of law aimed at annihilation: Guantanamo Bay, drone strikes, Abu Ghraib, extrajudicial killing, capture or kill lists, and so on.[36] However, the depoliticization of violence is complex and multivalent. To fully account for how homegrown terrorism is conceptualized, addressed, and managed, other avenues need to be explored.

In sharp contrast to the exceptional bodies confined to the cells of Guantanamo Bay, there are actual terrorists walking the streets of America today. Not the shadowy figures security discourses warn of, but those who have been convicted of terrorism-related crimes, have served jail sentences, and have been ultimately released. This includes Daniel McGowan, a convicted ecoterrorist; Rothschild Augustine, part of a group called the Liberty City Seven, who was caught up a sting operation and sentenced to seven years in prison; and two men from the Virginia Jihad Network, Khwaja Mahmood Hasan and Yong Ki Kwon, whose initial sentences were reduced (and who are now released) after reaching plea agreements and cooperating with prosecutors. Even John Walker Lindh, an American captured fighting alongside the Taliban, has a projected release date of May 2019. These instances point to a need to go beyond narratives of exception to make sense of homegrown terrorism.[37] There has been much debate over whether terrorism ought to be addressed through a war paradigm or as a problem of law enforcement. Critics of the war on terror have placed much focus on the war paradigm and how it has seeped into and/ or usurped the law. However, the depoliticization of violence has as much to do with the criminalization of terrorism as it does with the militarization of law.

While much attention has been (rightfully) given to the US PATRIOT Act in this regard, the process began decades earlier and produced a variety of implications. For example, the much-discussed "material support" statutes were amended rather than introduced by the PATRIOT Act; they were drafted in the 1994 Violent Crime Control and Law Enforcement Act (section 120005). This occurred two years after the Federal Courts Administration Act inscribed a distinction between domestic and international terrorism into criminal law. What is significant here is that while the previous inscriptions of terrorism into the US Code (in 1978 and 1987) were connected to foreign policy, the 1992 distinction is placed in Title 18 (chapter 113 B, section 2331), Crimes and Criminal Procedure, a markedly different focus. During the 1990s there were various attempts to further criminalize political violence with a variety of repercussions, some exceptional, others not. For example, the US Antiterrorism and Effective Death Penalty Act of 1996 established a list of "foreign terrorist organizations" and the ability to deport suspected terrorists based on secret information. Others facilitated practices that could hardly be characterized as exceptional. In the wake of the Oklahoma City bombing, the "terrorism enhancement" of the Federal Sentencing Guidelines (section 3A1.4) was enacted, under which a judge may significantly increase the sentence of an individual if his crime is deemed to be terrorism (we see examples of this in Chapters 1 and 3).[38] This is not to suggest that practices that could be characterized as exceptional have been abandoned. While the proposed Enemy Expatriation Act of 2012, which sought to grant the government the ability to strip individuals of their citizenship if convicted of a terrorism-related crime, initially failed—thought to have no chance of surviving a challenge on constitutional grounds—it has reemerged in more recent proposed legislation that I address in Chapter 3.[39] Nevertheless, the point here is that the criminalization of political violence sets up a particular mode of depoliticization that opens the door to discourses of radicalization.

Historically, every time terrorism entered (or threatened to enter) mainstream political discourse its valence of illegitimacy has been articulated in different ways.[40] But the marking of terrorism as inhuman and barbaric always begins, pace Badiou, with the manner in which it is emptied, or made "devoid of content." This process is evident in the definition found in the US Legal Code: "premeditated, politically motivated violence perpetrated against noncombatant targets by subnational groups or clandestine agents, usually intended to influence an audience." While terrorism is often used interchangeably with or is defined as "political violence," the two are hardly synonymous. Terrorism transforms the single space that separates the two terms (political violence) into an intractable gap, a distance already signified in the US definition by the insertion of "motivated." Political, in the context of terrorism, is thus always meant to be understood as being struck through, as ~~political~~, that is, as fundamentally illegitimate. The obliteration of the political is completed through the stress placed on noncombatants, those who cannot be rightfully constituted as targets of aggression.[41] The absence of legitimacy leaves in its wake only barbarism, irrationality, and evil.

In a peculiar maneuver, defining terrorism in US law voids the very motive fundamental to distinguishing it from other types of criminal violence, marking the complexity of its operation. Take, for instance, the 2006 Animal Enterprise Terrorism Act, which replaced the 1992 Animal Enterprise Protection Act. The result of a decades-long effort on the part of business lobbies, it is an example of the successful introduction of terrorism into new spaces of activity. The striking through of the political in domestic law opens an aporia in the "incorporeal transformation" of a criminal, arsonist, or vandal into a terrorist.[42] It is the political that differentiates these figures. Yet, when making sense of these crimes the political cannot be given significant weight. The political must be simultaneously invoked and refuted: "These individuals *claim* to be motivated by the deprivation of the earth, but what is *really* driving them?" In other words, without a legitimate political lens through which to decipher the motivation to violence and with the stakes becoming increasingly global, a void emerges: how to make sense of incidents in which Americans carry out terroristic violence against America? In effect, the ~~political~~ returns criminal motive to the level of the personal, but not in the same way as it relates to petty crime. The move back to the personal in the context of homegrown terrorism is not marked by a motivation of material gain. What remains is pathological.

Useful here is French philosopher Michel Foucault's interrogation of how psychiatry came to bear on law in the nineteenth century by addressing crimes that appeared to be "without reason" and "against nature"—two phrases commonly used to describe terrorism. Crimes, in essence, not preceded by a history, disturbance, or sign.[43] The psychologizing of such crimes—like that of a woman who killed and decapitated her neighbor's daughter, tossing her severed head out a window—injected into the fabric of society, a "dangerous individual." This dangerous element is similar to the "enemy of mankind" that emerged alongside and facilitated the terror of the French Revolution. Today, homegrown terrorism is discussed in similar terms. To be clear, my argument is not that homegrown terrorism is a crime without reason, history, or sign. As I show in the following chapters, these are precisely the claims made in government discourses. Rather, the history I am outlining illustrates how it has become possible to speak about homegrown terrorism in this way. While certainly not the same as the merging of insanity and criminality in Foucault's argument, what I argue here is that without the political to explain or make sense of violence, and yet a need to distinguish particular actions from petty crime, violence becomes unintelligible, monstrous, and irrational and a space opens up in which the (pseudo-) psychology of radicalization comes to bear on terrorism.[44]

Large amounts of government capital and academic effort have been placed into outlining, detailing, and defining the process of radicalization. Faiza Patel, co-director of the Brennan Center's Liberty and National Security Program, outlines two approaches to radicalization. On one end of the spectrum, proponents of radicalization almost all agree that there is no singular profile of a homegrown terrorist based on categorical schema such as race, ethnicity, class, gender, or religious upbringing. On the other, as political writer Arun Kundnani also illustrates, theories of radicalization are built on the assumption that violence originates from theological ideas.[45] In fact, many theories, but not all, do focus solely on jihadist violence.[46] Certainly, radicalization and the practices it underwrites are not equally distributed—the Double does not usurp the other, a topic I will return to below. Here, I am interested in the conjunction of the two approaches, and suffice it to say, models of radicalization however unequally deployed do not operate on the logic of the other exclusively. This is not to say that those "less reductive" theories are any less problematic; only that their multiplicity and messiness ought to be addressed. The theories posit a process in which a plethora of cognitive, affective, and experiential factors move someone from an unremarkable state and into one of bloodthirsty violence. These factors are conceptualized as personal, social, economic, and political (or more appropriately ~~political~~), from one's views on the war on terror to one's feelings of social alienation, from one's familial relations to one's socioeconomic status. Reflected in the "If You See Something, Say Something" campaign, in which the terrorist is often depicted as white, injected into discourses of terrorism is an idea that the threat America faces is not easily confined to particular categorical molds. Rather, threat is communicated as a distributed potential, as a dangerous element that can be triggered or put into action by the most ordinary of experiences or constellation of factors—which ultimately helps to strike out any political motive as legitimate. Sounding calls for monitoring, this narrative comes to signify not only "the rare and monstrous figure of the monomaniac . . . [but also] the common everyday figure of the degenerate, of the pervert, of the constitutionally unbalanced, of the immature, etc."[47] In effect, the figures are merged and the face of the foe is shown to mirror that of the citizen; the Double might materialize in the most ordinary of shapes.

The lineages that make up homegrown terrorism's genealogy are complex lines that contain overlapping and cascading notes. The territorial shifts of the refrain (from international to domestic to homegrown); the changes in security concerns from the Communist to the jihadist and beyond; exceptional and administrative modes of depoliticizing violence—none of these divisions are absolute, and the emergence of one, much like the move from the other to the Double, does not depend on the disappearance of another. Together the lineages constitute a historical triad from which to understand the emergence of the Double in its current forms and inflections. For Sigmund Freud, the Double simultaneously embodies what is "familiar and agreeable and . . . that which is concealed and kept out of sight."[48] A figure that takes the most ordinary of shapes (the everyday citizen) together with the most existential of threats (the monstrous terrorist), the Double is a dissonant melody, always out of key and in constant motion. The genealogy of homegrown terrorism does not produce the shape of the Double in any deterministic sense. The Double is an amorphous and complex figure. This history simply provides a backdrop from which to begin to theorize and make sense of the ways in which the Double is constructed in contemporary security discourses.

The Double

A cultural-literary motif employed in oral and written traditions across cultures and civilizations, the Double dates back to a twelfth-century BCE ancient Egyptian story, "The Tale of the Two Brothers." In it doubling is evident not only between the two brothers, but also in the externalization of the younger's soul, which takes on many changing forms. Shadows, reflections, and twins—the earliest manifestations of doubling that fascinated humankind—souls, lookalikes (doppelgängers), clones, suspected imposters, complementary characters, and psychological personality splits, these are the many expressions of the Double. Oscillating in and out of fashion, late eighteenth- to early nineteenth-century European literature marks the height of the Double's popularity.[49] Despite claims of its facile nature and that film had reduced its complexity, the Double has retained its peculiar draw. Notable twentieth- and twenty-first-century writers who employed it include Kafka, Borges, Nabokov, Saramago, Roth, and Pamuk, to name a few.[50] In intellectual circles the Double has been applied to an equally dizzying array of themes: Saussure's theory of the sign, Christian theology, Hegel's dialectic, Lacanian psychoanalysis, Derrida's work on language and representation, posthumanism, literary history, and the relationship of philosophy and literature more generally.[51]

The Double's seemingly endless iterations and uses present the daunting but necessary task of defining how it will be used throughout this book and how it relates to homegrown terrorism. While the Double's multiplicity has led some to describe the concept as "embarrassingly vague," malleability and amorphousness are its essence, its constitutive anxiety found in its shifting and porous boundaries.[52] The blurring of clear boundaries is precisely the core anxiety concerning incidents of Americans taking up arms against their own country and a productive force in strategies of security. Thus, the definition offered here does not reduce the multiplicity of the Double, but retains its core ambiguity. Also, since the nineteenth century—though some trace this back to Descartes's division of *cogito* and *res extensa*—the Double has been a predominantly psychological construct marking opposing tendencies, identity crises, and man's fundamental incompleteness.[53] While this book is primarily concerned with the Double in a collective context, the psychological inflection remains consequential. Claims that a Double is lurking and loose within the collective are dependent on assertions that the group's members are not only suspect but also susceptible to crises of identity. With these points in mind, the Double is *a trope that blends the familiar and the unfamiliar by placing within the familiar an amorphous sense of otherness, strangeness, and potential danger.*

The bright rays fell vividly upon the sleeper, and my eyes, at the same moment, upon his countenance. I looked;—and a numbness, an iciness of feeling instantly pervaded my frame. My breast heaved, my knees tottered, my whole spirit became possessed with an objectless yet intolerable horror. Gasping for breath, I lowered the lamp in still nearer proximity to the face. Were these—*these* the lineaments of William Wilson? I saw, indeed, that they were his, but I shook as if hit with a fit of the ague in fancying that they were not. What *was* there about them to confound me in this manner? I gazed;—while my brain reeled with a multitude of incoherent thoughts. Not thus he appeared—assuredly not *thus*—in the vivacity of his waking hours. The same name! the same contour of person! the same day of arrival at the academy! And then this dogged and meaningless imitation of my gait, my voice, my habits and my manner! Was it, in truth, within the bounds of human possibility, that *what I now saw* was the result, merely, of the habitual practice of this sarcastic imitation?[54]

Edgar Allan Poe's short story "William Wilson," from which the above passage is quoted, begins with a man who narrates his lifelong entanglement with his Double (who I will also refer to as "Wilson"). The Double's likeness to the narrator is at first made evident to the reader only through their common name.[55] Time and again the Double thwarts the narrator's mischievous actions. Their story ends with a single-blow murder-suicide in which the narrator kills Wilson, and, through a mirror that subsequently takes Wilson's place, realizes that he has mortally wounded himself. One of innumerable possible examples, Poe's story is a richly dense source from which to illustrate my definition and introduce key aspects of the Double. These include the identity markers deployed in conjuring the Double, its tie to media and communication technologies writ broadly, and, ultimately, its function in the context of homegrown terrorism.

The above passage describes the moment in which the narrator first recognizes the face of the Double as an exact likeness of his own. The Double often appears—and is predominantly thought of—as a lookalike.[56] This occurs slowly in Poe's story. The narrator discovers their shared physiognomy gradually over time and only once he examines the sleeping Wilson by candlelight. The closing scene leaves no doubt: "in my death, see by this image, which is thine own, how utterly thou hast murdered thyself." Dzhokhar Tsarnaev embodies this realization in the context of homegrown terrorism. But the Double does not solely, or always primarily, manifest in phenotypic duplicates or matching physiognomies. It can appear in vision (not limited to the face or physical body), voice, and manner. In "William Wilson," before the reader learns of the uncanny similarity between both faces, the narrator indicates not only physical likenesses—height, "general contour of person and outline of feature"—but also similarities in style of dress, gait, and the timbre of voice. Indeed, the conjuring of the Double in cases of homegrown terrorism is not exclusively based on physical markers but, paralleling the racism that pervades the war on terror, is centered on cultural markers as well as behavioral ones. Chapter 3 illustrates how officials and the media communicated a frightening recognition of "something of ourselves" in Anwar al-Awlaki—an American cleric affiliated with al-Qaeda killed in a 2011 drone strike—by highlighting his familiarity and command of American culture evident in the delivery and content of his lectures. In Chapter 1, Nidal Malik Hasan, the Fort Hood shooter, was said to be hiding in plain sight, camouflaged by his US Army fatigues (he was a military psychiatrist). These two cases illustrate how a variety of markers of likeness are invoked even in cases involving physiognomies that, throughout the war on terror, have consistently been made other.

The amalgamation of self and other in one individual, or the splitting of an individual, is often accounted for in media and official discourse through recourse to technologies that facilitate access to that which has been deemed foreign.[57] Paralleling Schmitt's assertion that developments in technology (including communication technologies) have changed the nature of conflict, the infiltration of America or radicalization of Americans by a malignant otherness is often attributed to communications media, particularly digital media. The Tsarnaev brothers were said to live out their second or shadowy lives on social media. The Fort Dix Five were said to be inspired by the digital output of Anwar al-Awlaki (Chapter 2), who himself continued to exist as a digital doppelgänger after his death in 2011 (Chapter 3). This is by no means a recent development in the Double motif. The ubiquity of the Double in nineteenth-century literature was also closely linked to anxieties concerning new technologies and the novel forms of contact they facilitated with distant others.[58] In Stevenson's *Strange Case of Dr. Jekyll and Mr. Hyde*, the electric light allows Hyde to roam the streets of London carrying out his vile desires—much like candlelight allows the narrator to finally see his Double in "William Wilson." In Mary Shelley's *Frankenstein*, new technologies produce a monstrous Double. Historically and today the Double (re)emerges in and through anxieties concerning the development of a "world of perpetual light."[59] Chapter 2 illustrates the ways in which a wide variety of media and communications technologies (e.g., books, airplanes, bombs, websites) placed in ubiquitous digital and analog networks (intimately connecting virtual spaces, foreign lands, and the living rooms of ordinary Americans) are implicated in the discourse of the Double and the securitizing practices it facilitates.

Bringing the Double into the context of the collective and, more importantly, the collective at war in its contemporary form begs the question of what exactly the invocation of the Double facilitates. What does framing an enemy as a circulating potential within ubiquitous communication networks and brought to life through experiences and pressures common to everyday life (as per theories of radicalization) do to notions of belonging? What is the utility of constructing a threat "like us" and proclaiming that this "highly energized and potentially dangerous" figure is loose within the collective?[60] An understanding of the function of the Double begins with addressing its status as potentially dangerous.

The simple appearance of one's likeness, whether in vision, voice, or manner, and however disorienting, does not fully explain the horror of the narrator's experience in "William Wilson"—tottering knees, lack of breath, and reeling mind. The Double motif is not a priori tied to terror. Not only was the Double once employed for comic effect, but in some of its earlier usages the figure signaled different variants of immortality. In Judaic tradition, the Double's appearance was considered proof of the soul's existence and thus man's immortality.[61] In the burial rights of Roman emperors, the use of and ritual around an effigy of the deceased signaled that "while the king may die, the King never dies."[62] However, what was once a guardian angel would come to be viewed as a harbinger of death. The presence of one's Double took on the meaning that one's soul had departed the body, signaling one's ultimate doom; hence, the reference to the Double as "the fetch" in Scottish folklore.⁶³ In literature, those who come across their Double, like the narrator of "William Wilson," eventually, and often quickly, meet their demise. Here, the "unfamiliar" is not simply another body or figure, but an otherness sensed in the presence of the familiar, in their conflation. When Freud states that the Double conceals something under the veneer of agreeability, the implication is that what is kept from sight is ominous, disturbing, and dangerous (its potency due to its inseparability from the familiar).

The Double, pace Freud, is underwritten by the logics of not only splitting and duplication, but also doubt and duplicity, giving the many forms of likeness embodied in the Double a peculiar valence. The Double is no mere facsimile.⁶⁴ In the pangs of discovering the Double's face, the narrator refers to Wilson's gait, voice, habits, and manner as "sarcastic imitation." However, he otherwise admits that through these, Wilson presents an "exquisite portraiture . . . [that] could not justly be termed a mere caricature." Moreover, in the climactic finale in which a mirror appears in place of Wilson, the narrator utters in response to the image in it, "Thus it appeared, I say, but was not." Here, the narrator communicates the ambivalence of the Double motif and how it works precisely to put into doubt any clear distinction between one and one's double. Doubt and duplicity are also evident in the multitude of terms the narrator employs to describe Wilson: brother, namesake, twin, companion, imposter, and antagonist.⁶⁵

In a collective context, particularly that of homegrown terrorism, the effect of the Double translates into an inability to tell friend from foe: "the phenomenological problem posed by [doubles such as Stevenson's] Hyde is that his deformity is unnamable. The monster cannot be expressly distinguished from normal forms," only intensifying the existential threat the figure presents.⁶⁶ The Double populates and generates what Schmitt calls "wider spaces of insecurity, fear, and general mistrust."⁶⁷ Like the narrator's unease about when and where Wilson might turn up—doubly reflected in the narrator's claim that their shared name is so unremarkable and ordinary that it is the "common property of the mob"—the discourse of the Double injects a similar anxiety into contemporary America. Family, friends, and neighbors of Americans who are charged with terrorism-related offenses or attempt to join ISIS exclaim in surprise at the revelation—"If he's a terrorist, he's the nicest terrorist I ever met in my life!"[68]

The Double unsettles and prevents closure: "what captures and entraps—what seems inescapable—is none other than an ever changing tendency to shift and defer, ad infinitum."[69] What this entails is, again, best illustrated in contrast to the functionality of the other. The other establishes clear boundaries and sutures a collective's identity. It circulates within what Foucault calls relations of disciplinary power. Discipline is a modality of power that lets "nothing escape," utilizing strategies of enclosure, confinement, and observation that materialize in a variety of spaces: the prison, the clinic, the asylum.[70] All of these disciplinary spaces divide the normal from the abnormal and structure what is permitted and what is prohibited. The present-day use of communication management units (which place extreme limits on contact with the outside world) in federal prisons, Guantanamo Bay, and various other black sites in which many brown, Arab, and Muslim men (marked as other) are held without charge or chance of release is a poignant reminder of the continuing relevance of disciplinary power, however modified by the logic of the exception.

The Double, on the other hand, could be said to simultaneously underwrite and exceed what Foucault terms biopolitical strategies of management that operate through a calculus of ratios and probabilities and in which pathologies are immanent rather than confined. Taking into account a whole constellation of variables, this modality of power is visible in theories of radicalization that, rather than always employing clear categorizations (though many do), consider a broad and ever-expanding list of cognitive, affective, and experiential variables in calculating what may take an American outside an acceptable curve of normality.[71] In search of and in anticipation of the dangerous individual, this logic of security "works on the future" and focuses on the uncertain and "tries to prevent [violence, crime, terror, etc.] in advance"—an urgency fed by the political costs of a terrorist attack occurring on one's watch.[72] The anticipatory calculus of uncovering an enemy that might materialize in the people and places one would least expect is an intrusive one. In "William Wilson," the true horror of the Double is uncovered only through covert action, penetrating the only private space Wilson has in the school—his bedroom. The narrator's discovery of the Double (in the sense that they share a physiognomy) occurs by casting a secretive light into a private space. In the context of homegrown terrorism, this practice takes two interrelated forms: first, sweeping modes of surveillance that penetrate into the most intimate dimensions of everyday life, such as the NSA's PRISM; second, the use of informants. Government informants, however, do much more than monitor and surveil; their function exceeds the biopolitical. Unlike discipline, which lets nothing escape, Foucault asserts biopower "lets things happen."[73] The Double requires that this be taken further and facilitates strategies that "make things happen"—it is a preemptory and "incitatory" figure.[74] Informants explicitly aid in the "radicalization" and mobilization of US residents and citizens, the practices and consequences of which are examined in Chapters 2 and 3.[75] The informant is himself a double—the inversion of the enemy-Double—illustrating just how the figure and discourse of the Double is not simply a threat to be confined, but a construct that is part and parcel of contemporary modalities of conflict.

If the Double marks the abandonment of the form of "originary [external] difference intrinsic to the Western logos," it does so in a temporary and oscillating manner and works in conjunction with other strategies.[76] Importantly, the Double does not negate the consequentiality of the other. The racism, violence, and discrimination faced by American Muslim and Arab communities serve as constant reminders. The move from the other to the Double, much like that of discipline to biopower and conventional to absolute hostility, is only a shift "in emphasis" (much like the imbricated histories that make up the genealogy of homegrown terrorism).[77] Moreover, forms of hostility overlap and biopolitical modalities embed themselves within the strategies of disciplinary power. The Double and other are contrapuntal figures and their relational trajectories play out side by side, intertwine, merge, and separate in complex ways. Indeed, the securitizing notion that titles this book could be written as "home|grown" to illustrate that it marks not simply the combination of foreign seed and native soil but an attempt to keep them separate through their conjunction. This relation is staged in popular fictional portrayals. In the widely popular series *Homeland*, the homegrown terrorist is a white Marine named Nicholas Brody who returns home after eight years in captivity. Yet, Brody's crisis of identity and involvement in a terror plot are closely tied to Abu Nazir, a proto-typical bin Laden figure (i.e., bearded, turbaned, Arab, and Muslim), with whom he developed a complex relationship through the latter's son (who was killed in a US drone strike). The program, in which a military hero "turns," plays out America's contemporary fears of homegrown ter-rorism. It is a phenomenon also visible in the before-and-after images that accompany news accounts of Americans who have tried to join ISIS.

Here, assertions that contemporary security positions the citizen as simultaneously suspect and spy must be tempered by the fact that this position is not equally distributed. That is, some are more suspect than others (Brody's radicalization is tied to, though not strictly at the hands of, the prototypical other). And while there have been recent cases of informant-led operations preventing violence against Muslim Ameri-cans, the rhetoric (and effort) of government officials illustrates that the practice is largely focused on America's mosques.[78] Moreover, the invo-cation of the Double is (an attempt at the) postracial in that it facilitates the distancing, at least rhetorically (through representations of terror via the white body), of the official government position from strategies of profiling, even as government agencies undertake such measures. Last, the brown-Arab-Muslim-other is irrevocably tied to the develop-ment and conjuring of the Double in contemporary security discourse (Chapter 1 dives deeper into the complex work carried out in marking an influence for political violence as "foreign"). Together, the Double and the other create a productive tension of deferral and closure, disrup-tion and suture. The two figures are deeply imbricated, and the Double is often a figure deployed strategically to uncover the potential other hiding within the populace. Nevertheless, the distinction between the other and the Double is crucial because, as I have outlined here, the Double exhibits significantly different forms of representation, fulfills a unique function, and signals distinctive relations of enmity and power. While the Double is by no means an equal opportunity concept, always inflected with the identity of whomever it is placed over, it captures the ambivalent play of otherness and likeness in discourses that warn of a threat that can mutate and materialize, a phenomenon somewhere in between infiltration and emergence, in the homeland.

Chapter Overview

The remainder of the book takes its cue from the genealogy presented here. I have attempted, however briefly, to retrace how the purview of counterterrorism in the United States has been (re)*defined* over time (*historically*) in a way that affects its *spatiality* and how the Double reemerges in discourses of security in this context. The following chapters are organized along these dimensions of homegrown terrorism/counterterrorism: definitional, historical, and spatial. These are not the only possible gateways for thinking through homegrown terrorism and counterterrorism, but they are tied to significant questions or problems concerning these phenomena. Discuss terrorism long enough and questions about its definition will arise. A constant issue in security, academic, and popular circles, the addition of "homegrown" into the mix only further complicates the matter. Also, terrorism is often invoked in an ahistorical tonality or has a way of obscuring important pasts. Thus, a history of anxieties of infiltration holds promise for making sense of the phenomena under the umbrella of terrorism in a more critical light. Last, in the late war on terror, anxieties concerning the collapse of spatial divides are increasingly visible in, for example, the construction of border walls.[79] Yet, boundary making in this environment is not limited to the border. Rather, it permeates social, cultural, and political relations, and, thus, examining the spaces of counterterrorism within (rather than at) US borders is a crucial aspect of understanding homegrown terrorism.

The three dimensions of homegrown (counter)terrorism that structure this book reveal more than just insights to the questions or anxieties from which they emerge. Each provides an entry point into further developing the figure of the Double and its place in security discourse. It is a potential I exploit by pairing the definitional, historical, and spatial with issues of identity, media, and citizenship, respectively. Certainly, these issues and the dimensions to which they are tied are intricately cross-stitched and overlapping; thus, the chapters are meant to be iterative in that respect. In other words, the pairings (definitional/identity, historical/media, spatial/citizenship) are intervals that cadence and cascade, and it is from the subsequent intersections and interstices that the Double emerges in all its complexity. The book is replete with doubles:

shadows, split personalities, clones, imposters, and doppelgängers. The Double as a heuristic construct here is not intended to reduce these manifestations into mere synonyms or different representations of a unified phenomenon. Rather, the Double ties these together in shifting ways that reveal the intricacies of today's anxieties, discourses of security, and modalities of conflict as well as how they come to bear on articulations and experiences of citizenship.

Chapter 1, "Identity and Incidence: Defining Terror," is concerned not with the formulation of a universally accepted definition of terrorism but with examining how three very different men and their violent acts were coded as terrorist: Daniel McGowan (ecoterrorist), Wade Michael Page (domestic terrorist), and Nidal Malik Hasan (homegrown terrorist). The chapter is structured along two definitional axes. The first is nominal (and suggestively ordinal) and examines the way identity constructs are deployed in efforts to mark an actor and his action as an existential threat, as "foreign." It is a maneuver performed through the super- or sub-imposition of the brown-Arab-Muslim-other atop or beneath the familiar—be they the white faces of environmentalists and racists or a US military uniform. For a threat to be existential it must also be reoccurring and persistent. Thus, the second axis is temporal and examines how each actor/action was constituted as an *incidence* rather than a mere *incident*. In this effort, I detail how each man was paired with a past doppelgänger—McGowan/Kaczynski (the Unabomber), Page/McVeigh (who carried out the Oklahoma City bombing), Hasan/al-Hazmi (one of the 9/11 hijackers)—and characterized as a rematerialization of a ghost that promises subsequent, cyclical, and perhaps even more destructive returns. Together, the two axes illustrate the complex interplay of constructs of familiarity and difference as well as temporality in recoding violence as terror. Therein, I illustrate how the Double, a figure positioned in the past and future, but never present—one deployed strategically by various actors—is the operational figure of anticipatory or preemptive politics, the failure of which only reinforces its necessity.

"Informants and Other Media: Networking the Double" places contemporary fears of radicalization in a productive comparison with Cold War fears of infiltration. By focusing on media, writ broadly, I show how these anxieties are both, at their base and despite their differences, fears of connectivity. Furthermore, they are made sense of—and simultaneously exacerbated and alleviated—through the lens of conspiracy. Thus, Chapter 2 is situated in two courtrooms over sixty years apart: the 1949 Foley Square trial in which eleven leaders of the Communist Party of the United States of America were found guilty of conspiring to teach and advocate the violent overthrow of the US government; and the 2008 trial of the Fort Dix Five, New Jersey men convicted of conspiring to kill US military personnel. I remap how an old surveillance medium, the paid informant, fostered, facilitated, and elicited social, technological, and ideological links between those accused and broader enemy networks (Communism and global jihad, respectively) in a manner that made conspiracy legible to publics and juries. Here, the Double is found in the network; neither here nor there, but always circulating. As such, the Double is epistemologically inseparable from the media implicated in the enemy network by the informant—books, videos, etc.—and the informant himself (as a surveillance technology). Here connectivity is simultaneously ill and remedy and the informant is a securitizing-Double, the enemy-Double's inverse, a conspiratorial figure that exploits connectivity in an effort to make conspiracy charges, a legal mechanism of counterterrorism, stick.

Counterterrorism materializes in more than just America's courtrooms. Chapter 3, "Opacity and Transparency in Counterterrorism: Belonging and Citizenship Post-9/11" examines two spaces integral to the production of counterterrorism spectacles: namely, the office of executive decision making and the US prison system, both largely kept from public view. The play of opacity and transparency in counterterrorism, inextricably linked to the spatial collapse of conflict, is visible in the two cases that inform this chapter: the placement of Anwar al-Awlaki on the infamous "capture or kill" list and the entrapment of four African American ex-convicts in a 2009 sting operation (the Newburgh Four). Both cases involve individuals readily made other, and yet what made their respective death and imprisonments so urgent was, I argue, their Americanness: al-Awlaki's cultural familiarity and American accent and the Newburgh Four's emergence from a quintessential American space—the prison. From there I examine the interplay of what is seen and left out of sight in counterterrorism, the articulations of belonging it fosters, and the already-existing second-class experiences of citizenship it exacerbates. The communication of the US drone program vis-à-vis hunting al-Awlaki as an open secret, a play of opacity/transparency, illustrates the fluid positioning of citizens as simultaneously spy and suspect. The resulting peculiar articulation of belonging—laughter, in the face of the drone strike that takes the life of a fellow citizen— illustrates the unequal distribution of this dual position. I develop this further through the Newburgh Four by illustrating how the largely unseen machinations of mass incarceration are integral to the production of the "successful" counterterror sting, which in turn only further oils the cogs of mass incarceration.

The book concludes by returning to the image with which it began, perhaps the most visible manifestation of the discourse of the Double in the context of homegrown terrorism. At the time of writing, the Boston Marathon bombing carried out by the Tsarnaev brothers is the only successful post-9/11 improvised explosive attack carried out on US soil by self-proclaimed jihadists. A metaphorical return to the originary Tale of the Two Brothers, the Tsarnaev case acts as a crescendo in which the themes of this book tie together. The case illustrates the failure of anticipatory politics, the complex interplay of articulations of otherness and likeness, and the consequences of the Double for thinking about belonging. Moreover, the Double manifests therein in digital media, in psychological splits, and as doppelgänger on the cover of *Rolling Stone*.

Above the cacophony of ball bearings, lost limbs, shootouts, messages scribbled in blood, and "fan-girls," a single note resounded with a peculiar resonance. The younger Tsarnaev's appearance in a space thought to be reserved for America's idols (though this is a historically inaccurate portrayal of *Rolling Stone*) was interpreted as an indication that the terrorist had been absorbed into the popular imagination beyond a nameless figure, an other marked for an unremarkable death in a high-budget Hollywood production. To conclude the book, I address the question of whether the image of the Double is in fact an enemy image or one of a different type and modality. From the Tsarnaev cover and its various appropriations I move to examining the double images (before and after) that structure how sense has been made of Americans who have tried to join ISIS. These images and their juxtaposition powerfully illustrate "home|grown" security discourse and the consequences of the Double's appearance on the scene of security. The strategic constructions of difference and likeness in threat itself, rather than in a clear us/other dichotomy, mark the usurpation of that binary. It is replaced by another nonbinary pairing—other-Double—that oscillates between deferral and closure, disruption and suture, engendering a cyclical movement, an ever-repeating coda that works to continuously defer the end of the war on terror.

Figure 2. *Time*, November 23, 2009.

1

Identity and Incidence

Defining Terror

December 7, 2005: Daniel McGowan was arrested in connection to a series of arsons. The arrest was one of a dozen, the culmination of the FBI's Operation Backfire, an investigation into acts of ecoterrorism.

August 5, 2012: Wade Michael Page, a known white supremacist, killed six at the Sikh Temple of Wisconsin. The FBI investigated the case as an act of domestic terrorism.

November 5, 2009: Major Nidal Malik Hasan killed thirteen fellow soldiers at the Fort Hood military base in Texas. Given Hasan's communiqués with Anwar al-Awlaki, the case was widely referred to as an act of homegrown terrorism.

"We cannot fully know what leads a man to do such a thing," President Obama said somberly as he relayed a request for Americans not to jump to conclusions in the wake of the Fort Hood shooting. Critics pounced, claiming that Obama, not a half year after his "New Beginnings" speech in Cairo, was playing politics with the lives of American servicemen and -women. Beyond the right's Islamophobia or disdain for Obama, the exchange illustrates a more general and much older problem: namely, that dubbing an individual or group as terrorist (or, in this case, not) is an inherently "political" act. Much bemoaned, academic after pundit after politician continue to attempt to construct a definition of terrorism that might move above such politics. One of the most widely cited is the "consensus definition" of terrorism studies scholar Alex Schmid:

> Terrorism refers to on the one hand a doctrine about the presumed effectiveness of a special form or tactic of fear-generating, coercive *political*

violence and, on the other hand, to a conspiratorial practice of calculated, demonstrative, direct violent action without legal or moral restraints, targeting mainly civilians and non-combatants, performed for its propagandistic and psychological effects on various audiences and conflict parties.[1]

Evident from Schmid's definition is that the so-called problem of politics associated with terrorism is not merely a matter of application (i.e., who counts as a terrorist) but is integral to the definition of terrorism itself. In his survey of academic definitions, "political"—that is, the nature of, or motive for, an act—is the second most commonly cited element of terrorism after "violence or force" (he conjoins the two in his definition). Thus, distinguishing the violence of crime, however heinous, from that of terrorism pivots on the ability to clearly determine whether an action is motivated by personal gain or politics—in moments of psychosis, it might be neither. So deeply ingrained is this thinking that in the aftermath of violence, news media coverage and government hearings are dedicated to uncovering the perpetrator's motivation and whether or not she intended for the act to send a message to an audience beyond her direct victim(s).

Yet, as information rolled in about Nidal Malik Hasan, determining the nature of his motive became no easier. Featured on the cover of *Time* magazine two and a half weeks after the shooting, "TERRORIST?" covers Hasan's almost expressionless eyes; the image taken from his military file. At this point, authorities and the public had learned that Hasan had communicated with a radical cleric. But they also learned of his potential psychological issues. In this chapter I do not engage in the futile labor of proposing a definition of terrorism that might somehow provide a way around this impasse.[2] Instead, I descend from the mythologized air above politics and into its ground, charting the maneuvers, tensions, and debates initiated by efforts to mark three very different individuals as (eco, domestic, and homegrown) terrorists—Daniel McGowan, Wade Michael Page, and Nidal Malik Hasan.

The three cases that make up this chapter reveal not only that the determination of the nature of a motive itself is a matter of politics, but more importantly, that it involves a peculiar kind of valuation. I argue that the transformation of violence into terrorism not so much depends on the illustration of a political motive (i.e., pro-life, race, the environment, social change, etc.), but rather hinges on characterizing that motive as ~~political~~; that is, as illegitimate, as foreign to ordinary politics, and, above all, as an existential threat to "our way of life" that must be anticipated and prevented. Thus, a shift in the crux of the definitional conundrum of terrorism—from searching for political motive to analyzing how actors are deemed a civilizational threat—reveals the close relationship between defining terrorism and identity constructs.

This chapter is structured around two definitional axes through which the three men were coded as terrorists. The first maps the manner in which the motives underlying the actions of McGowan, Page, and Hasan were demarcated as "foreign." Efforts to do so begin with the discourse of the Double, if in varying ways, claiming that within the familiar—be they the white faces of environmentalists and racists or a US military uniform—lurks an otherness that threatens (Western) civilization. While each case presents distinct narrations of otherness, they are all accompanied by invocations of the brown-Arab-Muslim-other. Through comparison or superimposition, this figure renders the otherness of each legible vis-à-vis their familiarity.

The second is temporal. *Time* magazine asked, "Is Fort Hood an aberration or a sign of things to come?" hinting that an answer to the single-word question that masked Hasan's visage depended on whether his act could be shown to be an *incidence* rather than a mere *incident*. In more general terms, if terrorism is part of a ~~political~~ project, it cannot, by definition, be a one-time act. Efforts to mark the men as terrorist involved tying McGowan, Page, and Hasan to past doppelgängers: Theodore Kaczynski, Timothy McVeigh, Nawaf al-Hazmi (one of the 9/11 hijackers), respectively. It is a definitional maneuver that sets in motion a Janus-faced discourse that projects and mutates a traumatic past into an imminent, yet not entirely determined, future. The logic here is that of a future-past (*futur antérieur*), but one that maintains a sense a Derridian unknowable future (the "to come," *à-venir*)—trauma, as Derrida states, proceeds from the future.[3] Each man, as the manifestation of a copy, the fulfillment of the future as past in the present, creates a cyclical lineage that promises subsequent copies and returns, though in perhaps even more destructive form. *Time* suggests as much. "A sign of things to come?" The titular question, thus, concerns more than one's status as a terrorist; an affirmative answer also includes the promise of things to come. It is a futurity "held in the present in a perpetual state of potential," made legible through a doubling in time.[4]

The Double reveals the complex and mutable interplay of identity constructs integral to recoding violence as terrorism as well as the temporal structure on which this incorporeal transformation depends. The Double is, in effect, the operational figure of preemption, a risk too catastrophic (and rare) to be subject to calculation and compensation. The Double, as existential threat, thus requires, as sociologist François Ewald puts it, that I, "out of precaution, imagine [rather than calculate] the worst possible, the consequence that an infinitely deceptive, malicious demon could have slipped into the false of apparently innocent enterprise."[5] Shifting the definitional problem of terrorism to a focus on how a wide breadth of actors, actions, and utterances are coded as existential threats illustrates how the Double is not simply a source of anxiety or another adversary to be captured and confined. Rather, the Double is internal to preemptive politics. It is an adversary that cannot—or, pace security thinking, ought not—be named, only anticipated.

Coding Terror (in Three Parts): Identity at the End of Civilization

Human-Hating Treehuggers

The largest domestic terrorism investigation in US history, Operation Backfire, focused on a series of arsons.[6] The operation hinged on the use of an informant, Jacob Ferguson, a one-time mainstay in the environmentalist movement in the US Northwest. Exploiting his heroin addiction, the FBI swayed him into service to avoid drug charges. For his handlers, Ferguson mapped out a cell of eighteen individuals with ties to a variety of groups known for taking "direct action"—i.e., arson, vandalism, sabotage, and demonstrations—against organizations whose activities harmed the environment and animal life. Referred to as "the Family," the cell was characterized by critics as a fiction cooked up by the combined imaginations of overeager FBI agents and a strung-out informant. Ferguson was flown around the country to stage "run-ins" with each individual and record their conversations; Daniel McGowan was one of the individuals he visited.

After his arrest, McGowan agreed to a noncooperative plea bargain (in which he was not required to testify against his codefendants) and admitted to his involvement in two arsons in Oregon in 2001. The trial judge applied a terrorism enhancement at sentencing and McGowan received a seven-year term, double the average federal sentence for arson. McGowan served his time in a communication management unit housed at the US Penitentiary in Marion, Illinois. It is a form of confinement developed specifically to house terrorists and one that severely limits one's contact with the outside world. He was released on June 3, 2013.[7] Throughout the process FBI officials unequivocally referred to McGowan and company as terrorists.

Ecoterrorism is not the conceptual offspring of 9/11. Ron Arnold, founder of the Wise-Use Movement, coined the term in a 1983 article for *Reason* magazine. His intent, on behalf of a consortium of industry interests, was to secure additional protections against (and vilify) environmentalists.[8] The concept's migration from the pages of industry pamphlets into mainstream political discourse was the result of intense industry lobbying. The campaign also worked to insert itself into academic debate; the first article about "environmental terrorism" to appear in the journal *Terrorism* was authored by an executive of Contingency Management Services.[9] Within two decades ecoterrorism became the FBI's top domestic terrorism priority. In 2003, the American Legislative Exchange Council published a pamphlet (amounting to model legislation) titled "Animal and Ecological Terrorism in America" in an effort to transform the Animal Enterprise Protection Act of 1992 into the Animal Enterprise Terrorism Act. The latter was ultimately ratified in 2006, preceded by a series of Senate and House committee hearings on ecoterrorism.

The radical environmentalist movement that industry sought to vilify is made up of a variety of groups, organizations, and networks. A few of the more recognizable names, those implicated in Operation Backfire, include the Earth Liberation Front (ELF), the Animal Liberation Front (ALF), Stop Huntingdon Animal Cruelty (SHAC), and Earth First![10] ALF, ELF, and SHAC are British imports that arrived in the United States in 1979, 1996, and 2004, respectively. ALF announced its presence in the United States by freeing five animals from the New York University

Medical Center.[11] Earth First! was founded in 1979 by Dave Foreman, a popular figure in the environmentalist movement who penned *Eco-defense: A Field Guide to Monkeywrenching* in 1985; his book details "ecotage," tactics for sabotaging machinery in order to disrupt industry activities. The groups are tied together in a number of ways: tactics, philosophy, shared members, and declarations of solidarity—not to mention being the co-subjects of government hearings, investigations, and reports.

James Jarboe, the FBI's domestic terrorism section chief, defines eco-terrorism as "the use or threatened use of violence of a criminal nature against innocent victims or property by an environmentally-oriented subnational group for environmental-political reasons, or aimed at an audience beyond the target often of a symbolic nature."[12] As a carbon copy of the FBI definition of domestic terrorism, the terms "environmentally" and "environmental" are scribbled in, either attached to or in place of, "politically" and "political." Republican Senator David Vitter, present at many of the hearings on the subject, lauded the application of terrorism to the actions of environmentalists. Echoing the testimonies of employees and executives who described the terror they felt as a result of direct action, he concluded, "I think it is absolutely appropriate. You look up the definition, and this is what terrorism is about. It is using violent and illegal activity to try to intimidate people, scare people into submission to go along with these extremist political agendas. That is basically the dictionary definition of terrorism."[13] Matters, however, were not so straightforward.

Despite causing approximately $110 million in damage in a suspected 1,100 cases, the actions of radical environmentalists have never resulted in a single death. The care taken by the movement's organizations to not "harm any animal (human or otherwise)" led some within government and elsewhere to chastise those who would equate direct action with terrorism as engaging in "excessive name calling."[14] While I address the attempts to deflect charges of terrorism below, what is at issue here is the manner in which direct action and its practitioners were marked as terrorist in light of a lack of fatalities. Arguments that one ought not call another a terrorist if there is no trail of dead implies that the identification of a political motive alone is not sufficient for recoding violence as terrorism. How was this impasse circumvented? What provided proponents of the institutionalization of ecoterrorism with an avenue through which to authoritatively and legally (i.e., in legislation) code environmentalists as terrorists?

The first maneuver involves including violence to property in the definition of (eco)terrorism. The owner of Superior Lumber, the target of one of the arsons with which McGowan was involved, described the destruction of his property as producing a feeling of terror.[15] Here, property is intimately tied to one's body and livelihood, the destruction of which could have devastating impacts. In government hearings, acts of property destruction were regularly compared to murder.[16]

If not wholly convincing, the movement's apparent disdain for private property acted as the basis from which arson and vandalism were delineated as fundamentally anti-Western acts, the motivation for which could only have a foreign or un-American source. In a statement to a House Subcommittee hearing on Ecoterrorism and Lawlessness in National Forests, one executive forcefully asserted that the environmentalist movement is

> disdainful of fundamental American values, including the rule of law, private property rights, free enterprise, and democracy. . . . [They] detest American businesses, our free enterprise system, our environmental policies, our use of animals for food and medical research, our judicial system, our elected officials, and many other American institutions and values.[17]

Others emphasized that radical environmentalists are, in essence, "human-hating treehuggers" who renounce "the view of the Greek philosopher Protagoras that 'man is the measure of all things.'" In effect, they want to "destroy civilization as we know it."[18]

Certainly various segments of the environmentalist movement align themselves with "the East"—a largely reappropriated and mythologized notion of a space and culture untouched by technology, which, among other things, speaks to the whiteness of which the movement has repeatedly been accused.[19] Various authors within the movement alternatively trace its roots to the Indian Vedas (1500 BC) that denounce the eating of meat, the Jains (circa 500 BC) who wore covers over their mouths so as to not accidentally swallow insects, and, later, Buddhists. Furthermore, they chastise the Abrahamic religions—Judaism, Christianity, and Islam, in equal measure—for claiming that god gave man dominance over the earth, which they see as the root of "an inherently irrational, exploitative, and destructive [Capitalist] system."[20]

Conversely, there is a contingent within the movement that aligns it with the very American philosophies of Ralph Waldo Emerson and Henry David Thoreau. They characterize environmentalist thought as the "most recent expressions of the centuries-old minority tradition in Western philosophy" that showcases and embodies the "highest ideals of Western society."[21] Others still connect their lived environment to US nationalism. In the 2011 documentary *If a Tree Falls*, which documents, in part, McGowan's story, Bill Barton of the Native Forest Council stumbles upon a felled old-growth tree and longingly muses that it "probably sprouted just about the time Columbus sailed the ocean blue."

To counter the potential that Americans might identify with the movement or its goals, its opponents further characterize the movement as anti-Western by conjuring the brown-Arab-Muslim-other: "They think they are heroes and crusaders for justice, just as the September 11 hijackers thought of themselves in this way." Moreover, radical environmentalists might prove even more dangerous. The movement's action against Huntingdon Life Sciences, whose animal testing practices broke various protection laws, succeeded in having financiers divest from the company. In his testimony before the Senate Committee on Environment and Public Works, the company's counsel claimed that in "attacking the integrity and independence of the US stock market system . . . [SHAC] had succeeded where Osama bin Laden had failed." In effect, within the familiar faces of these white Americans exists a "homegrown brand of al-Qaeda," a threat so dangerous to American interests and values that only a racialized terrorist identity construct could communicate its gravity.[22]

The Sound of Hate

On the morning of August 5, 2012, Wade Michael Page entered the Sikh Temple of Wisconsin in Oak Creek. He opened fire, killing six people. Another four were wounded before he turned his weapon on himself. One victim's relative recounted the massacre:

It was not the American dream of Prakash Singh, who had only been reunited with his family for a few precious weeks after six years apart. When he heard gunshots that morning, he told his two children to hide in the basement. He saved their lives. When it was over, his children found him lying in a pool of blood. They shook his body and cried "Papa! Get up!" But he was gone.[23]

After the initial confusion, which included reports of multiple gunmen and that the police had shot Page, details began to emerge about the shooter. He was a US Army veteran whose tattoo-covered body read "like a poster text for white nationalism."[24] Page had been a member of a white power skinhead organization. The Hammerskins—which includes a (self-characterized) clandestine group of supporters called Crew 38—formed in Dallas, Texas, in 1988 and is an integral part of the white power music scene. Himself a guitarist and vocalist in a variety of "hatecore" bands (e.g., Celtic Warrior, Intimidation One, Aggressive Force, Blue Eyed Devils, and End Apathy), Page had been on the radar of various watchdog agencies for some time. The FBI announced early on that it was investigating the shooting as an act of domestic terrorism.[25]

The United States has an endemic history of both systemic racial oppression as well as hate- and bias-motivated crime that includes intimidation, assault, vandalism, arson, and murder. The racist right to which the Hammerskins are tied is made up of a diverse set of organizations and networks. Sociologists Pete Simi and Robert Futrell divide the movement along four branches—the Ku Klux Klan, Christian Identity and neo-Pagan racists, Neo-Nazis, and racist skinheads. While not without their disagreements, conflicts, and debates, these branches have migrated, mixed, and overlapped in a variety of ways. Before the end of the Cold War connections between groups began to solidify under the banner of RaHoWa (Racial Holy War), facilitating the movement of individuals and iconography between groups. For example, the contemporary KKK is involved in the racist music scene and has itself "Nazified" through the adoption of Neo-Nazi symbols. Also, in the mid- to late 1980s skinheads began to incorporate Nazi ideals and were themselves recruited into other groups. The Hammerskins are a part of this mixture. It is perhaps ironic that one of their founding members met Tom Metzger (founder of the White Aryan Resistance) during a taping of the

Oprah Winfrey Show (February 4, 1988), which led to increased connections between the groups as well as the more active presence of the Hammerskins in the white supremacist movement as a whole.[26]

The distinction between hate crimes and terrorism is difficult to ascertain. The Southern Poverty Law Center, for instance, does not have a strict protocol regarding the distinct use of each term. Rather, it follows the FBI definition of "hate crime" and labels attacks it feels are politically motivated as terrorism on a case-by-case basis, admitting that there can be overlap.[27] Perhaps the crucial difference is to be found in the communicative aspect of terrorism. That is, one might hypothetically murder someone of a particular race, for example, motivated by prejudices one personally holds, and perhaps without the intent of sending a message to a broader audience. However, this distinction is problematic. First, divorcing personal prejudice from broader political, social, and cultural contexts is difficult if not altogether questionable. Second, a message is likely conveyed beyond one's victim regardless of one's intent, be it to those targeted by violence or those who are like-minded, and this audience need not be national or international in scope.

Rather than attempting to resolve this tension, it is more useful to examine what the tension itself reveals about the definitional problem of terrorism. The lack of concrete distinction between hate crimes and terrorism, the fact that there is always a semblance of political motivation in hate crimes, further illustrates that identifying a political motive is not in itself satisfactory in recoding violence as terrorism. Again, we return to the existential, even if at first glance, situating Page therein poses a quandary. The prevalence and institutionalization of racist violence within the United States begs the question of how such actions could be recoded as threatening the very essence and structure of American society—save a disingenuous denial of white supremacy. By what means does the racist violence integral to the establishment of the United States return in the guise of a transformational threat?

The redefinition of white racist violence from a mainstay of American politics to terrorism occurs through a rereading of the racist right's recent past. According to Heidi Beirich and Mark Potok of the Southern Poverty Law Center, the contemporary racist right is far removed from the likes of the Ku Klux Klan of the 1920s, which saw itself as a defender of culture and country. A decisive shift occurred at end of the Cold War:

without the Communist bogeyman, the US government became the racist right's foremost nemesis. They argue that, slowly ushered in and solidified through the Oklahoma City bombing, the racist right shifted from being a "restorationist effort" to constituting a "revolutionary movement" that pursues a fundamental transformation of the United States.[28]

Beirich and Potok released their report in 2009, the same year that a Department of Homeland Security report on the threat of right-wing extremism was decried as an attack on veterans and conservatism more generally. The backlash effectively gutted the branch of the department that dealt with right-wing extremism. I address this in detail below, but point now to how the aftermath of the Sikh temple shooting, and more recently the takeover of the Malheur National Wildlife Refuge in Oregon in early 2016, resulted in a revived interest (however momentary) in the workings of the racist and extreme right and how a movement the DHS called "paranoid" continues to plot "against America."[29]

By no means providing a characterization of the racist right that is universally accepted in the United States, Beirich and Potok attempt to solidify the transformation of racist violence into terrorism, to further position it as "foreign" so to speak. Their report does so through an indirect invocation of the brown-Arab-Muslim-other. The otherness of this figure is imbued into white racists by emphasizing statements of affinity made in the aftermath of 9/11:

> In case after case, extremists applauded the murder of some 3,000 of their countrymen. Billy Roper, then an official of the major neo-Nazi group National Alliance, said it best in an email to all 1,400 of his members. "The enemy of our enemy is, for now at least, our friends," he wrote. "We may not want them marrying our daughters, just as they would not want us marrying theirs. We may not want them in our societies, just as they would not want us in theirs. But anyone who is willing to drive a plane into a building to kill Jews is alright [sic] by me. I wish our members had half as much testicular fortitude."[30]

White supremacist web forums have featured, and not infrequently, discussions regarding whether or not Arabs are "white," with a variety of opinions on the matter. More recently threads focused on Muslims dominate discussions therein of what constitutes an existential threat to white America. Regardless, it is through the suggested affinity quoted above that statements by the racist right, such as "that government [one led by Barack Obama] is not our government," are given resonance as existential threats.[31]

The argument here is not that groups such as the SPLC are wrong in labeling racist violence as terrorism. Surely, in the current political climate, there is a strategic utility to marking violence as terrorism in order to garner needed attention. Nor is it to deny the immense terror inflicted by white supremacists (and this terror is too often denied). There are, however, serious limits to dealing with racism and racist violence in the United States through the lens of terrorism. Specifically, it begs the question as to whether conceptualizing the racist violence experienced by communities of color through a formulation of terrorism that effectively severs violence from its complex contexts—reducing the source of violence to "evil" or a "foreign" entity—can address the continued institutionalized character of that violence, particularly given the statist nature of present-day conceptualizations of terrorism (which I address below). Nevertheless, the immediate purpose here is to show the manner in which identity is deployed in efforts to communicate and redefine violence as terrorism. More than a political cause, it is violence with an aim to bring an end to society as we know it, a claim communicated through the figure of the brown-Arab-Muslim-other and the clash of civilizations baggage with which it comes, however seemingly questionable or counterintuitive the coupling might be.

The Horror at Fort Hood

On the afternoon of November 5, 2009, Major Nidal Malik Hasan, an Army psychiatrist who had joined the military out of high school, entered the Soldier Readiness Center at Fort Hood, Texas. Wearing his military uniform and brandishing a semiautomatic pistol and a revolver, he opened fire. Unleashing over a hundred rounds, he killed thirteen and wounded thirty-two of his fellow servicemen and-women. In the melee, Hasan was shot several times and was paralyzed from the waist down. In August 2013 Hasan was convicted of thirteen counts of premeditated murder, dishonorably discharged, and sentenced to death. In the immediate aftermath, as rumors circulated about Hasan being troubled by his imminent deployment to Afghanistan, President Obama urged Americans to avoid making premature conclusions about the nature of the crime, for which he received much criticism.[32] Despite the FBI's conclusion that Hasan had no significant ties to terrorist groups, the shooting is widely referred to as an act of homegrown terrorism.

The DHS definition of homegrown terrorism places focus on those who work "in furtherance of political or social objectives promoted by a foreign terrorist organization, but [are] acting independently of direction by a foreign terrorist organization." Thus, Hasan's status as a "lone wolf" acting outside of official structures of command or control, that is, his lack of material ties did not preclude the application of the terror label. In lieu of these—and before it became public knowledge that Hasan had contacted Anwar al-Awlaki—identity markers were used to substantiate his ties, however nonmaterial, to a foreign interest. (The contents of those emails would become known only later; those and Hasan's own later statements regarding his motive I address in the next section.)

Within hours of the shooting, media pundits, politicians, and readers were quick to jump on what was for them the neat realization of their racialized fears of terrorism. "I think the name Malik Nidal Hasan might give you a clue," stated one *New York Times* reader referring to the debate about the nature of the incident.[33] Others stressed Hasan's "heritage" or "roots" (i.e., he was born to Palestinian parents) over his American birth. His faith, illustrated by his dress and beard (which was later forcibly shaved), was a key focal point of speculation.[34] His search for and ultimate failure to find a "pious" wife rendered him a childless bachelor, which was in turn construed as a failure in fulfilling his religious duty. Implied here is that, emasculated in the eyes of his god, Hasan found another way to assert his masculinity and satisfy his religious obligations. Even his good deeds, such as forgiving his neighbors who often taunted him and vandalized his car, were taken as indicators of a dangerous piety. One reader put it most plainly, "He wasn't connected with a 'terrorist' group! Actually, he was—it is called Islam."[35] All this was made even more troubling given that his parents were reported to be not particularly devout, signaling a purposeful move to the "other side" of the existential conflict in which America is embroiled.

Yet, for the Webster Commission, tasked with reviewing FBI procedure after the attack,

> Nidal Malik Hasan's transformation into a killer underscores the dilemma confronting the FBI. Hasan was a licensed psychiatrist and a U.S. Army Major with fifteen years of military service. He was a member of two professional communities—mental health and defense—whose missions include protection against violence. He worked at Walter Reed Army Medical Center and other facilities in close and constant contact with other U.S. military personnel, including fellow psychiatrists. He was a religious person. He had no known foreign travel. Other than his eighteen communications with Anwar al-Aulaqi, he had no known contact and no known relationships with criminal elements, agents of foreign powers, or potential terrorists.[36]

In the cases of McGowan and Page, the brown-Arab-Muslim-other was invoked in order to communicate that within familiar visages exists a threat of such severity that it justifies the label of terrorism. The form that the discourse of the Double takes in the Hasan case presents the inverse: of the threatening other hiding in plain sight, disguised as it were in military fatigues. Reinforced by notions of Islam as an inherently political and violent system of beliefs and laws, doubt was placed on whether a Muslim could faithfully serve in the US military. "A Muslim American soldier kills American soldiers. I'm shocked. Shocked," one reader wrote sarcastically, while another framed it in a matter-of-fact tone: "What a split identity_-[sic] Arab (Muslim) American soldier (combatant). Talk about a person in a job for which they were not suited."[37] For those on the conspiratorial right—pundits who believe that the Oklahoma City bombing was carried out with Saddam Hussein's help, that Obama is secretly Muslim, and that the Muslim Brotherhood has infiltrated all levels of the US government—it was clear that Hasan's allegiances lay with sharia law, which dictated "that the faithful must engage in jihad."[38] Hasan's refusal to shave his beard was, in effect, an indicator of his militancy, of his extremism, and of where he placed his loyalty. (And, surely, the insistence to forcibly shave it at trial was an impotent gesture of asserting control—that even the other must follow protocol.) The implication here being that admitting Muslims into the military provides lone wolves with sheep's clothing. For many, Hasan's identity was proof enough that "the western civilized countries of the world . . . [must take] realistic approaches to the condition of cancer, Muslimism, existing in the world." Framed as a matter of "self preservation," at stake is no less than the "future of the republic."[39]

* * *

The coding of all three men as terrorists did not go uncontested. In the immediate aftermath of the Fort Hood shooting voices in the media and its readership avidly rejected the application of reductive stereotypes to Hasan. For instance, in response to the reader (quoted above) who suggested that Hasan's name indicated that he was in fact a terrorist, another retorted, "Does the name Timothy McVeigh give you a clue? Or how about Theodore Kaczynski?" Still another reader pointed out the racialized character of terrorism discourse: "When a white guy shoots up a post office, they call that going postal. . . . But when a Muslim does it, they call it jihad."[40] Here, Hasan's "torn psyche" is attributable not to some inherent incompatibility between Islam and serving in the American military, but rather to the racism Hasan experienced while in the service. In efforts to vilify one's enemy, epithets such as "camel jockey," "haaji," and "raghead" had become part of soldiers' everyday lexicon. Because Hasan experienced this firsthand, some saw the incident as a tragedy remedied only by more inclusivity rather than as a betrayal that warranted a purge.

There were also questions of mental illness, in both the Fort Hood and Sikh temple attacks. In Page's case, media reports pried into his economic and relationship woes (the latter framed differently than those of Hasan). In the years leading up to his violent attack, his home—already once refinanced—went into foreclosure. After a move to Milwaukee, his girlfriend broke off their relationship. Soon after, Page stopped showing up for work. In the same vein, his violent act was repeatedly and widely referred to as a case of mistaken identity (which, of course, insinuates that violence against Muslims is somehow more understandable). This led those within the white supremacist movement to reject Page as "sick" or an idiot on the fringe of the movement.[41] A thread started the day of Page's rampage on the white supremacist site Stormfront captured the movement's sentiments:

> Let me guess, the story will be that he went to a Sikh temple to get revenge for 9/11, thinking that it was a Mosque.

> Just as I thought when I heard the news: some low IQ White who doesn't know the difference between Sikhs and Muslims.[42]

Some members even suggested collecting money for the victims. The label that represented his band also distanced itself from Page. Claiming it strove to promote a positive image, it removed his band's merchandise from its website because it did not want to profit from the tragedy (which suggests that it could readily have done so). Here, either explicitly or otherwise, Page was placed on the fringe, either mentally ill or deficient.

The morning after the Fort Hood shooting, the *New York Times*' Bob Herbert penned an op-ed, "Stress Beyond Belief," in which he argued that breakdowns like Hasan's were a sign of an overstretched and overworked military, with some troops serving multiple tours and little being done to address the resulting psychological effects.[43] Despite the fact that Hasan had not yet been deployed, it was thought that his imminent deployment terrified him, particularly after counseling so many others who returned with posttraumatic stress disorder (PTSD) and other afflictions. Readers commented that Hasan's break was a sign of the unsustainability of US neo-imperialism, a foreign policy structured around natural resources and the greed of the military-industrial complex. The racism Hasan experienced in the military also contributed to his deteriorated mental health. In response, the *New York Times*' David Brooks claimed that arguments about mental health were driven by "political correctness" and prematurely ruled out the "possibility of evil."[44] One of Brooks's readers reiterated his dismissal of any explanation for Hasan's violence outside of the clash of civilizations narrative more succinctly: "Calling guys like Nidal Hasan 'nuts' is like calling a member of the Nazi party a nut—its simplistic and overlooks the actual problem which is Islamic political ideology."[45]

The invocation of the brown-Arab-Muslim-other is evident not only in efforts to code actors as terrorists, or to reject other plausible explanations of violence, but also in attempts to deflect the application of the label of terrorism. This line of articulation is evident throughout the documentary *If a Tree Falls*. The film catches up with McGowan on the anniversary of 9/11, walking the streets of New York City:

> Of course I am going to get off of house arrest on this day, of all days, it'll be today, you know? It's really sad for me to have all these feelings about my home being attacked, my city being attacked. I mean, when I tell people that I'm accused of being a terrorist, whether it's "eco" or "domestic" in front of it or if it's just straight terrorist, it's ludicrous to me, it's surreal and, most people that know me are, like, "what?" No one's accused in my case of flying planes, bombing things, trying to hurt people, none of these things, no one's accused of that.

Earlier in the film, McGowan refers to terrorism as a "bogeyman word" that is applied to those with whom one disagrees. Yet, in the passage above he reverts to a seemingly obvious distinction, one predicated on unspoken cultural and racial stereotypes. A *New York Times* reader echoed this sentiment by stating that "labeling of ecologically motivated monkey-wrenchers as 'terrorists' . . . is disrespectful to the memories of those who perished at the hands of real terrorists on Sept. 11."[46] While McGowan and company at times invoke right-wing extremists as terrorists, often the "real terrorist" is embodied in a racial/ethnic/religious/cultural other. Either way, the argument is that to put radical environmentalists in the same "category as Osama bin Laden and Timothy McVeigh . . . weakens the word terrorist."[47]

Conversely, white supremacists also bemoan the implication that they are terrorists, claiming that "Jewish-controlled" watchdogs do not cover left-wing groups with the same fervor. Other conservative writers have also voiced this criticism (while avoiding the explicit anti-Semitic overtones), stating that groups such as the Anti-Defamation League and Southern Poverty Law Center overuse the term "terrorism" and have a tendency to vilify their opponents (a critique squarely in line with current white supremacist discourse).[48] Perhaps unsurprisingly, those on white supremacist message boards ultimately blamed Page's stupidity on the "Jewish-controlled media." Despite resorting to established white supremacist paranoid myths to deflect charges of terrorism, online discussions turned their focus to the brown-Arab-Muslim-other.

The Hammerskins online forum conspicuously lacks any threads concerning Wade Michael Page or any posts at all for that matter on August 5, 2012, or the days following. On the other hand, the world's most popular white supremacist site, Stormfront—which has been linked to a hundred deaths in the United States alone—hosted ample discussion.[49] The implication of Muslims as the "real terrorists" already found in the mistaken identity narrative popular in white supremacist discourse is made explicit: "Sikh people are OK and, while they might not belong in the UK or America, they know better than anyone, the dangers of Islam . . . [and in] *the struggle for civilization*, Sikhs are mainly on our side—valuable against Islamic primitivism."[50] Prior to the massacre, members of the Hammerskins forum reacted to a Department of Homeland Security public service announcement titled "The Drop Off" in a similar way. In the dramatization, a white cab driver stops in front of a commuter station. The white woman who gets out of the cab walks into the station and drops off her purse, while the driver arms a bomb in the trunk. Receiving this as an antiwhite message that distorts the "truth" about terrorism, one member wrote in an August 20, 2011, thread, "Fact there were 122 people indicted last year on charges of terrorism in the US, out side of the fact they are terrorists what do they all have in common? . . . Every one of them was a Muslim. So of course lets be on the lookout for well-dressed white ladies."[51]

The three cases here are coded as various types of terrorism—eco, domestic, and homegrown. Ecoterrorism is a variety of domestic terrorism, evident in its poached definition. While domestic and homegrown are often used interchangeably, in the official DHS definition what distinguishes them is whether or not the perpetrator is working in furtherance of a foreign entity or ideology. In short, officially, homegrown is a label exclusively meant for jihadists. Refocusing the definitional problem of terrorism from political motive to existential threat reveals a common denominator. The variety of uses of the brown-Arab-Muslim-other illustrates that—in addition to the continued problem of Islamophobia and the ingrained nature of the clash of civilizations thesis—a sense of otherness communicated in identity constructs is integral to marking all three men as terrorists in a way that blends with strategic invocations of likeness.

In the aftermath of the Fort Hood shooting, a military spouse reflected on the push to mark Hasan as foreign, which we can extend to all three cases:

> I think that some need to believe that an attack such as this has to be about something Muslim, Jordanian, terrorist—pick your label—something foreign to touch us where we are supposed to feel most safe. . . . The alternative—that this war, or even the idea of this war, might make our cherished ones desperate and nearly unrecognizable . . . is too much to bear.[52]

The invocation of "something foreign" is certainly a mechanism through which a collective might avoid having to face its own monstrous tendencies. This foreign entity is also integral to coding violence as terrorism; in her comments terrorism is that something foreign, as is the brown-Arab-Muslim-other that, as I outlined in the Entrance, is intimately tied to (counter)terrorism discourse. Her comments, however, also hint toward the complex uses of the brown-Arab-Muslim-other in an interplay with other identity positions. The "something foreign" is superimposed onto familiar spaces "where we are supposed to feel most safe." McGowan, Page, and Hasan are constituted as doubles; white physiognomies or military fatigues mask an otherness that threatens civilization. For McGowan and Page, the brown-Arab-Muslim-other is superimposed in order to make the threat they pose legible; for Hasan, he is framed as the prototypical other hiding in plain sight. While the effects are certainly different, this process illustrates the centrality and usability of identity in defining terrorism as well as the limits of formulating threats in ways that do not resort to racialized frameworks.

The process of redefining violence as terrorism is closely tied to its anticipation; the terrorist threatens civilization and, thus, must be prevented in advance. If, as Ewald asserts, society is required to imagine the worst, these cases highlight that this responsibility falls not just on the state and its apparatuses, but also on citizens, NGOs, and private business. Identity constructs and their interplay are an important part of this anticipatory reckoning. Not only must the worst be imagined, but it must be imagined beyond the usual suspects and scrutinize spaces populated by anarcho-hippies, skinheads, and military personnel. In other words, threat must be imagined as emerging from spaces beyond those structured by binary stereotypes; uncovering otherness, thus, ominously maintains a strategic sense of the familiar. Neither the process of anticipation, nor that of coding terrorism is presentist in nature. They involve a temporal lineage and speculation, to which I now turn.

Doubles Future-Past

For sociologist Ulrich Beck a dependence on the "past encourages anticipation of the wrong kind of risk."[53] It is an observation that certainly applies to post-9/11 air travel security and the ways certain provisions have been quickly outmoded by the imagination of those who sought to bypass them. Only three months after the Twin Towers fell, Richard Colvin Reid (the Shoe Bomber) made it onboard a Miami-bound plane in Paris with explosives packed into his shoes, which he failed to detonate. Unsurprisingly, passengers from then on have been required to remove their shoes for screening (unless they are at an airport during a Thanksgiving Day rush). Here, security plays catch-up, responding to things that have already occurred, as if the past can force the future to cohere to a particular modus operandi.

The past, nevertheless, is integral to the definitional transformation of violence into terrorism. In a February 2002 hearing on ecoterrorism, the FBI's James Jarboe was pushed on his definition of terrorism. He responded:

> If the motivation [of an actor] was to induce over [sic]—a long-term change in the Government or political entities, or social environment with a political agenda at the heart of the motivation, then it would become—come under the terrorist umbrella. *If it's just a one time act, irritation at an individual, or a specific one instance without looking at the long-term social change, then it would not.*[54]

In Jarboe's argument, for violence to constitute terrorism it must have significance beyond the impact of a single bomb. Terrorism cannot be a one-time act, but rather must be part of a series of events that threaten society, both past and future. (Jarboe is equivocal about in which direction one ought to look to make such a determination.) In effect, each action, whether that of McGowan, Page, or Hasan, must be codified as an *incidence* rather than a mere *incident*. Each incidence is a rerun or a copy of a previous act and each man the doppelgänger of another.[55] If each man is already the return of a ghost, the recurrence of the past in a once-future present, then each also forebodes yet another return.

This temporal logic of the Double, the future-past (*futur-antérieur*), is indispensable to both the definition and anticipation of terrorism because it provides a future "about which one can speak definitely because it is already past."[56] The past, however, is not always put to use in the overcoded and narrow way that Beck suggests. The future as past does not mean that the projected future cannot or is not expected to exceed the past in its intensity or detail. In effect, the deployment of the future-past and its doubles furnishes an opaque and alarming conceptualization of the future: inevitable, yet not without uncertainty. The future-past of the Double, thus, only further inscribes terrorism as an existential threat. Beyond a one-time act, it is a persistent threat that requires vigilance. None of this is to suggest that this mode of anticipation *actually* prevents violence. It fails. But, its failure works only to reinforce its necessity.

Theodore Kaczynski

The invocation of al-Qaeda in order to communicate the existential quality of the threat presented by radical environmentalists was one strategy through which to circumvent the fact that the movement has never left a dead body in its wake. To this maneuver, there is a complementary temporal one that reaches into the future by way of the past and facilitates arguments that it is only a matter of time until the movement kills. The potential and imminence of a future death at the hands of radical environmentalists has been articulated in several ways. First, officials, executives, and commentators read into the movement signs that forebode an escalation in tactics and the likelihood of fatalities.[57] For example, ELF's homepage features a burning structure that, for one commentator, hauntingly invokes the group's "spiritual ancestor," the Ku Klux Klan.[58]

Second, the absence of casualties is framed as a matter of luck rather than planning. The groups associated with the movement adopt an open-source structure. ELF openly promotes its lack of "central leadership or chain of command. Each cell . . . [is] autonomous and an individual could join or drop out at will. Anyone could call him or her self a member of ELF."[59] ALF is similarly structured: "Any group of people who are vegetarians or vegans and who carry out actions according to ALF guidelines have the right to regard themselves as part of the ALF."[60] (In effect, the groups also conjure the Double, a strategy I will discuss below.) Thus, the argument proceeds as such: while ELF and ALF distribute guides that teach others how to carry out direct action, they exert no direct control over unknown sympathizers and, thus, cannot be certain that strangers will show the same level of precaution.[61] The lack of hierarchical structure also leaves the door open for particular strangers to be connected to the movement. Enter Theodore Kaczynski.

Kaczynski, known as the Unabomber, killed three people during a bombing campaign that lasted almost two decades. The shadow of the Unabomber is cast over radical environmentalism in efforts to mark its potential to kill. Kaczynski's actual connection to the movement, however, is by and large tangential if not nonexistent. By his own admission, he disdained the left and cared little about environmental issues:

> I don't even believe in the cult of nature-worshipers or wilderness-worshipers. I am perfectly ready to litter in parts of the woods that are of no use to me—I often throw cans in logged-over areas or in places much frequented by people; I don't find wilderness particularly healthy physically; I don't hesitate to poach.[62]

It is thought that he tacked on an environmentalist strand to his manifesto to give it wider appeal. Moreover, claims that Kaczynski wrote a letter to a reporter congratulating ELF and ALF for their actions and that he had chosen two of his victims from an Earth First! "hit list" are unsubstantiated and highly contested claims.[63] Yet, Kaczynski is repeatedly characterized as, at least, one of the loosely affiliated sympathizers that authorities fearfully anticipate: Ron Arnold, who coined the term "ecoterrorism," wrote a book on ecoterrorism and the Unabomber; a pro-hunting lobby, Putting People First, produced a press release titled "Unabomber Linked to Radical Environmentalism"; and Craig Rosenbraugh, a onetime spokesperson for ALF, was asked at a government hearing if he considered the Unabomber to be a "prisoner of war."[64]

The movement's own open-source structure and its opponents' (however spurious) invocation of the Unabomber are used to support anticipatory claims that it is "only a matter of time before their parade of terror results in loss of human life."[65] Thus, the government cannot "sit aside and wait until someone is killed with an IED [improvised explosive device], and you know it is going to happen."[66] Here arguments that use the past—in conjectural ways—service the future-oriented gaze of anticipatory politics. This gaze makes future violence imminent through the return of the Unabomber. Simultaneously, it maintains an uncertainty in who exactly will constitute this reincarnation and its intensity. McGowan and company were just a few in a lineage of repetition, and their lower level of violence in no way dispels the potential for future escalation. In his testimony in front of a 1998 hearing on ecoterrorism, the president of the pro-industry Alliance for America, Bruce Vincent, summed up what drives anticipatory logic: "'What if' and 'but' are the two words of terror in this discussion. They are small words, but they are powerful and palpable."[67]

Timothy McVeigh

The much-maligned 2009 Department of Homeland Security report, *Rightwing Extremism: Current Economic and Political Climate Fueling Resurgence in Radicalization and Recruitment*, was not itself novel. Both the FBI and SPLC published reports on the military's "white power problem" in 2008 and 2009, respectively.[68] These documents in a sense foreshadow the coming of Page, with the conclusion of the SPLC report ominously titled, "The Future." Outlining and anticipating a rise in right-wing extremism, the DHS report, much like the others, bases its argument on the fact that conditions in 2009 mirrored those that gave rise to Timothy McVeigh over a decade prior. These overlapping factors included a prolonged economic recession, a difficult job market, and a large population of veterans returning home affected by the horrors of war (with the election of a black president adding fuel to the fire). At the time of its release, conservative pundits and lawmakers quickly denounced the report claiming it disrespected veterans and effectively equated conservatism with terror; Janet Napolitano, who at first defended the report, later withdrew it and apologized to veterans.[69]

In the aftermath of the Sikh temple massacre, the press turned its attention back to the 2009 DHS report, comparing aspects of Page's life to the troubling factors outlined therein. A few accounts commented on Page's economic difficulties, but most focused on the connection between his military service and his racism (save any discussion concerning the structural place of racism in the US military enterprise). While likely harboring racist beliefs before his enlistment, Page was thought to have become "a true convert after joining the Army in 1992."[70] His final posting was in 1995 at Fort Bragg, which then served as the home base for unabashedly vocal white supremacist soldiers who flew Nazi flags, played music that endorsed the killing of minorities, actively recruited soldiers for their cause, and led KKK training exercises. Beyond sharing a particular military experience, Page was also tied to McVeigh through the images and text that covered his body. Particular attention was paid to the number 14 tattooed on his upper left arm:

> The "14" itself is particularly telling: It's a reference to "the 14 words" [We must secure the existence of our people and a future for white children], a racist credo first set down by David Lane, the cofounder of a white nationalist terror group known as The Order. (The Order—whose name was inspired by a similar group immortalized in William Luther Pierce's racist novel, *The Turner Diaries, a favorite of Timothy McVeigh's*—has been active for nearly 30 years and was implicated in the 1984 murder of Alan Berg, a liberal Jewish radio host.)[71]

Here, Page is not simply tied to the broader movement (which he was clearly a part of) but, in effect, is positioned as a copy of McVeigh. As the return of the past, Page is but one iteration of a threat that continuously portends its own future return.

The future beyond Page, the potential of McVeigh's continuing return, is located in the racist right's methods of recruitment and its organizational structure. The Hammerskins organize Hammerfest, a yearly white power music festival, which is referred to as "a virtual Woodstock of hate rock."[72] Hammerfest is only one event within a broad music scene that is supported through online sharing and informal performance spaces such as backyard parties. American leaders of white supremacist groups initially came across white power music in the United Kingdom and sought to make use of it in the United States for their cause.[73] On the radar of law enforcement and civil rights organizations since the early 1980s, the music simultaneously provides the movement with entertainment, a mythology, violent imagery, and a major source of funding—Resistance Records, a prominent white power record label, once reported one million dollars in annual sales.

Music has often erroneously been posited as single-handedly catalyzing violence in America.[74] Nevertheless, music is undoubtedly a key feature in the construction of the hypermasculine identity of the white supremacist movement. And unlike the music implicated in the Columbine Massacre, for example, hatecore's style, lyrics, and imagery—as well as the band names (e.g., Jew Slaughter, Grinded Nig, Angry Aryans, and Ethnic Cleansing)—are more explicitly geared toward mobilizing listeners to, if nothing else, identify their enemies; they mirror what Democratic Senator Durbin called the movement's own "propensity for violence."[75] This propensity materialized in Page. Headlines read "Inside the Creepy World of 'Hate Music,'" "Hatecore Music Is Called White Supremacist Recruiting Tool," "Wisconsin Killer Fed and Was Fueled by Hate-Driven Music."[76]

The potential of music molding Page is compounded by the open-source structure the movement utilizes. The Hammerskins describe themselves as "a leaderless group of men and women who have adopted the White Power Skinhead lifestyle. We are blue collar workers, white collar professionals, college students, entrepreneurs, fathers and mothers."[77] Web forums like Hammerskins.org and Stormfront.org surely facilitate a non-hierarchical mode of entry and exchange, though not without their own protocols (e.g., the Hammerskins are wary of surveillance and warn that any account on the site that does not regularly post will be terminated). Moreover, the individuals who populate the movement are said to blend into society seamlessly, a point reiterated in response to some media reports that characterized Page as a "typical" white supremacist. On the day Page was identified, one "sustaining member" of Stormfront wrote:

> You know it's curious—every single one, without exception, of the racially-aware/White Nationalist-minded people I personally know are the most unremarkable, and least "extreme" people one could meet!! *They are in no way distinguishable from any other White American*—and in many cases, their own friends and family are probably totally unaware of their political/ideological outlook.[78]

Here, like radical environmentalists, the racist right invokes the Double. The adoption of this lifestyle and worldview does not require white supremacists to shave their heads and cover their bodies with tattoos.

In 2009 Beirich and Potok warned "a perfect storm is brewing." Economic conditions, military disillusionment, and increased racial tensions, combined with an open-source structure and a musical hook with which to attract individuals (who may be indistinguishable from the general populace) forebode the cyclical return of McVeigh, of which Page was but one copy. Moreover, the gathering clouds are made up of an increasing number of hate groups, patriot organizations, and armed militias, reactionary assemblages to the Obama presidency (and now further galvanized by a white supremacist Trump administration). In the plethora of opinions and investigations that made up the effort to understand Page, one perhaps best captures the anxieties of a future-past that is imminent, yet indeterminate in detail. In an op-ed for the *Washington Post* a US Army veteran and self-described former white supremacist asked himself, "Could I have been Wade Michael Page?" He could muster only one answer: "It makes me sick to say that I don't know."[79]

Nawaf al-Hazmi

Senator Joe Lieberman referred to the Fort Hood shooting as "the most destructive terrorist act to be committed on American soil since 9/11."[80] Tying incidents to 9/11 does more than simply act as a benchmark—based on body count or otherwise—against which to assess the severity of violence. The coupling transforms an event into an incidence, one in a series of events threatening Western civilization, a foreboding of a return of the mythical originary trauma through which Americans make sense of contemporary life.

Allahu Akbar! For conservative pundits who described it as a "battle cry"—one heard by military brass in the battlefields of Afghanistan and Iraq—these two words confirmed Hasan's ties to al-Qaeda.[81] For some *New York Times* readers the utterance was proof of not only an ideological affinity, but a calculated effort.[82] The connection to 9/11 was only reinforced when it was revealed that Hasan had sent a number of emails to Anwar al-Awlaki.

In the course of six months, between December 2008 and June 2009, Hasan had sent Anwar al-Awlaki eighteen email messages, the first through a "Contact the Sheikh" tool on al-Awlaki's personal website. He wrote asking if al-Awlaki considered Muslim American soldiers who carry out violence against Americans to be undertaking jihad and if dying in the process granted one martyrdom status. Later notes included his thoughts on Iran, the Palestinian-Israeli conflict, and Hamas. After four unsuccessful attempts to illicit a response from al-Awlaki, Hasan sent a succession of three notes asking for alternate avenues through which to donate money to him. The third, which reads much like spam from a fictional Nigerian prince, informs al-Awlaki that a five-thousand-dollar scholarship is to be awarded in an essay contest titled "Why is Anwar al-Awlaki a great activist and leader?" and that "we" want him to present the award in person. Three days later he receives a short response in which al-Awlaki says it would be impossible for him to fulfill the request and that he would be "embarrassed" by the award in any event. Hasan followed up later that day, telling al-Awlaki that despite "everyone . . . giving me the green light with tentative reassurances" the contest had been cancelled. The FBI's investigation determined that Hasan had no contact or ties to any other extremist individuals or groups. Hasan ends the email offering help—that "goes without saying . . . should be legal and in accordance with U.S. Law and Allah"—and telling al-Awlaki that he is looking for a wife (this was a common theme in media reports about Hasan's damaged psyche). Al-Awlaki responds only once more, informing Hasan that he cannot offer any advice on how Hasan can help, but closes by stating, "Tell me more about yourself. I will keep an eye out for a sister." This would be al-Awlaki's final note to Hasan. This despite the latter's attempts to illicit a response by sending notes about a public opinion poll on Muslim Americans, again offering financial help, and the ethics of suicide bombing.[83]

Certainly, one can read into Hasan's emails signs of the psychological instability that readers and media pundits discussed (and that others dismissed). Regardless of how al-Awlaki's persona might have influenced or allured Hasan, he had all but ignored Hasan's attempts at a meaningful exchange. After the attack, however, al-Awlaki called Hasan a "hero," describing him "as a man who took his Muslim faith seriously, and who was eager to understand how to interpret Islamic sharia law."[84] Al-Awlaki also claimed that he acted as Hasan's confidant. By virtue of the fact that Nawaf al-Hazmi, one of the 9/11 hijackers, also considered al-Awlaki to be his spiritual leader, al-Awlaki's claim on Hasan positioned the latter as a copy of those who carried out the 9/11 attacks.[85]

Hasan's name is listed in *Inspire*, al-Qaeda in the Arabian Peninsula's online magazine, which began publication in June 2010 and with which al-Awlaki was involved. Not only does each issue memorialize a string of prisoners, but it is the vehicle through which they promise a future return. The magazine promotes "Open Source Jihad," a regular installment based on the writings of Abu Mus'ab al-Suri's sixteen-hundred-page *The Global Islamic Resistance Call*. Al-Suri has been referred to as the "architect" or "mastermind" of global jihad who once scolded bin Laden for catching "the disease of screens, flashes, fans, and applause."[86] Al-Suri is a methodical thinker who wrote his treatise over fourteen years. In it he asserts that al-Qaeda does not accept America's definition of terrorism, which, as an abstract concept, can have either positive or negative connotations depending on the context.[87] Al-Suri distinguishes between two types of terrorism—blameworthy (*irhab madhmum*) and praiseworthy (*irhab mahmud*). The former is "the terrorism of falsehood (*irhab al-batil*) and force of falsehood (*quwwa al-batil*) . . . which inflicts harm and fear among the innocent without a true cause . . . [it is] the terrorism of . . . invaders . . . and unrightful rulers." The latter is the opposite— "terrorism by the righteous that have been unjustly treated . . . [and] is undertaken through terrorizing and repelling the oppressor."[88] *Inspire* also attempts to facilitate individual jihad by publishing hit lists and articles on weapons maintenance and construction.

Anxieties concerning the potential for other reincarnations of martyred men are compounded by *Inspire* magazine's call for ordinary Muslims—and anyone willing to adhere to their reading of Islam—living in the West, regardless of race or nationality, to take up arms.[89] Al-Qaeda, thus, also invokes the Double. *Inspire*'s original editor, Samir Khan—also an American and killed alongside al-Awlaki in 2011—penned, "I am proud to be a traitor to America," in which he places the responsibility for his actions on the United States and its foreign policy. Similarly, al-Qaeda argued that Hasan was recruited not by the group or by al-Awlaki, but by America's crimes, which promises the continued supply of new recruits from the West.[90]

* * *

Each man is a copy of a past terrorist, effectively placing each into a series of events that makes the label of terrorism applicable. Moreover, each incidence or iteration in the series forebodes its own return. McGowan/Kaczynski, Page/McVeigh, Hasan/al-Hazmi. The former in each doubling is the return of the past in the once-future present. Each return, as a return of the past at a later date, forebodes its own future return. This cyclical future-past, in which the Double appears and reappears as ghost, copy, or doppelgänger, is a fundamental component of recoding violence as terrorism, as an existential threat that requires an anticipatory vigilance, itself caught up in this temporality.

The Fort Hood shooting spurred a variety of reports and hearings, including the Webster Commission Report, the Pentagon's *Protecting the Force: Lessons From Fort Hood*, the Committee on Homeland Security and Government Affair's *A Ticking Time Bomb: Counterterrorism Lessons from the US Government's Failure to Prevent the Fort Hood Attack*, and the Subcommittee on Oversight, Investigations and Management's *Lessons from Fort Hood: Improving Our Ability to Connect the Dots*. These documents all focus on the failure of the state's anticipatory security apparatus. Their recommendations included technological integration that would allow for information to be more widely shared and accessible between agencies while maintaining protocols of access by clearance level. Moreover, while there needed to be more horizontal integration, the reports recommended a clear policy concerning a hierarchy of responsibility or "ownership of the lead" in order to ensure timely responses to potential red flags (such as those raised by Hasan's communications to al-Awlaki).

Perhaps the most stressed recommendation in the reports concerns the need for nuancing what in practice constitutes a red flag. The

Department of Defense report states that "policy regarding religious accommodation lacks the clarity necessary to help commanders distinguish appropriate religious practices from those that might indicate a potential for violence or self-radicalization" and that a baseline of traditional religious practice must be established. This was echoed in the Committee for Homeland Security report. In effect these reports use loosely coded language effectively blaming "political correctness" for the tragedy—had Hasan's overall behavior (beyond his academic performance), including expanded character references, been adjudicated as a whole, his clearance might have been downgraded. The implication being that this was not done due to oversensitivity. The manner in which such a practice to distinguish between extreme and normal expressions of one's faith could be established, let alone in a way that maintains constitutional guarantees, is left to the imagination of the reader. Indeed, it opens up a space into which one can inject one's own prejudices or those already part and parcel of counterterrorism. The crux of the reports is that in light of self-radicalization, the security apparatus desperately needs ways to uncover individuals' "*potential* for violence." The Committee for Homeland Security report recommends that the FBI and DoD ought not limit a red flag to overt statements and actions toward terrorism, but include the various factors that signal one's move toward radicalization; in effect, the report's call for "new ways to discern potentially violent behavior" requires either (or both) intrusive surveillance or the further implementation of reductive and racist models of radicalization.[91] What is most telling in these reports is that nowhere does the failure to anticipate terrorism come to suggest something fundamentally amiss with the belief that time, effort, and money ought to be spent on sussing out potential extremists. Rather, however politicized a failure might become, the failure of anticipatory politics at its base works to reinforce, if not intensify, its own necessity.[92]

This unshakeable need for anticipation is closely linked to how terrorism is defined or coded. Deeming an actor, action, or utterance to be terrorist requires that they be marked as existential threats. And while, as the three cases illustrate, the responsibility of anticipating a threat falls beyond the state—to NGOs, watchdogs, citizens, business lobbyists— the manner in which groups are coded as terrorists also has a particular legitimizing function. In constituting the essence of the terrorist threat to be existential—one that promises a continuing return—the state becomes the guarantor of the status quo, of continuity in the most reductive sense of the word. Terrorism Studies as a field contains within it debates regarding whether or not the state can be a terrorist, but maintains a predominantly statist orientation. If the definitional problem of terrorism pivots on the gravity of the civilization threat, it is unsurprising that the state is often effectively excluded from consideration (which also highlights the limit or pitfall in addressing the root of violence against people of color and other minorities through the lens of terrorism). Thus, lawmakers can not only dismiss accusations of terrorism on behalf of or by the state, but also ride out its failures to anticipate terror.

A Threat with No Name

The inability to profile an enemy, to clearly mark the boundaries of where she resides, is the constitutive anxiety surrounding homegrown terrorism. Moreover, it is an anxiety exploited by the movements to which McGowan, Page, and Hasan are linked, an observation that in no way morally equates these movements. Each promotes an open source or leaderless structure. White supremacists generally trace this back to Louis Beam, an American white supremacist and KKK member who coined the term "leaderless resistance" and first outlined the workings of the strategy in a 1983 article. Others assert that the racist right adapted the approach from left-wing revolutionary groups. And al-Suri traces what he refers to as individual jihad (*al-jihad al-fardi*) to the Prophet Muhammad's companion Abu Basir.[93] The material utility of this approach lies in avoiding detection and arrest, aspects all three movements explicitly promote. However, its strategic value does not end with issues of command and control. It also has another communicative utility found in the very claim that one's members, sympathizers, and operatives blend seamlessly into the crowd. The Animal Liberation Front claims that "anyone in your community could be part of ALF without you knowing. This includes PTA parents, church volunteers, your spouse, your neighbor, or your mayor." Skinheads have long been urged to adopt conventional appearances, and as an owner of a white power music label claims, "Our customers, you couldn't pick them out of a crowd. They are the captain of the football team, the cheerleaders, just regular suburban kids." Al-Suri urges would-be warriors to act in a manner so as to be able to remain "present in the West in a natural way."[94] This practice (rhetorical and actual) denies authorities a profile. Moreover, it suggests that beyond being a strategy to avoid detection, the effort to blend in also serves to communicate a sense of power that the movements, in actuality, lack. In *Inspire*'s list of prisoners, included are individuals who have never had any contact with the group or downloaded any of their material such as the Fort Dix Five, who, save one, had no idea they were part of a terrorist plot (none knew that it was one led by an informant). Notwithstanding this, a movement with a claimed and/or suspected multitude of followers indistinguishable from the general populace is more formidable an adversary than one that can be neatly located.

This line of articulation is reproduced in the media and in academic and government discourse. Radical environmentalists/ecoterrorists are described as "nebulous . . . and purposefully disorganized"; as having no formal organization, lurking in the shadows and having no typical recruit.[95] Aryans are invisible and "hide amongst us"; Page "was one of thousands."[96] Hasan's former neighbor expresses this quandary well: "You think you know a person by seeing them, by how they act, but sometimes you're wrong"; another adds, "He looked normal."[97]

What then, ultimately, is the Double in this context? Temporally, the Double is never present, but always lurking in the past and future, existing only in a potential that is made legible through the future-past. Alexander Galloway and Eugene Thacker intimate this point in their theorization of networks. In their discussion of the network as a weapons system they touch on the topic of enmity: the "name of this distributed new enemy is 'terrorism.' . . . [However,] in the same breath, we see the statement that our new enemy is networked and distributed to such a degree that *it cannot be named*."[98] In short, the Double is a never present adversary.

Defining terrorism, or recoding violence as terrorism, has little to do with political motive. The FBI's John Lewis was asked if he considered Right to Life and other antiabortion groups terrorist organizations because they have, like ecoterrorists, committed arson and, unlike ecoterrorists, have killed for a political cause. He responds that one "of the reasons that I hesitate [to designate them as such] is because there are law-abiding individuals in some of these groups, that spend their day trying to do the right thing."[99] In short, the cause of antiabortion groups, for Lewis, is not an existential threat to the United States specifically or the West in general. In this chapter I have shown how the designation of an actor, action, or utterance as an existential threat is made visible by interrogating two axes of coding terrorism: identity and incidence. The first rests on accusations that an otherness that threatens our way of life hides behind and is distorted by familiar faces or military fatigues. These accusations are made legible and actionable not through expositions on political motives, but through invocations of identity constructs, oscillating between their blurring and consolidation. The second rests on constituting each man as a once-future, now-realized copy of a past other. Each man's manifestation as such promises another iteration, a future-past that signals a perpetual potential, adding to the grave nature of a terrorist threat. In short, to transform violence to terrorism, it must be coded as foreign (within the familiar) and as a forever returning threat that aims at the destruction and/or transformation of the way "we" live.

The Double manifests in a variety of iterations in this process: as a familiar face, as an other hiding in plain sight, and as a future-past copy. The Double simultaneously encompasses the mechanisms and maneuvers through which terrorism is made sense of (coded or defined) and makes legible/localizes the perpetual potential that is the constitutive anxiety surrounding homegrown terrorism (all in an attempt to preempt or anticipate it). The Double as an adversary that cannot be named is part of a structure of enmity that facilitates a set of practices utilized by a multitude of actors with varying relations to one another. The Double not only is deployed by those positioned as terrorist, but has productive functions in counterterrorism efforts as well.

This requires some explanation. There is a fundamental qualitative difference between stating "We are at war with the Germans" and stating "We are at war with terrorism"—which correspond to Schmitt's ideas of conventional and absolute enmity, respectively. The former *names an enemy* in that it clearly situates one's adversary in a bounded space (i.e., Germany). The latter *delineates a threat* through what could be best described as a perforated line, one that can shift and expand, requiring one to include in anticipatory calculations spaces one might not initially suspect: lumberyards, Sikh temples, military bases. It reflects the blurred boundaries that characterize contemporary warfare and the ways that a variety of actors conjure it and react to its invocation. It requires more fluid ways of making sense of one's adversary. One of these is, as Galloway and Thacker suggest, through the concept of the network. An enemy that cannot be named circulates. In the following chapter I turn to this networked articulation of the Double, its historical reoccurrence, and its function and form in counterterrorism.

2

Informants and Other Media

Networking the Double

On October 15, 1949, New York's *Daily Mirror* ran the headline "Victory for America." At Foley Square in New York the day before, Eugene Dennis and ten other leaders of the Communist Party of the United States of America (CPUSA) were found guilty of conspiracy to teach and advocate the overthrow of the US government by force or violence under the Smith Act.[1] Almost six decades later, on December 22, 2008, a twenty-two-year-old naturalized American named Mohamad Ibrahim Shnewer along with Serdar Tatar and three brothers (Dritan, Shain, and Eljvir Duka) were convicted of conspiring to kill US military personnel at the Fort Dix military base in New Jersey.

In moments of national crisis, conspiracy charges become weapons in the ostensible struggle for security. Fears of Communist infiltration and jihadist radicalization form the backdrop of Foley Square and Fort Dix, respectively. Foley Square centered on the 1945 reestablishment of the CPUSA, a move that came after its disbandment and transformation into the Communist Political Association a year prior was publicly criticized by Jacques Duclos, the French Communist leader. Its reformation raised fears that American Communists were committed to a worldwide Communist plot. The Fort Dix case was triggered when a Circuit City employee contacted authorities about a video a customer had asked him to convert to DVD. In it, men were shooting guns at a firing range and speaking in Arabic. Two paid FBI informants would later befriend and implicate five of the men in a terror plot.

The use of the conspiracy charge is rarely uncontroversial. In sharp contrast to the celebratory announcements that the conviction of the CPUSA elite sent a strong message to Moscow, W. E. B. Du Bois wrote, "Nothing in my life has so shaken my belief in American democracy . . .

[the trial] marks the nadir [of] our hysteria and the determination to throttle free speech and make honest thinking impossible."[2] And, when New Jersey attorney general Christopher Christie praised law enforcement for preemptively stopping men who "wanted to be jihadists . . . a new brand of terrorism where a small cell of people can bring enormous devastation," critics called the plot "manufactured."[3]

In this chapter I use the historical resurfacing of the conspiracy charge vis-à-vis the Double to examine the relationship between connectivity, media/technology, and enmity. What makes the conspiracy charge an apt site for this inquiry is that it depends on establishing links between at least two individuals; in other words, it requires that the enemy be networked, directing focus to the surveillance technologies deployed in the process of networking and the media implicated in the resulting assemblage. Certainly, both now and then, an array of actors were/ are connected in a variety of ways. However, the network here is not an object of study but a method. By examining the effort exerted in making the shape of a network legible to juries and publics, I illustrate how the Double is made sense of through and in relation to media, as both threat and an answer to that threat.

In the contemporary moment, the network is certainly the structuring diagram of collective dreams and nightmares. Aspirations of increased peace brought about through the olive branches of connectivity persist in various circles despite having largely given way to epidemiological fears concerning the viruses and poisons (ideological, biological, and affective) to which connectivity makes us vulnerable. The network is a "weapons system." Al-Qaeda is a "network of networks."[4] ISIS has skillfully exploited networked social media to spread conflict beyond its declared borders. These assertions are often displayed in frozen images of dots and lines, as in Jytte Klausen's Western Jihadism Project (Figure 4), an example of the most distributed of computer scientist Paul Baran's network diagrams.[5] The most recent deployment of the network metaphor and diagram in the realm of security certainly owes much to the popularization of RAND researchers John Arquilla and David Ronfeldt's netwar doctrine in policy circles in the 1990s.[6] However, as the CPUSA conspiracy case suggests, the use of the network in both thinking and doing security predates the contemporary war on terror.

In 1934, Elizabeth Dilling, a fervent right-wing anti-Communist, published her infamous *The Red Network*, listing some 1,300 alleged Communists and 460 suspect organizations (including Albert Einstein and the ACLU).[7] The book was popular, though not as influential as Dilling herself claimed. Nevertheless, the same metaphor was one that found resonance in the Internal Security Act of 1950. The act names the "Communist network in the United States" as part of a "world Communist movement" that spreads through "treachery, deceit, infiltration into other groups (governmental and otherwise), espionage, sabotage, terrorism, and any other means deemed necessary."[8]

The threat of the red network was visualized in a starkly different way than the sparse geometric diagrams circulating today. The 1938 pamphlet produced by the Catholic Liberty Service, "How Communism Works" (Figure 3), depicts the Communist network as an octopus. The "cartographic land octopus," a popular image in maps intended to convey existential threat, first appeared in the last third of the nineteenth century.[9] It is not difficult to see why the cephalopod was an attractive creature on which to structure imaginaries of Communist threat as it possesses: an ability to camouflage; an aptitude for obfuscation found in the cloud of ink it emits on command, obscuring its movements; a powerful grasp provided by the two rows of suction cups found on each of its eight arms, which are themselves autotomizing, making her resilient to defeat and setback; and a bite largely hidden from sight containing a toxin used to paralyze its prey (producing the intoxicated Double).

There are dangers in using the network to understand complex social and political phenomena. Not only does the "network graph problematically [freeze] the temporality of [events]," but the concept is so ambiguous that French philosopher and sociologist Bruno Latour admits it ought to have been abandoned long ago.[10] In a more direct assault on the metaphor, sociologist Mark Erickson asserts that the network graph "explains nothing" and "reducing everything to network hides things from us, and makes us think we have been precise when we have been vague" (the very characteristics that make it compatible with the conspiracy charge).[11] There are perhaps even more pitfalls in deploying the network in a comparative context. Certainly the Cold War and the war on terror, with their accompanying diagrams, are not identical in design or consequence. There are a variety of important differences. The octo-

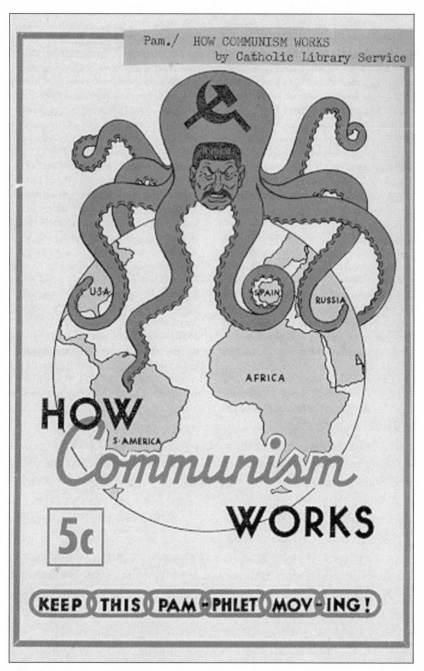

Figure 3. Catholic Library Service, 1938.

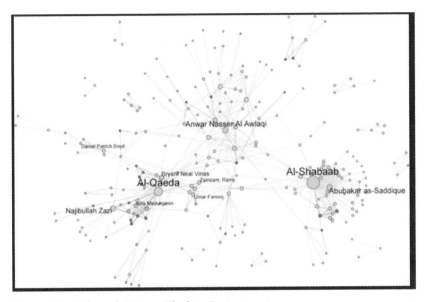

Figure 4. Jytte Klausen's Western Jihadism Project, 2006.

pus, resembling a centralized network, has a clear head/center (Stalin/ the Soviet Union) that most contemporary visualizations of networked adversaries lack, suggesting increasing decentralization and dispersion. Moreover, unlike the cephalopod diagram of the Cold War that exists in and on the globe, contemporary network diagrams are often, like the one above (Figure 4), mapped in the ether of the cloud. But it is this last difference that is the impetus for my inquiry. The network as octopus makes plainly visible the work that goes into networking, into thinking and practicing security in and through the network in a manner that contemporary geometric visualizations tend to obscure.

My interest in the Double vis-à-vis the network comes from the manner in which the figure was articulated in the Cold War. Thus, the first part of the chapter outlines just how the Double was conceptualized in security discourse in an America on the cusp of McCarthyism. The Foley Square trial marked a pivotal turning point against the backdrop of continuing hearings in front of the House Un-American Activities Committee and rising hysteria. Building on and contrasting to the notion of the Double of contemporary counterterrorism, a comparative examination of the Cold War Double further develops the figure's spatiality: as neither here nor there, but circulating through and in relation to a variety of media. Fears of infiltration and radicalization are not synonymous. They are historically specific and differently structured, one with an identifiable head, the other more amorphous. Nevertheless, both represent fears of connectivity.

The second part and bulk of the chapter shifts to how the Double was networked at Foley Square and Fort Dix. Often, when security and networks are mentioned in the same breath, the focus turns to the ways in which a variety of groups exploit social media in structure and content. In *The Shock of the Old*, the historian of technology David Edgerton argues that by focusing on new technologies in conflict, we miss the continued significance of the horse, that is, existing technologies of continued, if revamped, significance and consequence. In the context of security that old horse is the informant, a surveillance medium as old as political power itself that came into widespread use with the professionalization of the police in nineteenth-century Europe.[12] Here, I repurpose Arquilla and Ronfeldt's netwar doctrine into a heuristic through which to examine the informant's role in cultivating, curating, and eliciting the social, technological, and ideological links that tie his targets to a conspiratorial networked threat. An examination of the work of the informant reveals how the enemy network takes shape, how it is made legible, and how a variety of media are conceptualized therein and to what effect—all in relation to the Double.

The enemy that cannot be named is instead mapped in its movement through the circuits of a network, the shape of which is not self-evident. This suggests that the circulating-Double is epistemologically inseparable from the media it circulates in relation to as well as the surveillance practices used to make all of this legible. Further revealed through efforts to network the enemy is that the Double embodies more than a threat. The informant is the enemy-Double's inverse, a sheep in wolf's clothing—or perhaps a wolf in wolf's clothing. Thus, the Double is an ·incitatory figure in the work of anticipation and, ultimately, preemption.[13] While the other must be confined, the Double must be flushed out, a process that is not revelatory but productive—the Double "makes things happen." In other words, the enemy network is not something the informant simply infiltrates, but is ontologically and epistemologically inseparable from it. In the informant's work we see that conspiracy is not simply a counterbalance to fears of connectivity embodied in the

Double, but that conspiracy, as a security mechanism, depends on the productive exploitation of connectivity through the informant. Indeed, both conspiracy and connectivity are defined by the type of paranoia associated with the circulating-Double—not omnipotent, but potentially anywhere. The Double underwrites connectivity as a general feature of enmity, both anxiety and remedy; as the Catholic Liberty Service instructs, "Keep this pamphlet moving."

Seeing Double/Seeing Red

The media coverage of the Foley Square trial was largely structured around long-held notions that positioned Communism as antithetical to the American spirit, as its other. The *New York Post* wrote that the trial had revealed the "true nature of Communist loyalty . . . [which was] to a foreign capital rather than a revolutionary cause."[14] A sentiment soon after nested in the Internal Security Act of 1950, to be a Communist was to "repudiate [one's] allegiance to the United States." Even those who thought the trial absurd and saw the threat posed by Communist fifth columns as no more than a "bad joke" couched their arguments in this binary. After the convictions, journalist Max Lerner asserted that Communism had "no roots in the American soil, no appeal to the American mind."[15] In contrast to today's narratives of fundamentalism and hyper-religiosity, the foreign character of Communism depended on highlighting its atheism. In the lead-up to the trial, a concerned citizen wrote to the *Washington Post* that the country would come to see Communists as agents bent on destroying the concept of "the relationship of man to God . . . which gave birth to the American system and its institutions."[16] This was a regular theme at the House Un-American Activities Committee (HUAC) hearings on Communist infiltration of minority groups, held in the summer of 1949 as the Foley Square trial was in full swing. Prominent priests and rabbis appeared before the committee to affirm that their faith inoculated them from the toxins of Communist thought.[17] Inside the courthouse, the prosecution asserted the credibility of its star witness, Communist-turned-informant Louis F. Budenz, by stressing his return to the Catholic Church. (He dedicated his memoir, *This Is My Story*, to "Mary Immaculate, Patroness of Our Beloved Land.")[18] A tense exchange during a long aside on March 31, 1949, demonstrated the thorny nature of this distinction. One of the defense lawyers, Abraham Isserman, in an objection regarding the introduction into evidence of piecemeal and decontextualized passages of Communist texts, remarked, "Certainly you couldn't try any ideas of, say, Christianity by quoting a few passages out of the Bible." Judge Medina, the presiding magistrate, retorted sharply, "I really think that is a comment that you ought not make. How you can compare what we have been hearing here with the doctrines of Christianity is beyond me."[19]

The Second World War intensified fears of Communism within the United States, of the "rachitic child dropped on the U.S. doorstep by the Russian Revolution."[20] Certainly, much of the suspicion was directed at non-Americans. Against the backdrop of stoked fears of infiltration and fascist fifth columns, as early as 1939, 87 percent of Americans were in favor of a requirement for all noncitizens to register with the government, something the Smith Act of 1940 institutionalized.[21] However, there was also a considerable effort aimed at Americans. HUAC, established in 1938 under various commissions, became a standing committee in 1945 and was tasked with investigating subversive and un-American propaganda activities "instigated from foreign countries or of a domestic origin." The committee paid particular attention to Communist infiltration of minorities, education, entertainment, and government. The Smith Act, in addition to targeting foreigners, also sought to punish anyone who "willfully advocates, abets, advises, or teaches the duty, necessity, desirability, or propriety of overthrowing or destroying the government of the United States . . . by force or violence"; the trial of the CPUSA leaders would be the first in a series.

Despite the neat abstract division of American and Communist, the Communist was not easy to pick out. Philosophers Michael Hardt and Antonio Negri argue that during the Cold War the boundary between "inside" and "outside" began to unravel.[22] The cover of a 1948 New Jersey Manufacturers Association cartoon book captured this anxiety and serves here as an entry point into understanding the other-Double relation that took shape in post–World War II America:

> There is an ominous shadow looming over you, over your family, over your home, your job, your church—over your whole life. . . . This shadow

which comes from across the ocean, threatens to destroy <u>your</u> liberty, the liberty that cost so much in blood and sweat, and suffering. . . . What is this shadow? What is behind it? The dark shadow is Communism—and behind <u>Communism</u> is A PLOT TO STEAL THE WORLD!

The above caption accompanies an illustration of a shadow that covers Europe (as if invoking Marx), stretches across the Atlantic and creeps onto the northeastern seaboard. Behind the shadow is what one of the Foley Square defendants, Benjamin J. Davis Jr., critiqued as an unfairly depicted "lustful figure" with his feet firmly planted in the Soviet Union.[23] The shadow is one of the earliest manifestations of the Double, both an evil twin and a sign of potency (the loss of which portends imminent death). The casting of Communism's shadow represents a more amorphous and perhaps even more sinister threat than the Soviet Communist.

The mutability of the shadow that loomed over America was evident in the "miscellany of ordinary-looking U.S. citizens" that sat at the defense table at Foley Square. Thus, as a later Armed Forces propaganda film would instruct, "in recognizing a Communist, physical appearance counts for nothing." A Communist may be any race, ethnicity, and gender (the latter made clear by the film's interchangeable use of male and female pronouns in referring to Communists). Even more disconcerting was that the Communists' "chameleon-like" abilities were not incidental but thought to be a key part of their strategy, evident in their actions and words.[24] Again, at a HUAC hearing on the infiltration of minority groups held at the height of the trial, Lester B. Granger, director of the National Urban League, was asked, "Where can the line be drawn between Communist-front activities and Negro progressive activities?" He replied that at "certain times you can't draw the line . . . [that you] can't tell the difference," and that the kernel of any distinction between the two lies in whether the action was of a moral or political character.[25] And, as *Time* magazine noted, when Eugene Dennis outlined the principles of the CPUSA in the courtroom, "those principles sounded no more radical than Harry Truman's Fair Deal, no more revolutionary than the teachings of Abraham Lincoln."[26]

If, as Richard Nixon would later remark about Alger Hiss, "that men become Communists out of the best of motives," the conundrum presented by the shadowy-Double in red concerned how to understand one's transformation.[27] For example, how was one to make sense of the metamorphosis of Francis X. Waldron Jr., a regular American from Seattle "with his wavy brown hair, his snappy clothes and his electric smile . . . as handsome as a junior Arrow Collar Man" into Eugene Dennis, the general secretary of the CPUSA? *Time* magazine's profile traced Waldron's story from when he received all of his father's worldly goods from the hospital in which he died: "a crumpled leather cigarette case, a Seattle streetcar token, and a worn 25¢ piece." Not long after, "Frankie went to Europe, probably stopped in at Moscow, went to South Africa, on to China, then back to Moscow." By the time he found himself in a Shanghai apartment, "seedy-looking and burning-eyed, with a shock of wild hair . . . so far as he was concerned, Francis X. Waldron Jr. was dead and buried. Not a trace of him remained, not even a Seattle streetcar token."[28]

Time's profile of Dennis suggests that the Double is a fundamentally circulating figure, neither here nor there, but in motion. This narrative was articulated differently in the Fort Dix case. The Duka brothers' supposed involvement in the Fort Dix plot shocked members of their community. One neighbor expressed his surprise: "They were your everyday Muslims . . . I would have believed they were aliens before I'd think they were terrorists." Even the Circuit City employee who contacted authorities admitted, "if you saw the defendants at a strip mall in Jersey, you wouldn't look twice."[29] And, while each individual implicated in Fort Dix had a reported attachment to places outside of the United States (e.g., Shnewer to Palestine and Jordan, the Dukas to Albania, and Tatar to Turkey), what was most concerning to authorities was each one's virtual travels, through digital networks that led him to jihadist propaganda.[30] Ultimately, as much with Foley Square as with Fort Dix, the circulating nature of the Double is tied to communications technologies. Much like the way in which the electric light allowed Dr. Jekyll's double to roam freely, the neither here nor there positionality of the Double— not everywhere but potentially anywhere—is made sense of through and in relation to a variety of technologies, old and new. The emergence of the Double in security discourse cannot be separated from how threat is conceptualized through a network of people, places, and media.

Networking the Double

"Whoever masters the network gains the advantage." This is Arquilla and Ronfeldt's central dictum in their influential *Advent of Netwar*. In addition to emphasizing the exploitation of network structures offensively, they also stress the necessity of making sense of one's adversaries as networks, which requires a deep understanding of its nodes and edges.[31] There are three fundamental types of edges in their diagram: technological, social, and narrative (or ideological). This is the framework through which I retrace the informant's work.

The "parade of trusted 'communists' who revealed themselves in the courtroom as FBI agents" at Foley Square were matched by the small cadre of informants, agents, translators, and experts who took turns on the witness stand at the Fort Dix Five trial.[32] My primary focus is on the efforts of a pair of informants in each case, and the supporting roles played by expert witnesses. Louis F. Budenz, a labor organizer turned Communist turned expert informant, made a career of testifying at government cases against Communists. As much as his return to Catholicism lent him credibility, he leveraged his experience as the managing editor of the *Daily Worker*, the CPUSA's newspaper, to position himself as an expert of all things Communism. Herbert Philbrick volunteered to become an FBI informant after he reported the Communist leanings of a youth group he had joined. Fulfilling what he thought to be his patriotic duty, he made his way through a variety of groups. He broke his cover the day he took the stand at Foley Square, April 6, 1949.

Federal agents approached the primary informant of the Fort Dix case, Mahmoud Omar, in 2006 after they were apprised of the Circuit City DVD. Omar was acquainted with one of the men in the video, Mohamad Shnewer. Omar, who had entered the United States illegally and had a history of fraud convictions, was enticed into service for the FBI by the hope of obtaining legal status. While it is unclear as to whether this materialized, the FBI did help him get clearance to visit family in Egypt and return to the United States (despite being undocumented). The agency also paid him and covered his expenses. In total, he earned approximately $238,000. Besnik Bakalli, an undocumented Albanian, was deployed later to befriend the Duka brothers on account of their

shared ethnicity. In addition to the two informants, the networking of
the five men to global jihad depended on the testimonial performance
of Evan Kohlmann, known as the Doogie Howser of terrorism, who has
made a living off of providing "expert analysis" on the link between jihad
and the Internet. Kohlmann scours the Internet for jihadist propaganda
and maintains a database. Lacking fluency in Arabic (most of the videos
he analyzed were in Arabic, and he depended on translations), he bases
his credibility on his bachelor's and law degrees as well as his certificate
in "Islam and Muslim Understanding" from the Prince Walebtatal Center for Muslim Christian Understanding at Georgetown University.[33]

These two historical moments are as different as the network diagrams
that define each adversary. Yet, examining how the social, technological, and narrative/ideological links were cultivated, curated, and elicited (and made legible) in and through the informant reveals more than
just the continued relevance of the informant in security practice. First,
more than just a listening post—as the NYPD refers to its informants—
that is, a passive sensor capable of collecting uncontaminated data, an
analysis of the informants' own accounts and performances on the stand
uncovers a more active function.[34] Second, retracing how the enemy
network is given shape in trying conspiracy illustrates both the relation
between the enemy-Double and the media that circulate within this network as well as the place of the Double in security, rather than simply
its object-enemy.

Comrades/Brothers

Social ties are a key dimension of the netwar doctrine. Arquilla and
Ronfeldt directly connect the strength of social ties to a network's effectiveness. Of course, this depends on what is meant by effectiveness.
Sociologist Mark Granovetter theorized long ago not only that weak ties
were important for the mass diffusion of information but that a weak
tie is more likely to connect individuals from different groups.[35] As Latour
argues, the strength of a network overall "does not come from concentration, purity, and unity, but form dissemination, heterogeneity, and the
careful plaiting of weak ties."[36] Nevertheless, what Arquilla and Ronfeldt
identify as the base of social ties, mutual trust and a sense of identity, are
certainly necessary for holding a network together, particularly one that

aims to act out in the physical world. They argue that these are strongest in the "clan ties" of "ethnically based" groups. In the digital age, notions of "remote intimacy" act as a stand-in for the seeming lack of direct social ties between homegrown terrorists and those for whom they claim to work.[37] Undoubtedly, both al-Qaeda and ISIS attempt to foster a sense of shared identity across national and ethnic groups in and through their propaganda efforts. The work of informants in this regard depends on the context in which they are placed. For instance, while there (still) exists a Communist Party in the United States, there is no comparative organization of jihadists. The common thread that runs through informants' work across these different moments is that for informants to be able to do their work, to function as they are supposed to—and to establish the necessary credibility they exploit on the stand—they must cultivate trust and a shared identity at a local level.

Formed in 1919, the Communist Party of the United States of America was frequently, if not constantly, the object of suspicion or active repression. As the primary organization through which American Communists developed and deepened a sense of shared identity, it organized a variety of clubs, schools, and classes, none of which were particularly secret. For instance, the party headquarters was listed and could be reached by phone. Yet, the landscape of social spaces that concerned authorities was far broader. Subsection 3(1) of the Internal Security Act defined an organization as "a group of persons, whether or not incorporated, permanently or temporarily associated together for joint action on any subject or subjects." Effectively, informal study groups and book clubs constituted nodes in a larger conspiratorial network, one defined not just by institutions but also by more fluid social relations.

Budenz and Philbrick came into this social setting in very different ways. Budenz was a labor organizer who was arrested on multiple occasions for his activities. He joined the Communist Party in 1935, a moment he described in detail in his memoir. As he sat in front of a boarded-up warehouse at the foot of the Williamsburg Bridge in Brooklyn, he read an account of Georgi Dimitrov's speech at the Seventh World Congress of the Communist International in the *Daily Worker*. His excitement regarding what he saw as a move that gave American Communists more autonomy led him to the party. He characterized his work for the Communist Party as always strained, trying to balance his faith and his belief in the cause of labor. He claimed to have left the party once he no longer saw this balance as tenable, returning to the Church in 1945; it was then that he began to cooperate with the government as an expert informant. During his time in the party, Budenz worked for a variety of Communist newspapers. He eventually worked his way up to the position of managing editor of the *Daily Worker* in 1940. The paper's offices were located on the eight floor of 50 East 13th Street in Manhattan, just a floor below the party headquarters. There he established a rapport with Eugene Dennis and Jack Stachel, who was the newspaper's editor. He conferred with them about the paper's content either by making the trip up to the ninth floor or through a direct phone line. He also lectured on Communist journalism for the party.[38]

Herbert Philbrick took another path. He joined the Cambridge Youth Council in 1940 and soon after became alarmed by what he saw as the increasing leverage of Communist thought in its ranks. According to this memoir, he approached the FBI despite doubting his anxieties. When the FBI validated his concerns, he volunteered to work for the agency as an undercover informant. Two years later the FBI suggested that he join the Youth Communist League and approved of his secret move into the Communist Party. Philbrick reported on what was discussed at party meetings and who attended; he provided the agency with the literature that circulated therein. As an advertising executive, Philbrick worked on pamphlets for the party, taught at a Communist school, acted as an educational director for some subgroups, and was entrusted with reestablishing a party group in Wakefield, Massachusetts. He was also an alternative delegate at the July 1945 Convention of the Communist Political Association of New England. Both Philbrick and Budenz were at one time well-entrenched and trusted members of the circles in which they ran.

Despite their differing paths into the party—Philbrick's being more directly guided by the FBI—their work on the stand was similar. Both men not only described their place within the network but, more importantly, characterized the social ties that held the Communist network together in a manner that lent itself to conspiracy: as hierarchical and secretive. Much of the trial was focused on illustrating that the CPUSA was a Moscow-controlled conspiratorial group; while the party certainly had international ties (e.g., the Communist International), the reconstitution of the party (after it had been the Communist Political Association under Eric Browder's leadership) was framed as an unchallenged order rather than the result of a more complex political process within the United States. Both men framed their experiences in ways that illustrated such control at the micro level within the party. Budenz characterized his conferences with Dennis and Stachel as a "continuous supervision" and equated other meetings to "the lecture of a teacher to a class."[39] Philbrick, who wrote in his memoir that he "was never free from close scrutiny," added on the stand that those who wanted to participate in panel discussions at group meetings had to organize their materials in advance, suggesting that their words required approval (rather than giving other participants a chance to familiarize themselves with material).[40] Budenz communicated the control within the party most alarmingly during his cross-examination. He was asked why he did not simply resign and leave the party instead of making a public spectacle of his exit—the defense accused Budenz of owing the party money and leaving as he did to avoid paying his debts. In response, Budenz conveyed the prosecution's characterization of the CPUSA in a single phrase, "You can't escape from the Communist Party that easily."[41]

Branding the CPUSA as part of conspiratorial movement also depended on articulations of secrecy, which the informants claimed to have uncovered. Both Budenz and Philbrick described various party meetings as being held in secret. Yet, Budenz admitted that the "secret schools" for training party leadership were regularly reported on in the *Daily Worker*, which, as the defense pointed out, openly worked to increase its readership—efforts Budenz himself described as "very strenuous." Much of Budenz's secretive characterization rested on the lack of detail with which he conveyed his experiences. One particular meeting was held in "the winter of 1939 or 1940 . . . after the Hitler-Stalin Pact," the location of which was a basement "in a building in Chicago, a big building." Budenz attributed his vague recollection to vast number of secret meetings he had attended. Similarly, when Philbrick was asked if branch meetings were open to the public, he replied, "Not in the generally accepted sense of the word, no." He went on to claim that the only nonmembers in attendance were potential, and thoroughly vetted, recruits.[42]

The indictment included "others unknown," and both men also testified to this fact by stressing the use of "party names," aliases to avoid identification.[43] In his memoir, Philbrick recalls the first thing he was told by a fellow Communist when becoming involved with the Youth Communist League: "Naturally, your membership will not be known publicly. . . . You needn't be afraid of that."[44] On the stand, he went on to describe his interactions with shadowy figures, "a man named Pete," and others who went by single names.[45] These individuals were, in effect, the "fellow-travelers" and "crypto-Communists" that were often the subject of inquiry in front of HUAC.[46] The defense argued that the use of subgroups and assumed names needed to be put into context. Given the stigma and consequences that came with identifying as a Communist, many individuals in their membership feared losing their jobs. The anxiety was particularly acute in 1948 when the Mundt-Nixon Bill was being considered in Congress. It would have required any member of the Communist Party to register with the attorney general. In his memoir, Budenz articulated that regardless of the historical circumstances, secrecy was, in practice, fundamentally un-American. Moreover, Philbrick neatly tied the use of false names to the hierarchy of the party. In response to accusations that he had in fact proposed the use of assumed names at one meeting (to further his work for the FBI), he claimed that the practice was an order that "would come from above some place. It wasn't up to us to decide that."[47]

* * *

Mahmoud Omar and Besnik Bakalli were not tasked with infiltrating al-Shabaab or al-Qaeda. For the Circuit City employee who received a videotape showing a group of men firing guns and speaking in Arabic, it was the stuff of post-9/11 television. Programs like *24* and *Sleeper Cell* featuring jihadist fifth columns preparing to strike the homeland, though the one he thought he witnessed was clearly very sloppy if the supposed cell had in fact entrusted incriminating material to a complete stranger.[48] (Jihadist sleeper cells are virtually nonexistent in the American context.) The resulting deployment of informants seemed to closely follow the netwar doctrine. Omar was sent to befriend Mohamad Shnewer not only because Omar knew him, but because the two men shared nominal markers of identity: both Arab and Muslim. Similarly, Bakalli, like the Duka brothers, was a native Albanian. Bakalli was befriended by the brothers when they saw him sitting at the Dunkin' Donuts they frequented, speaking on his phone in Albanian loud enough for those around to hear as instructed by the FBI. Instead of plugging into already-existing organizations, Omar and Bakalli worked to develop social relationships with their targets by developing trust through performing acts of friendship and fostering a sense of family.

Omar had met Shnewer at the latter's family store in 2005 but had not befriended him until instructed to do so by the FBI in 2006. Omar, sixteen years Shnewer's senior, began to assert himself as an older brother—"You know that I am like your older brother," he was once recorded saying—or father figure, regularly referring to Shnewer as "my son." When asked by the defense if he was trying to create a sense of comfort one usually feels around family, Omar replied plainly, "That's the only way to get him to trust me and talk to me."[49]

Omar solidified his position as Shnewer's quasi-guardian through persistently warning Shnewer to avoid someone called "American Mahmoud"—a nickname the men used for an acquaintance named Joe DeStefano to distinguish him from Omar, the "Egyptian Mahmoud." American Mahmoud candidly spoke about violence and jihad even at the wedding of Eljvir Duka to Shnewer's sister. This, Omar said on the witness stand, rubbed him the wrong way. The defense pressed Omar about American Mahmoud. If Omar's job was to report suspicious activity to the FBI, why had he not told his handler about American Mahmoud? The defense suggested that the FBI had in fact told him to warn Shnewer about American Mahmoud to further secure his trust. Irrespective of the motivation, Omar did precisely that and asked the Duka brothers to similarly warn Shnewer.

As his work progressed, Omar worried that the Duka brothers and Serdar Tatar did not trust him, the impetus for deploying Bakalli. Tatar, twenty-three years old at the time and with aspirations of becoming a police officer, reported Omar to the Philadelphia Police Department after Omar repeatedly pressured him to get a map of the Fort Dix army base. Afterward, Tatar recorded a conversation with Omar in preparation for when he expected the FBI to call. And when agents—who were aware of Omar's operation—finally came to his door, they downplayed the threat.[50] There were indications, however, that Omar had developed a good relationship with the Dukas, particularly Tony (Dritan's nickname). Omar did favors for the brothers, fixing their cars (he was a mechanic) and taking them to car auctions (as a dealer he was able to give them access to government auctions); he once loaned Eljvir money to buy a car when the latter was in trouble financially. Omar also bonded with Tony by claiming to understand, like Tony, the harsh realities of growing up "on the streets" (the truthfulness of Omar's claim is unclear). Over time, signs of friendship and trust multiplied. Omar was invited to Eljvir's wedding and to join the brothers on fishing and paintball trips. At times he was invited without Shnewer—who had introduced Omar to the brothers—because the Dukas, for the most part, did not like Shnewer. Most importantly, the brothers expressed trust at key moments of the operation. Tony felt nervous about purchasing guns illegally through Omar, even if he had wanted them only for use at a gun range. Ultimately, despite his reservations, Tony told Shnewer, "I trust you brother."[51]

Bakalli came later, posing as a fellow Albanian who was going through a divorce and experiencing financial trouble. He told the brothers that he was forced to leave Albania because he had killed a man who had raped his sister. As their friendship grew, Bakalli would regale the Duka brothers with (fake) war stories about fighting with the Kosovo Liberation Army. After some time, he began to regularly eat dinner and drink coffee with the Dukas. Later, he asked the brothers to help him be a better Muslim, to which they agreed. It is then that jihad became a more frequent topic of discussion at Bakalli's seemingly naïve behest.[52]

The only person with whom Omar discussed a plot was Shnewer (he did ask Tatar for a map, but did not disclose any details, hoping instead that Shnewer would speak with him). Exploiting their mentor-mentee relationship, Omar had convinced Shnewer to assign him as the leader of the plot: "And if you appoint me as the Amir [sic], leader, I should be able to tell you which, uh, uh, plan could be done, what can be executed, who should be present and what are your possibilities."[53] In this passage, Omar transformed his position of authority and respect into one of a military advisor. As such, Omar constantly pushed Shnewer to plan an attack, berating him for being all talk and no action—the Dukas knew Shnewer to be a big talker who rarely fulfilled his promises and thought him likely to be emotionally disturbed. Omar demanded deadlines for assembling a team, attempting to move the process along by constantly bringing up Eljvir in conversation with Shnewer: eleven times on August 2, 2006; thirty-four times on an August 4 to 5 fishing trip; thirty-one times on August 11; fifty times on August 13 and 14; forty times on August 20; twenty-five times on August 30; twenty-five times the next day; forty-five times on September 14; and thirty-seven times on September 19.[54] To satisfy Omar's demands Shnewer told him that the brothers were on board, which always turned out to be false based on Omar's own interactions with the Dukas. Omar also insisted Shnewer perform surveillance, which Shnewer never did save the one time he was accompanied by Omar. He attempted to goad Shnewer into action by complaining that the latter's skittishness about buying weapons was making him look bad in the eyes of a (fictional) Baltimore arms dealer. Similarly, Bakalli attempted to use his currency as a supposed freedom fighter to rile the Dukas into action, telling them that without acting one is a coward.[55] Both men, though Omar more than Bakalli, worked to cultivate social ties not in an effort to infiltrate an existing cell, but in a manner that would constitute their targets as the "Fort Dix Five."

By recalling how they cultivated social ties, or as in the case of Foley Square in using their position to characterize the social ties of a group, the informants began to populate the enemy network with a variety of nodes. Budenz and Philbrick present a network consisting of party leaders and countless shadowy doubles that move in a variety of spaces over which the network is laid: the offices of the *Daily Worker*, the Communist Party headquarters, and more ephemeral spaces such as living rooms, basements, and bookshops. The hierarchical social ties may suggest a direct mode of control, but as the details of both the technological and ideological ties come into focus, they reveal a more complex structure. The arms of the Red Octopus are not completely under the control of its head. In a more dispersed environment, Omar and Bakalli worked to constitute a cell through social ties, to draw a dot on the geometric plane of jihad that could be labeled "the Fort Dix Five." Just as Omar pushed Shnewer to act in ways that would establish the cell, so too were the informants instrumental in establishing the technological ties that would connect this cell to other nodes in global jihad.

Books/Videos (and a Pizza Delivery Map)

The shape a network takes is, to some degree, a function of the communications technologies utilized therein. Arquilla and Ronfeldt argue that netwar is afforded its capacity "by the latest information and communication technologies—cellular telephones, fax machines, electronic mail (email), web sites, and computer conferencing."[56] However, care must be taken not to fetishize technologies and cut them off from the social relations in which they are situated. By focusing on the work of the informant, I intend to denaturalize the role of technologies that are implicated in conspiracies by showing how their use and characterization are the result of much effort. In other words, I am interested in outlining how the communications technologies situated in international Communism and global jihad—broadly defined to include that which either is used in or facilitates the transfer of information—are positioned as what Latour calls "actants," objects whose mere presence can change a state of affairs. The positioning of books and videos as actants in an enemy network is made visible in the intense focus placed on their transfer, exchange, and circulation in the courtroom. The edges established by the movement of these media are facilitated and made legible as such by the informant.

Throughout the second Red Scare various modes of communication were thought to aid the reach of the Red Octopus. Similar to the red flag that traveling to Pakistan or Yemen raises today, traveling to the Soviet Union or another Communist nation was similarly incriminating. The prosecution at Foley Square made a point of stressing the defendants' "almost yearly trips to Moscow."[57] A common theme in the HUAC hearings, those summoned to appear in front of the committee were also questioned about long-distance phone calls. Within the United States, the means of communication between American Communists were also of concern. On the stand, Philbrick gave an account of how small subgroups would communicate with the party apparatus largely through human couriers. Each subgroup would elect a member to represent them at the next level of the chain of command, and so on.[58]

Yet, of most concern was neither air travel nor the telephone, but an even older means of information transfer: the book. On March 29, 1949, Judge Medina reminded the courtroom that part of the conspiracy charge concerned the fact that the "defendants would publish and circulate and cause to be published and circulated books, articles, magazines and newspapers advocating the principles of Marxism-Leninism."[59] The defense contested the manner in which the books were introduced as evidence:

> Indeed, frequently, with a triumphant flourish the prosecution produces the "very book" (another one is obtainable at any public library) that was used by the witness in his class. . . . The ever-present goal of the prosecution is to create the impression with the jury that these books are dangerous weapons, *secretly smuggled from reader to reader* and produced at the trial only as a result of the daring of the government informer.[60]

The circulation ("secret smuggling") of Communist texts was a principal issue at trial in addition to their content, and the informants had much to do with making apparent their exchange and circulation as secretive and sinister.

Budenz's testimony began with a series of simple questions. Did he receive a particular text from Jack Stachel (his boss at the *Daily Worker*)? Did he recognize another? The texts in question included Moissaye J. Olgin's "Why Communism?," "Program of the Communist International," Stalin's *Foundations of Leninism*, Lenin's *State and Revolution* and *Imperialism*, among others. After providing an affirmative answer, select portions of each text would be introduced as evidence and read aloud in the courtroom (and onto the record, at Judge Medina's request). Beyond acting as a passive conduit, a circuit that by answering in the affirmative allowed a text or book to be read into evidence, Budenz also played a twofold active role on the stand. The first was to provide a personal account, constituting proof of the circulation and exchange of the texts within the Communist network. In doing so he was sure to characterize any transfer of texts, whether passing through the hands of the defendants or not, as incriminating them:

Q: Did Mr. Stachel give you any copy of Dimitrofff's [sic] speeches at the Seventh Congress?

A: Not directly.

Q: Well, did he give you any copy at all directly or indirectly?

A: He gave it to me indirectly in the sense that we all received it and the Political Committee approved of it and he was a member, but he did not personally give me a copy, so far as I remember.[61]

Second, in order to make the circulation of texts an issue of conspiracy, Budenz, along with Philbrick, worked hard to dehistoricize the works in the face of defense assertions that the texts' focus on "historical conditions" signaled a necessity for interpretation, rather than literal reading. On the stand, Philbrick equated any text that was considered "just a historical document" with one the party would "pay no attention to," implying that the only works considered timeless and worthy of circulation were those read to the letter.[62] It was a characterization reinforced by Budenz and Philbrick's repeated referral to the Communist texts in question as "manuals" and "textbooks"—complementary to the prosecution's assertion that the Russian Revolution acted as a "blueprint" for the CPUSA.[63] The act of possessing Communist texts was evidence of Communist "thought control" and of participating in their circulation, of being, along with the text itself, a link in the chain of conspiracy.

Much of the prosecution's argument suggested that the books were on trial as much as any individual—a regular charge from critics of the trial.[64] In his closing argument, chief prosecutor John F. X. McGohey attempted to dispel this charge. However, belying his own effort, McGohey's remarks make more explicit that which Budenz and Philbrick's testimonies more subtly suggested, revealing the positioning of texts as actants (and thus part of the conspiracy being tried):

We are not concerned with the innocent use of books or papers or publications. We are concerned with the use of such material as an instrument in the commission of a crime. Now let me give you an example: A chisel, a hammer, and a baseball bat on the shelf of a store. They are perfectly innocent objects; perfectly innocent. But if three men intent upon robbing a home take those objects and use them as a means to gain entry into the home, as a means to subdue the occupants of the home, and as a means of opening the cabinets and the closets, then of course these objects are no longer mere innocent objects . . . and how silly, how silly it would be for the defendants in such a case to argue, as these defendants have argued here, that the baseball bat, or the hammer, or the chisel were on trial and not the criminals who used them.[65]

What is effective about McGohey's analogy is that the objects to which he compares a book can easily be imagined in their "innocent use"—a chisel is for sculpting, a hammer for building, and a baseball bat for playing a sport. Yet, in strategically leaving these uses unsaid and describing the objects as nonthreatening only when "on the shelf"—all the while suggesting robbery and murder—any benign use of a Communist text becomes unimaginable. His juxtaposition implies that taking a Communist text "off the shelf," simply putting it into circulation, constitutes an act of aggression, conspiracy, and potential murder. Throughout the trial, in the testimony of the informants and the arguments of the prosecution, what mattered was not the manner in which either informant had witnessed a book being taught, or any interpretation that any of the defendants might have articulated (whether encouraging the violent overthrow of the US government or not). Rather, it was the texts themselves that transformed the reader/teacher into the "voice of the Kremlin."[66] Here, the book, not the teacher, is the intoxicating agent that changes the state of an individual. Thus, to put them into circulation— through production, exchange, "teaching," recommendation, or "secret smuggling"—is tantamount to teaching or advocating the violent overthrow of the government.[67] The book, as actant, is in effect constituted as a suction cup on the Red Octopus's arm, extending Moscow's dangerous reach.

* * *

The Fort Dix sting operation was triggered by a DVD, foreshadowing the prominence of jihadist videos both in the informants' work and as evidence at trial. Digital media occupy a central position in theories of radicalization and discourses of homegrown terrorism, posited therein as indirectly (and at times directly) connecting an individual to like-minded individuals, providing a space in which one might immerse oneself in an alternate narrative-reality and, ultimately, portending one's turn to violence. Mohamad Shnewer did indeed download a few jihadist videos. He also offered his password to Eljvir Duka for a website on which one could view Anwar al-Awlaki's translation and interpretation of Yusuf al-Uyayri's "The Constants of Jihad" (a lecture that is also available on YouTube). Both Shnewer and Tony Duka were recorded on occasion praising al-Awlaki for providing "raw and uncut" commentary.[68]

The significance of Shnewer's actions and words in this regard was hardly self-evident, a problem not lost on the prosecution. Procuring the services of Evan Kohlmann, a self-proclaimed terrorism expert, the prosecution used his testimony to convey to the jury exactly how the possession of jihadist propaganda connected the defendants to global jihad. Aside from describing and interpreting the content via translations (to which I will return below) Kohlmann explained the significance of the videos' authors or stars. Much like the admission of Communist texts through Budenz at Foley Square, Kohlmann made apparent the importance of a variety of figures in the jihadist network—Osama bin Laden, Anwar al-Awlaki, Ayman al-Zawahiri, and Adam Gadahn. Also, in sifting through what he characterized as Shnewer's "very wide compendium" of some of al-Qaeda's "most significant" videos, Kohlmann made a point of stressing their "high resolution."[69] In effect, the clarity of the images served to analogize the clearness of the link between the Fort Dix Five and global jihad.

For Kohlmann, the act of downloading and, thus, extending the circulation of jihadist propaganda presented an even more sinister possibility. Shnewer had used LimeWire, a now defunct peer-to-peer file-sharing client program, to download videos. In his testimony, Kohlmann stressed that LimeWire had a chat function. During his cross-examination, Kohlmann was pressed further on the subject:

> Q: Right. The answer is you've not been presented with any evidence
>   that [a direct chat] did occur, correct?
> A: I—I wasn't able to recover it. The answer is I don't know. Again, I
>   want to be very clear here because there might be. I don't know.
> Q: All right. So when you don't know something, you can't say that it
>   did occur, correct?
> A: I can only say—I can only say—say it again. The only thing I can say
>   for sure through the Limewire [sic] was the high resolution jehadi
>   [sic] propaganda videos were specifically selected, were searched for,
>   selected, picked and downloaded from other supporters of jehad [sic]

on the internet. What else they may have—what other communications, I don't know, but there was a communications link.[70]

Despite the lack of any forensic evidence that the defendants had directly chatted with anyone, Kohlmann maintained that the men might have established contact with those from whom they were downloading videos. He framed these shadowy avatars—here Communist Party names are replaced by screen names—as "other supporters of jihad," suggesting that the defendants had found their kin online.

As much as an online community of others facilitated Shnewer's procurement of jihadist videos, the role of the informant in establishing this technological link cannot be understated. Omar provided Shnewer with the technological means to store and share the videos, a burner drive paid for by the FBI. The burner drive was intended to allow Shnewer to make physical copies and hand them to Omar, facilitating something similar to what we saw at Foley Square; the informant intercepts (and makes visible) the exchange of actants. More significantly, the effect of Omar is evident in the way Shnewer's online activity sharply changes once Omar is in the picture:

[Shnewer downloaded a] total of two, three, four, five videos, before . . . relating to and interacting with Omar. Now, let's see what happens in June of 2006; four videos. July of 2006, 13 videos. August of 2006—and this is when Omar's really pouring it on. . . . Let's look at the downloads in August of 2006 from his [Omar's] pushing and prodding and inducing. 30. September of 2006; 44.[71]

In all, 96 of the 101 videos found on Shnewer's hard drive were downloaded during the time his relationship with Omar was growing.[72] Just as Omar pushed Shnewer for plot details and deadlines, he further exploited their mentor-mentee relationship by constantly pressuring Shnewer for more videos and DVDs, often berating his mentee for taking so long to fulfill his requests. Here, the informant is much more than a passive listening post, but an indispensable actor in solidifying a defendant's technological links to global jihad.

At this juncture, the efforts of Kohlmann and Omar come together in a remarkable way to belie the active role of the informant. Kohlmann testified that the videos do more than motivate an individual; they fundamentally instill a sense of obligation in the viewer without further guidance or contact. Effectively, Kohlmann characterizes the videos as actants.[73] While this cannot be completely separated from the content of the videos, the prosecution (like at Foley Square) stressed their circulation. What is important here is that positioning the videos as agents of radicalization absolves the informant of any responsibility, rendering his pushing and prodding in the context of the social/familial relationship he had cultivated as ultimately unproblematic. The informant's cultivated intimacy is denied significance and his role is maintained as passively making legible the men's technological links to global jihad rather than curating edges between the men and other nodes. In effect, possessing the product of an al-Qaeda operative connects the men to the network; exchanging the videos among themselves constitutes the Fort Dix Five as part of a conspiracy in league with al-Qaeda.

Without an established cell or organization to infiltrate, Omar and Bakalli also utilized technology to establish the Fort Dix Five as a conspiratorial cell (supplementing the social ties they cultivated). Omar was fully aware that a conspiracy charge would not stick if he had only discussed a variety of plot points with each defendant individually. Thus, he attempted to facilitate the use of technology between the men in order to generate proof. For instance, Omar instructs Shnewer to call Tony and ask about how many guns he wanted from Omar's dealer (something Omar had already directly discussed with Tony).[74] Omar also pressured Shnewer to conduct surveillance, utilizing technologies that one might expect a terrorist to use in planning an attack (e.g., cameras and cell phones), creating a forensic trail of images and video. Aside from one short outing with Omar—during which neither took take any images or video—Shnewer never again went on a scouting mission. Compounded by Shnewer's constant lies regarding the Dukas' involvement, Omar complains to the Dukas (in a conversation captured by his own wire) that Shnewer is bullshitting him. While on the stand Shnewer's attorney asked Omar about this incident: "Were you now starting to form the impression, and excuse my language, that Mohamad was bullshitting you in his interaction?" Omar ignores both the evidence and his cultivated relationship with Shnewer by simply stating, "It was very easy for Mohamad to tell me I have nothing to do with this issue and I don't want to do anything."[75]

The wires worn by Omar and Bakalli, as well as the CCTV cameras planted in Omar's home, were key accessories in giving the impression that the informants in the case were mere listening posts. Omar, for example, was instructed to never be with his targets without his hidden wiretap. However, the active character of the informant's work is found in that both Omar and Bakalli switched off their recording devices, at times on their own accord, at others on instruction. Their active function became even more pronounced when Omar's accompanying technology failed and he resorted to becoming a medium himself, in two very different senses. First, Omar conjured connections (much like Kohlmann's potential online chats). Omar insisted, "I'm the one who lived every minute and every second in all this case and I know everything about this case and everything about this case is in my head."[76] When asked in turn about a trip the men took to the Poconos and whether any plot to kill military personnel or otherwise was discussed, he accounted for each of his blind spots (and those of the technology that accompanied him) by repeating, "In front of me, didn't happen." Here, Omar is maintaining that, based on his deep knowledge of the men "in his head," it was possible that such exchanges might have been made outside of his ear's (or mic's) range.

Second, in the absence of direct connections, Omar took on the role of middleman. One of the centerpieces of the investigation was a pizza delivery map. Shnewer had repeatedly failed to provide Omar with a map of the Fort Dix base, which he was supposed to obtain from Tatar, whose family owned a pizza shop in the base's general vicinity. Omar resorted to directly asking Tatar. Tatar, despite having reported Omar to the authorities, eventually came through (on November 28, 2006). Omar's efforts then turned to gathering the men in his home, in front of his CCTV cameras, to discuss the map and "plot" together (Tatar was still unaware of the details of any plot). When this meeting also failed to materialize—largely due to Shnewer's obfuscation—Omar then simply handed Shnewer the map directly on December 29, 2006. In effect, the only piece of physical evidence involving planning was exchanged through Omar. Once in possession, Shnewer did not share the map with anyone else. What is peculiar about this exchange is that Shnewer, who was capable of downloading videos, did not simply use Google Maps, which would have provided a much more accurate and detailed map. Barring this, Omar had to improvise and establish an exchange that would help constitute a conspiracy.

In curating technological ties—exchanging books, downloading videos—informants further made legible the nodes of the enemy network. This includes the Communist and jihadist elite. More importantly, the work of the informants constituted the books and videos as nodes of a curious sort—latent, circulating, and imbued with a particular power. In effect, the books constitute a series of suction cups on the Red Octopus's arms, which could be put into motion and latch onto another space or individual. The videos, on the other hand, made up a constellation of latent nodes waiting to be downloaded, uploaded, and copied. These media are not stationary, but move through circuits of exchange, either in the movement of the Red Octopus's arms or in the vague orbital trajectories of geometric lines in pure space.[77] And once put into circulation, they have the power to change the state of the affairs. A Communist text or jihadist video travels from one node to another, changing the internal makeup of each as it moves along. The threat posed by the Double, the anxiety it imbues, and thus the Double itself is inherently tied to these actant-objects. The Double is made sense of in, through, and in relation to these media. Positioned as actants in security thinking, these objects also guarantee their own recirculation. These dangerous objects threaten to intoxicate individuals, transforming them into (Communist or jihadist) automatons that will further replay the exchange through a potentially endless chain of party or screen names.

The relation between the various ties in networking the enemy is complex. Already indicated above is that social ties are used to generate technological ties. The implication at Foley Square was that the trusted position of the informants is what led to the exchange of books through them. At Fort Dix, the cultivated familial relationships provided the leverage through which to curate technological links to jihad and the supposed cell itself. While I have attempted to discuss technological ties (via books and videos) separately from their content—and, indeed, the very fact of their circulation and exchange is a key part of the prosecution of conspiracies—doing so always already hints at the centrality of ideological ties in networking the enemy, to which I now turn.

Double Talk/the Perfect Cover

Arquilla and Ronfeldt assert that narrative, which they interchangeably refer to as a common story, doctrine, or ideology, is vital to maintaining and, thus, understanding networked groups who lack ethnic or "clan" ties. Mirroring this line of thought, perhaps the most decisive work of the informant is that of showing the perpetrators to be true believers, that their motive can be articulated in and through an anti-American narrative or ideology. A shared narrative communicates an (in)human connectedness, filling in the gaps left by a lack of clear social and technological ties or their ambiguity; intertwining narrative in the social and technological also makes them more flexible and robust. The ideological is the lifeblood of the Red Octopus as well as its venom, it is also the plane on which a geometric network can be drawn, supporting and running through all of the nodes and edges therein. The work of the informant in this regard involves translating and interpreting the words and actions of their targets as part of "the narrative."

The defendants at Foley Square were avowed Communists. Yet, despite the general disdain toward Communism in public discourse, the men had to be tied to a more specific narrative. Ostensibly, it was not a crime to assert that capitalism is fundamentally unjust. Thus, while the exchange and circulation of Communist texts surely constituted ideological links, the task of linking the defendants to a conspiracy required that their expressions of Communist thought (and those in the texts) be characterized as signaling a belief in the inevitability and desirability of the violent overthrow of the US government. The informant was indispensable in this regard, acting as a translator of Communist discourse.

A common refrain at HUAC sessions stressed: "[when] Communists and their kind talk about 'democracy' and 'equality,' they are using *double talk*. They use good words in their own topsy-turvy way, to cover up bad intentions."[78] The double talk of Communism had a name—Aesopianism. Originally advanced by J. Edgar Hoover in his March 1947 testimony in front of the Thomas-Rankin Committee, the theory was based on a single excerpt from Lenin's *Imperialism* and an editorial footnote therein. In the passage, Lenin outlines why coded language was a necessity for revolutionaries in Tsarist Russia; it was a means to avoid censorship. He called this Aesopian language, after the ancient Greek fabulist Aesop.[79] In his memoir, Budenz admits that some of the secrecy practiced by the Communist Party in the United States has historical roots, stemming from anti-Communist efforts such as the Palmer Raids between November 1919 and January 1920. However, for him it is ultimately a strategy in extending the reach of the Red Octopus. Judge Medina not only allowed the theory to be advanced at trial, but regularly expressed opinions that aligned with it. On March 25, 1949, he commented that Communists had a "curious way of expressing themselves in . . . articles and resolutions. . . . It seems to me like a special jargon." He later added, "words that seem to have a common meaning, at least to me, are sometimes used differently [by Communists]."[80] The chief prosecutor closed the trial similarly arguing that "tricky phrases, high-sounding platitudes" were used to cover up sinister meanings.[81]

Judge Medina made the role of the informants in revealing the true meanings of Communist language explicitly clear. Intervening in the prosecution's direct examination of Budenz, he told the witness, "I am going to read this section [article 8, section 2 of the Communist Political Association's Constitution]. . . . And then you are going to tell us what it meant."[82] The informants were thought particularly suited to the task largely because of the social ties they established within the Communist Party. Budenz wrote in his memoir that his position as managing editor of the *Daily Worker* made him "well versed in 'the Communist code' by which to unravel and interpret . . . [the] ideological and involved language" deployed by Communists.[83]

Budenz provided what was perhaps the most important definition of the trial, that of Marxism-Leninism. He did so against a dissonant backdrop made up of the repeated and vociferous (and overruled) objections of the defense. For Budenz, Marxism-Leninism (also referred to as the "Leninist line") held that "scientific socialism" clearly indicated that socialism could

only be attained by the violent shattering of the capitalist state, and the setting up of a dictatorship of the proletariat by force and violence in place of the state. In the United States this would mean that the Communist Party of the United States is basically committed to the overthrow of the Government of the United States as set up by the Constitution of the United States.[84]

Budenz also conveyed to the courtroom that the charges of "revisionism" levied against Eric Browder in the Duclos letter were really a condemnation of Browder's abandonment of a Communist policy that requires American (and all) Communists to turn imperialist war (of which they accused the United States) into civil war.

Philbrick would later testify that concepts such as "the proletariat" were defined in such a way as to allow individuals who did own property—he uses the example of a small shop owner—to identify as part of the struggle against capitalism. Thus, Aesopianism not only supposedly served a "protective" function against revealing the violent intentions of Communists, but was also a way to lure others into the Communist Party. Budenz, who describes in his memoir how he was partially a victim of this strategy, was asked during cross-examination:

Q: Did the Communist Party during that ten-year period put out pamphlets on rent control?
A: Yes, sir, among other subjects.
Q: On price control?
A: Yes, sir.
Q: On supporting the efforts of organized labor to organize?
A: Yes, sir.
Q: On supporting the efforts on the part of trade unions to obtain wage increases?
A: Yes, sir.
Q: Supporting efforts on the part of trade unions to obtain recognition in collective bargaining?
A: Yes, sir. *They took advantage of every grievance.*[85]

The above exchange is indicative of how both informants testified that the CPUSA was not actually concerned with any issue beyond its end goal of overthrowing of the government. Ultimately, any release, document, or statement that promoted peace, reform, or any other cause was, according to Philbrick, "public literature," that is, literature intended for "public consumption." He followed by providing convoluted accounts of how nonpublic ideas were communicated within the party. This was based on his recollection of what a member *meant* when she directed others' attention to a particular section of a particular book in a class (interpreting, for example, that the distinction between just and unjust wars mentioned in some Communist texts, like most anything, indicates the necessity to transform imperialist war into civil war).[86] Budenz similarly offered serpentine explanations of how Communists, sympathizers, and those susceptible were directed to the party's intended message. For instance, Budenz described an article he wrote for the *Daily Worker* in April 1945 in which he recommended an article in *Political Affairs* (*The Communist* until 1944) by John Williamson, who himself recommended that his readers pick up Stalin's *The History of the Communist Party in the Soviet Union*. Budenz relays the danger in this seemingly benign connection: "every Communist knows that when you being to read [Stalin's book] you begin to commit yourself to the Leninist line."[87] Again, the book is positioned as an actant, simply its possession—before its content—is an indication of conspiracy.

The defense attempted to illustrate that Lenin saw Aesopian language as a "cursed, slavish tongue," but necessary in the face of repression. They also worked to highlight how various Communist texts stressed the need to be keenly aware of historical conditions and, thus, did not communicate a predetermined or eternal necessity for violence. Against these efforts the translation work of the informants set a trap that transformed most anything into an ideological tie to a violent interpretation of Communism; it is one that the defense recognized. In other words, the work of the informants transformed "any evidence offered by the defendants to answer the charges against them [its efforts against 'racial, national and religious discrimination, against Jim Crowism, anti-Semitism, and all forms of chauvinism'] . . . into 'proof' of their guilt."[88]

* * *

At the beginning of Evan Kohlmann's testimony, the prosecution asked him, "Could you please describe to the jury al-Qaeda as an organization versus al-Qaeda as an ideology?"[89] Kohlmann went on to present an account of what was once an organization like any other, but forced to dramatically change after its base was destroyed and many of its leaders killed in the US war in Afghanistan. While al-Qaeda persisted as a smaller organization, it then began to emphasize that those who share their beliefs, feelings, and grievances could become members by downloading their materials and acting on those instead of attempting to travel to Afghanistan or Pakistan. Kohlmann builds on the discourse pushed by various pundits who (erroneously) claim that an anti-American or jihadist narrative—"the narrative"—is at the core of the transformation of Americans into terrorists; the narrative of "the narrative" is itself built on simplistic notions of a binary clash of civilizations and its accompanying Islamophobic tropes (i.e., they either refuse to understand "us" or simply cannot).[90] Nevertheless, the work at trial largely centered on showing that what the men said and did was ideologically in sync with al-Qaeda's anti-American narrative; the informants worked hard to elicit from the defendants words and actions that a cadre of experts then labored to fashion into a coherent narrative.

One of the first witnesses called by the prosecution was an FBI translator who defined "jihad" for the court (to the objection of the defense) as "holy war"—in addition to "inshallah," "fatwa," "Allahu Akbar," and other phrases.[91] Often, when the men used jihad in this way, it was in response to a provocation by one of the informants. In one heated conversation Omar was able to elicit the intended response. Shnewer told him, "If we are going to fight these people, we will not fight them based on racism. We are not fighting them for anything but for Allah's sake. Glory and praise to him almighty because they have persecuted Muslims everywhere."[92] However, in many other instances Omar could not produce the same effect. For example, in a discussion with Serdar Tatar (and without disclosing the existence of any plan) Omar emotionally states that he wants to make the United States pay for what they supposedly did to him personally. Tatar responds in shock rather than in agreement or sympathy.[93] Thus, delimiting "jihad" on the stand was particularly important given that both Omar's wiretap and Bakalli's revealed the multiple ways the defendants used the term. In one recorded discussion, Tony Duka describes "big jihad" as a struggle against one's own "lusts." Similarly, Shnewer, when asked by Omar to define "jihad," responded that it was an internal struggle against one's own urges.

Against the equivocal utterances elicited from the targets, there were efforts both within and outside of the courtroom to mold the men's words into more legible ideological ties. After Shnewer provided Omar with a nonviolent definition of jihad, Omar attempted to lead Shnewer to a more violent definition, going through a litany of scenarios, hinting at the necessity of violence.[94] The majority of such efforts drew on the videos found in the men's possession and their content. In the courtroom, the defense asserted that while disturbing and insensitive, the act of watching jihadist videos did not equate with planning an attack on America. The prosecution ostensibly agreed but added that "when taken with [the defendants'] conversations, [the videos are] powerful evidence of their motive . . . [and] explain why the defendants did what they did."[95] Thus, part of Kohlmann's role was to match the words of the defendants with the content of the videos that they downloaded. The turn to content indicates that the technological ties used to position the Fort Dix Five in global jihad are always-already ideological. Kohlmann testified that much of what came out of Shnewer's mouth in his recorded conversations with Omar were verbatim reproductions of the videos' content. For the prosecution, Shnewer's words were proof of the effect of the videos as actants and of an ideological affinity, rather than attempts to impress an older father figure who was repeatedly asking him for more videos and eliciting discussions about jihad. The social ties of the enemy network are here imbued with an ideological current that subverts the significance of the affective connections (of friendship and family) the informants cultivated.

In addition to eliciting comments on jihad, Omar found ways to establish ideological ties by other means. Omar offered to get the men weapons, AK-47s and rocket-propelled grenades (RPGs), by connecting them to his (fictional) arms dealer in Baltimore. The weapons were chosen strategically. On the stand, Kohlmann referred to the AK-47 as one of al-Qaeda's "most preferred weapons" whose operatives regularly extolled its virtues.[96] Beyond being frightening, the weapons conjure images of insurgent fighting in Afghanistan and Iraq. The transfer of—and desire for—these weapons signaled an ideological link through a shared modus operandi.[97] Again, the informant was key in establishing this link beyond introducing the men to a fictional arms dealer. When Shnewer made it clear that he could not afford the weapons, Omar first lowered the price and later offered to pay for the weapons, reminding

Shnewer that he was dedicating ten thousand dollars of his own money for their "mission." Also, the men never once requested RPGs, and once the Dukas saw them on the list, they quickly rejected them. The men had experience firing high-powered rifles at the gun ranges they would visit and wanted their own so as not to have to wait their turn on outings. When the men made the purchase, Tony Duka was recorded saying, "Now we don't have to wait on line to shoot in the Poconos."[98] Surely the purchase was illegal, but to further fashion the act into a sign of ideological affinity, the seemingly innocent purpose of the purchase (i.e., for use at a gun range) was characterized—much like the actions and words of Communists—as having a sinister meaning.

The defendants often played paintball and went to gun ranges on their trips to the Pocono Mountains in Pennsylvania. The prosecution framed these trips as training sessions. Shnewer had in fact explicitly referred to the trips as such. However, not only was he the only one to do so, but the very idea of training came from Omar. Drawing on his own story of being a veteran of the Egyptian army, he assured Shnewer that he could provide the younger Shnewer with the skills necessary for a mission. Similarly, Tony Duka's assertions that paintball was like real war and that the US Army used it for training were not only cued by Omar, but were really a reiteration of what Omar had said to strike up that particular conversation. On the stand, Omar further drove home the characterization of the men's activities as training, repeatedly referring to paintball guns as "fake guns," claiming Shnewer preferred them because they attracted less attention. Almost in unison, Kohlmann made strained efforts to justify his characterization of any visit to a gun range as "training." In response to defense assertions that shooting at a range is a legal activity in which many Americans participate, Kohlmann responded that that is what makes it the perfect cover.[99] He did this with many incongruities and seemingly benign acts, illustrating them as dangerous through conjuring other homegrown plots. Beyond creating a prototypical mold that the Fort Dix Five seemed to fit through a scattered assemblage of cherry-picked examples, Kohlmann helped convey a paranoid sense that anything benign was potentially threatening. A simple U-turn was a "counter-surveillance maneuver."[100] Even balloons signaled jihad: "Balloons were recovered. Balloons mixed in with ammunition. Recovered from Dritan Duka's house, were some balloons. Little party balloons. And in most cases, in most situations that would just be an odd fact. A curious fact. But not in this [case]. And not with these defendants. Those balloons have a deadly sinister meaning."[101] Here, the balloons the brothers used for target practice come to signify soldiers' heads and a visit to a gun range takes on an ideological meaning, training to kill American soldiers (mimicking what the men watched in jihadist propaganda). Dispelling this would be extremely difficult. According to the prosecution, the laughter and joking caught on surveillance tapes of the defendants during their supposed tactical training ought not be misconstrued as a sign that they were in fact not training and that they were simply on vacation. Kohlmann backed this up when he stated that even Ayman al-Zawahiri had joked around and laughed throughout the recording of one of his propaganda videos.[102]

Returning to the videos that played such a pivotal role in the trial. Omar failed to have Shnewer or any other "member" produce a fatwa—which an FBI translator defined as "an Islamic ruling or edict"—for their "mission." Seeking religious sanction for their plot would have surely solidified their affinity with al-Qaeda. At trial Kohlmann filled in this ideological gap by suggesting that Anwar al-Awlaki's "The Constants of Jihad"—a video the men had in their possession but that forensic evidence made clear they had never watched in its entirety—constituted a fatwa. Not only did the men become part of al-Qaeda as Kohlmann asserted, but they also received sanction from its ideological leaders "without even speaking to [al-Qaeda] directly even once."[103]

Kohlmann's statement indicates the manner in which the ideological links shape the network diagram of each historical moment. The ideological grants the Red Octopus, despite its legible center, a level of movement and distribution, its arms wandering in a semi-autonomous manner from space to space, potentially infecting unsuspecting organizations that become fronts, their words another Aesopian vehicle for the octopus's venom. In the distributed geometric constellation of global jihad the ideological provides a guarantee of uniformity without recourse to direct control. The ideological interweaves with the social and technological, making them legible as part of a network and conspiracy. The ideological and its accompanying potential of spreading a network into the most innocuous of spaces illustrates the common thread of paranoid thinking of both conspiracy and connectivity, an interstice in which the Double's rhizomatic trajectory—not everywhere but potentially anywhere—finds expression.

Conspiracy/Connectivity

The homegrown terrorist, the DHS definition indicates, works without direction. As such, Omar characterized his work as getting into the heads of his targets, reflecting the pseudo-psychologizing of contemporary radicalization theories. Indeed, the lack of "explicit evidence" (read: direct links) did not bother Judge Kugler, who presided over the Fort Dix criminal trial, in also denying the men's subsequent appeal of their life sentences.[104] And in the immediate aftermath of CPUSA convictions, upheld by the Supreme Court in *Dennis v. the US*, and as McCarthyism came into full swing, accusations occurred in concert with the belief that directives (between Communists) "hardly needed to be transmitted."[105] Articulations of Communist "thought control" were inflected with religious rhetoric, reflecting fears at the time of how the atheist ideology "burned into the souls of some Americans like a hot skewer."[106]

Read properly, these assertions about America's adversaries illustrate the move of paranoid thinking of connectivity not just from the pathological to the logical, as theorist of digital media Wendy Hui Kyong Chun posits, but also to the legal in and through conspiracy. Times of national crises are accompanied by the increased use of conspiracy charges, as deployed in Foley Square and Fort Dix. Conspiracy is itself based in the paranoid thinking of connectivity, seen in the leverage and leeway given to the prosecution in making particularly loose and imaginative connections. A successful conspiracy conviction simultaneously assuages the paranoia of connectivity by outing the Double through conviction while exacerbating it by proving the paranoiac right—the Double, future-past, guarantees its own potentially more destructive return. The Foley Square convictions only served as proof that "it is hard to tell where these seeds of the Russian theory have sunk into the soil or what new crops may spring."[107] But the conspiratorial movement of the Double is also utilized in "proving" conspiracy through the informant. In other words, security simultaneously fears and exploits connectivity, in the twin figures of the hidden enemy and the informant. This chapter has focused on how the informant's work shapes the enemy network through cultivating, curating, and eliciting connectivity in a way that is legally legible. I conclude here by elaborating on how connectivity maps onto conspiracy, on the relation of the informant to the shape of the enemy network, and what both reveal about the Double.

In outlining the work of the informant in times of national crisis, my intention was not to suggest the accuracy of the netwar doctrine, but to repurpose a popular security framework as a heuristic from which to uncover how enemy networks take their shape and the effort that goes into such a project. Albeit in differing ways given the network diagram native to each moment, informants cultivate social relationships, curate exchanges through and of communications media, and elicit and translate ideological links through which to implicate their targets in a broad international or global conspiracy. I have traced the variety of links separately, but conceptually the edges of the enemy network cannot be thought of as distinct. Rather, they are stitched together over the same trajectories. In the Fort Dix case, the informants exploited their social connections to curate technological links. Moreover, the technological links that resulted—an increase in downloading jihadist videos—were always-already ideological; the ideological links, often elicited strategically by the informants, simultaneously helped to determine the quality of one's communication patterns and reduced the significance and legal consequence of the informants' cultivated social ties, which they couched in the language of familial bond. At Foley Square, both Budenz and Philbrick moved through the Communist Party apparatus—"I had passed the first stringent tests, and now I was entrusted with new and larger responsibilities," wrote Philbrick in his memoir.[108] Once established in the organizational and social makeup of the party, their positions therein allowed them to act as conduits through which Communist media changed hands, often producing the "very book" that moved through them as proof of conspiracy. Moreover, their social ties lent them the credibility to translate Communism's tricky phrases and Aesopian language, which in turn was a key part of their effort in making the social and technological links they helped constitute legible.

In the face of countervailing evidence and the lack of direct ties, the "success" of the work of the informant is closely linked to conspiracy law.

In US jurisprudence there is no objective test regarding a conspiracy's boundaries, whether in time (duration), space (geographic specificity), or subject matter (target or aim). Moreover, the agreement at any conspiracy's heart need not be formal. That is, not only can one's assent be tacit, but each individual party need not be aware of the identity of her accomplices or even how many there are. Omar—to the FBI while in the field, on the stand and in interviews afterward—explicitly stated that the Dukas were not involved in any plot. But, because evidence of directive is not requisite to proving the existence of a conspiracy and "whether an agreement exists depends on the facts and inferences appropriately drawn from them," even an informant's admission against inclusion can be overridden.[109] Despite his statement about the Dukas, Omar did much on the stand that was crucial to establishing such inferences. By stitching the ideological into the social and technological, by making all of the enemy network ties legible through the lens of ideology (international Communism or global jihad), the informants provide a malleable subject matter capable of encompassing an innumerable amount of actions and utterances. In doing so, they also furnish a movement whose potential covered the globe (if in different ways) and was bent on destroying "our way of life," thus placing it on the plane of eternal time (the Double is never present but always past and yet to come). Indeed, the ideological links conceptualized as running through not only the social and technological but the very plane on which each network was diagrammed are at the heart of the paranoiac reasoning of conspiracy prosecution.

It is certainly tempting to leave the analysis here, to reduce the work of proving conspiracy to the invocation of threatening ideologies, whether international Communism or global jihad. And certainly, the informant was instrumental in doing so. Moreover, the anti-American narrative provides accompanying identity constructs that transform a vast swatch of individuals into potential coconspirators (those associated with an other) and malleable enough to implicate many more (intoxicated or radicalized doubles). However, there is more at work here. The informant's efforts depended a great deal on what Chun calls the "fantasy of connectivity," asserting, "paranoia stems from the reduction of political problems into technological ones."[110] Positioning media, books and videos, as actants fulfills precisely this function, shifting focus away from complex historical-political contexts (and the cultivated social contexts created by the informant) and onto the circulation of media. Technical connectivity or mere circulation, as much as articulations of ideology, act as enablers and proof of conspiracy. Moreover, what media scholar Jose van Dijck terms the "ideology of connectivity" conflates this potential for technical connectivity with (in)human connectedness, suggesting a quality of tie that is neither simply technical nor ideological but also affective (on the stand Kohlmann often referred to the emotions displayed by those who watched jihadist videos).[111] Last, the fantasy of connectivity posits a freedom analogous to buying and selling, one that dedifferentiates users, obscuring their social position. In the contexts at hand, particularly that of Fort Dix, the logics of connectivity work to further downplay the social relationship cultivated by the informant: "It was very easy for Mohamad to tell me I have nothing to do with this issue and I don't want to do anything," Omar said on the stand, suggesting that regardless of the nature of their relationship, Shnewer bought into global jihad.[112] In short, inasmuch as anxieties concerning anti-American narratives fuel the paranoid thinking of security, so too do fears of connectivity. The notion that "everything is connected" has deviance at its core, according to Tung-Hui Hu, a historian and theorist of digital media, "circuits—or people—that are unreliable and untrustworthy."[113] Here, there is a circular relationship apropos of the paranoid thinking of connectivity and conspiracy. The conspiratorial ideologies used to connect adversaries (and thus flesh out the Double) depend on fantasies of connectivity, which simultaneously always-already contain a conspiratorial rot that maintains connectivity as a fantasy that can be mobilized in the service of security, particularly in the conspiracy charge.

In the paranoid circularity of conspiracy and connectivity, the Double as more than enemy emerges. The informant, the enemy-Double's inverse, the wolf in wolf's clothing enters into this cycle, himself not always able to distinguish friend from foe; Omar and Bakalli had no idea that the other was also an informant. And from this work, drawing on dedifferentiating tendencies of ideological narratives and connectivity, the informant produces the shape of the enemy network in a form legible to publics and juries. I have attempted to make visible this process, often hidden under the innovative flash of the new, by examining this old technology that is deployed into the conspiratorial circuits of connectivity. Certainly, in each moment the informant-Double's productive work is different. In the contemporary crisis, the octopus has become a constellation floating in ideological ether, and, thus, the work of the informant has become more taxing. Rather than infiltrating organizations and characterizing them as cells in a conspiratorial network (which is itself fundamental to producing the enemy network as a legible threat), the informant cum fledgling jihadist must attempt to form a cell from which to link individuals to global jihad. Curating radicalization is much more labor-intensive than infiltration, perhaps an irony in an increasingly automated world.

Yet, the octopus and the constellation are both afforded a certain amount of movement and control—perhaps because the Cold War marked a move toward distributed modes of organization or because a truly distributed network is a fiction. Regardless, the characteristics of these networks are packed into the actants that are said to circulate within, carriers of ideology and means of connectivity. In this sense, the Double as both an enemy figure and informant cannot be epistemologically separated from these media. The Double as circulating—not everywhere, but potentially anywhere—threatening to materialize in the people and places one would least expect, is inherently tied to the actants of a network. In the next chapter, I turn to spaces of contemporary counterterrorism, which, in an attempt to freeze the movement of the enemy-Double, are themselves caught up in the play of opacity and transparency, producing novel articulations of belonging and exacerbating already-existing experiences of second-class citizenship.

Figure 5. Drone strike in Baghdad, April 10, 2008. This is a composite of two screen shots from a Department of Defense video posted on YouTube.

Figure 6. Surveillance footage from the Newburgh sting.

3

Opacity and Transparency in Counterterrorism

Belonging and Citizenship Post-9/11

On September 30, 2011, an American named Anwar al-Awlaki was killed in a drone strike in Yemen. The drone images shown (Figure 5) are not from that operation, but from a similar one in Iraq. Footage of the al-Awlaki strike was never released, perhaps because it showed the extrajudicial killing of a US citizen. The camera of a surveillance helicopter (Figure 6) hovering over the Bronx, New York, on the evening of May 20, 2009, focused in on four African Americans (James Cromitie, David Williams, Onta Williams, and Laguerre Payen) in the midst of carrying out a supposed terror attack. Minutes later federal agents arrested the men who would come to be known as the Newburgh Four. The footage and the arrest were made possible by a paid FBI informant who lured the men into the plot.

Both videos illustrate the spaces in which counterterrorism materializes, or at least those shown to the public: faraway lands and everyday American streets. Videos of drone strikes, which have collectively garnered tens of millions of views, are uploaded onto YouTube by the Department of Defense, ostensibly in an effort to be more transparent about its (openly) secret program. The same could be said for the images of FBI sting operations. Yet, even with their release, much is hidden. The humanity and status as citizen of the targets are pixilated away and the horrors of war mediated into more a palatable infrared form of visual representation—thus, while the *particular* video of al-Awlaki's killing is classified, the dedifferentiation of what Lisa Parks calls the drone's "vertical mediation" allows any one video to act as a reasonable stand-in.[1] The specificity of the location is thus also mediated away into exotic deserts and anywhere USA, spaces that become interchangeable and overlapped. Moreover, any video in isolation leaves unseen the complex processes involved in its production. Beyond the network of communication infrastructure populating and orbiting Earth, the two cases in this chapter bring our attention to two other spaces integral to the production of counterterrorism spectacles, spaces largely invisible to the public eye: the increasingly solitary office of executive decision and the American prison system.

My interest in the operational spaces of counterterrorism stems from the spatial terms deployed vis-à-vis homegrown terrorism. In the previous chapter I showed how the Double is made sense of as a figure in circulation, networked, neither here nor there. In light of this continuous motion the spatial dimension of counterterrorism is best described as one of collapse, the boundary between foreign and native becoming difficult to discern. This collapse is further visible in various phenomena: in the drone, whose pilot sits in front of a screen in a trailer outside of Las Vegas, Nevada, or Langley, Virginia, or at a base in Somalia or the United Arab Emirates, while the machine stalks and kills targets in Africa, the Middle East, and South Asia; in the fact that operations against US citizens are carried out both abroad and at home; and in the declaration of the American home front as a battlefield in the war on terror via the National Defense Authorization Act. In the debates in response to the latter, critics worried about how the act would facilitate the infringement of individual rights, while supporters claimed that those who had nothing to hide—those who truly belonged—had nothing to worry about. These debates closely link the spatial dimension of counterterrorism to notions of belonging and citizenship in contemporary America. This chapter examines this link, but from a different perspective.

My focus on American spaces of counterterrorism—the institutional configurations of executive secrecy and mass incarceration—takes its cue from how the spatial collapse of homegrown terrorism is articulated in a tense unison in al-Qaeda in the Arabian Peninsula's *Inspire* magazine and the multiagency "If You See Something, Say Something" campaign (See/Say Something campaign hereafter). Both warn of the Double, a threat that might materialize in the places one would least expect. Al-Qaeda claims she will become completely visible only in the ephemeral flash of terror; government authorities assert they could pick her out of the crowd if only given enough access to information. A notion already suggested in the efforts to network the enemy, what is of particular interest in this cacophony of threats is the way in which the Double is constructed. Beyond the unidirectional infiltration of the native by the foreign, what is articulated is an uncanny recognition of something American in contemporary jihad, communicated as a promise in *Inspire* and as an ominous warning in the See/Say Something campaign. I argue that both al-Awlaki and the Newburgh Four were framed as particularly worrisome threats (deserving of death and life in prison, respectively) through an articulation of precisely this type of uncanny recognition: in al-Awlaki's American accent, idiomatic English, and effortless ability to traverse cultural spaces; in the Newburgh Four's (supposed) emergence from a quintessential (racialized) American space—the prison.

The second half of the chapter begins with the exhortations of Department of Homeland Security head Janet Napolitano, in harmony with the See/Say Something campaign, calling for citizens to keep watch in the face of the threat that may come from their fellow Americans. Effectively positioning each individual as both suspect and spy, the cases in this chapter illustrate how this double identity is not distributed evenly. To show this, I begin not from the assumption that the shape of counterterrorism practice could be understood as a reaction to a foreign threat that has infiltrated the United States. Rather, I play on assertions regarding the Americanness of jihad and focus on how long-established American institutional configurations shape counterterrorism and how their entanglement therein produces articulations of belonging and experiences of citizenship. The al-Awlaki and Newburgh cases, which have both been used as examples regarding the effect of counterterrorism on citizenship, present unique incarnations of this phenomenon.

Instead of discussing the legality of the extrajudicial killing of Anwar al-Awlaki, I focus on the manner in which his placement on the capture or kill list and the drone program, in general, were communicated to the American public. It is a communicative strategy best understood as the open secret, which at once acknowledges (if partially) and denies, releases (e.g., drone videos) and withholds (e.g., details about how one is marked for death), and communicates trust and suspicion without clearly or explicitly marking who is trusted and who is not. Mirroring the spatial anxieties of counterterrorism, this strategy cannot be properly understood without being situated within a long-standing institutional configuration that accelerated under the Reagan administration, that is, executive secrecy. In the open secret's play of opacity and transparency, a peculiar articulation of belonging is produced: laughter. I argue that the laughter in response to questions about al-Awlaki's death and the drone program acts as a complex, if fleeting, vocalization of one's belonging.

The Newburgh case provides further insight into those who cannot laugh in the face of counterterrorism practice and its accompanying secrecy. The announcement of the capture of four violent men, career criminals whose antisocial tendencies found an outlet in jihad, fit the Prislam narrative conveyed in various government circles. Prislam is the fear that convicts, who convert in prison, are vulnerable to the lure of a violent form of Islam; in short Prislam is framed as an unholy alliance of criminality and jihad. I flip the script of Prislam by connecting counterterrorism practice to mass incarceration, its constitutive racism, and its institutionalization of a cyclical movement of individuals between two spaces largely hidden from public view: the prison and the depressed city. It is this institutional configuration, I argue, on which this informant-led operation depended. And, given how mass incarceration disproportionately affects African Americans, I show how counterterrorism practice can work to exacerbate already-existing second-class experiences of citizenship, in its intersection and exploitation of the machinations of mass incarceration.

Citizenship, more than holding a passport or having a nationality, establishes one's membership in a community in a complex interplay of identity, participation, and rights.[2] It involves expressions of belonging as well as the manner in which one is able to assert one's rights, both of which have been and continue to be doled out unequally. In his analysis of the unequal experiences of citizenship endemic in America history, political scientist Rogers Smith highlights that many Americans have long been denied their "personal liberties and opportunities for political participation . . . on the basis of race, ethnicity, gender, and even religion"—categories that he argues are at the core of the political identity of Americans, their "stories of peoplehood" and "imagined communities."[3] In times of war, unequal experiences of citizenship are often tied to the ways in which the nation's enemy has been portrayed. This trend does not end with the Double. The double position of suspect/spy is not equally distributed. The examination of the play of visibility and invisibility, transparency and opacity, spaces shown and spaces hidden in counterterrorism communication and practice illustrates how America's political structures and institutions, through which counterterrorism practice moves, shape the form that the Double takes before the public's eyes and its unequal effects.

As American as . . .

The multiagency See/Say Something campaign predates al-Qaeda's *Inspire* magazine by almost a decade, but, as if holding a joint news conference, both warn of an adversary that threatens to materialize within US borders in the people and places one would least expect. Al-Qaeda in the Arabian Peninsula published seventeen issues of *Inspire* between 2010 and 2017. One of the publication's primary functions is to facilitate violence (or at least give the impression that it has the ability to do so). By promoting "Open Source Jihad" the magazine leaves the choice of where terror might materialize to individual whim rather than organizational planning. But the magazine does provide aids, including illustrated manuals for weapons training and manufacturing as well as hit lists that mark particular individuals for assassination. These include Terry Jones, the Florida pastor behind "International Burn-a-Quran Day," and more high-profile figures such as Bill Gates. More often than not, however, its suggested targets are much more nondescript and generic (e.g., borders, financial institutions, government buildings, military bases, harbors, railroads, etc.). Even more vague is its encouragement to target civilians in general by hitting populated areas, causing car accidents, starting forest fires ("Arson Jihad"), or carrying out workplace violence.[4] This vague and never-exhausted list acts as a threat, one that underwrites al-Qaeda's warning to its adversaries that the "question of 'who and why' should be kept aside. You should be asking 'Where is next?'"[5] This also happens to be the message communicated in the See/Say Something campaign, whose most recent incarnation includes a series of videos titled "Protect Your Everyday."

A ten-minute Department of Homeland Security public service announcement features an array of mundane and innocuous spaces in which the terrorist might appear: shopping malls, dimly lit parking garages, the subway, nondescript neighborhood streets, sanitized hospital labs, industrial storage facilities, and the like.[6] In one scene, a man enters a parking garage and notices that the lens of a security camera has been spray-painted over. He then spots several individuals (all covered in dark clothing) exit a white van, drop its keys on the ground, and leave the garage on foot. Avoiding detection by shrinking into his car seat, he then calls authorities, "Hello? Listen, I don't know if this is anything, but what I just saw looked *really* suspicious." The video represents well how the terrorist is never portrayed as a stereotyped other in the campaign. Rather, the terrorist double is either white, masked (often by a hoodie or other clothing), or ambiguous. Through a display of press clippings and footage, the same video also parades a miscellany of threats, including Ted Kaczynski, Timothy McVeigh, Colleen LaRose (aka Jihad Jane), Faisal Shahzad (who attempted to set off a car bomb in Times Square), and Joseph Stack (who flew a small plane into an IRS building in Texas). Against this diversity of threats, the video instructs Americans not to make judgments based on race, language, gender, or religion.

Inspire communicates an image of a potent threat by manufacturing a sense of collective identity that similarly does not depend on a typical member profile. Seeking to foster a "borderless loyalty," the magazine calls out to every "building, slum, desert, house," directing its communications not only to Muslims in the West, but to anyone willing to adhere to its political quasi-theology.[7] This imagined community is given a history by comparing it to figures from the past and commemorating events. In this work, homegrown attacks in the United States are central to their narrative; for example, the Boston Marathon bombing is reframed as the Battle of Boston.[8] In the back of most every issue, *Inspire* lists a dispersed legion of prisoners held by the West. These tributes include those whose arrests predate the magazine's existence and others who had no contact with the magazine or organization, whether directly or indirectly (including the Fort Dix Five). In short, al-Qaeda appropriates events that can be labeled jihadist; several of these are American.

This leads into what has been a topic of conversation since *Inspire* first appeared. Stoking fears of radicalization, most concerning for officials is that *Inspire*, as one commentator put it, "feels so very American":

> A canny blend of photos, feature stories, insider details, snappy news
> bits and verse-quoting theological justifications for terrorist attacks, all
> of it calculated to appeal to American Muslims who grew up on glossy

magazines like *Details* and *GQ*. It is also notable for its collegiate sense of humor, which includes a mention of the fact that the plotters dropped a copy of Charles Dickens's "Great Expectations" into one of the bomb packages—a detail illustrated by a close-up of the novel's paperback edition. . . . [All] a seeming attempt to appeal to the sensibilities of Muslim hipsters.[9]

The *Wall Street Journal* wrote that the magazine's most unnerving pages are those in which it "remixes old-school jihadist tropes for an English-speaking Western audience . . . [particularly] the aspiring suburban jihadist."[10] *Inspire* posits this suburbanite as a reluctant superhero through the visual language of videogame culture.[11] It glorifies martyrdom through Hollywood-style poster spreads. Beyond flashy graphics, *Inspire* also covers a variety of social issues read as relevant to Americans such as materialism, poverty, and climate change—the first issue featured a piece by Osama bin Laden titled "The Way to Save the Earth."[12] Furthermore it stresses not only the persistent prejudice faced by American Muslims and Arabs but also the continued effects of institutionalized racism on African Americans, appropriating the horrific murder of Trayvon Martin, for example, to buttress its message. More than promising paradise, the magazine presents its political ideology as a solution to some of America's most pressing problems.

Surely, the surprise expressed in media accounts in reaction to what is seen as *Inspire*'s American or Western style can be read as emerging from widespread Orientalist assumptions about a backward, antimodern, and unsophisticated other. However, the recognition of something uncanny in the publication also signals anxieties over a particular adversary: the Double. *Inspire* is thus feared to be the stuff of traitors. In a 2010 statement that uncannily mirrors that of Eric Holder quoted in the Entrance, Anwar al-Awlaki made this explicit: "Men and women in the West who were born in the West, raised in the West, educated in the West, whose culture is that of the West, who have never studied or met with any 'radicalized' Imams, and never attended any radical mosques are embracing the path of Jihad."[13] The magazine, in fact, features articles penned by American defectors. Al-Awlaki's experience has been serialized in "Why Did I Choose al-Qaeda?" Samir Khan—another American killed alongside al-Awlaki (officially not targeted and classified as collateral damage) and *Inspire*'s original editor—penned, "I am proud to be a traitor to America." This, and the sheer amount of American cultural references within its pages, is clear evidence for Peter Neumann, director of the International Centre for the Study of Radicalisation, that "the people who are producing the magazine are clearly American. We don't know for sure, but it would surprise me very much if not 80 per cent of the contributors to the magazine were American." His remarks echo those of former DHS head Janet Napolitano in a 2011 speech: "Indeed, one of the most striking elements of today's threat picture is that plots to attack America increasingly involve American residents and citizens." Al-Awlaki put all this in more concise terms, asserting that jihad "is becoming as American as apple pie."[14]

In a tense harmony, American counterterrorism officials and their adversaries announce the collapse of clearly bounded spaces of enmity. It is against this backdrop that threats are positioned as particularly worrisome by invoking the manner in which there is an air of the familiar in what ought to be strange, in their uncanny comfort with American culture or their emergence from quintessentially American spaces. Two cases that were described in precisely these terms, albeit in very different ways, were that of Anwar al-Awlaki, who seemed to have fulfilled his own prophecy, and the Newburgh Four, a group of four African American ex-convicts caught up in an informant-led FBI sting operation.

. . . Apple Pie: A US Citizen in America's Crosshairs

> Silent and cold. At twenty thousand feet, the temperature is minus ten degrees Fahrenheit. At almost a thousand miles per hour, sound cannot keep up. Heat and noise struggle in the turbulence. Three miles away, seven thousand miles from American soil, an American citizen driving an empty road has ten seconds to live. . . . This American citizen has become an enemy of the United States. In response . . . his government added him to a kill list, targeted him, and launched a military operation against him. The Hellfire finds its mark. The heat and noise catch up.[15]

Anwar al-Awlaki and his companions had just eaten breakfast five miles from the town of Khashef in Yemen's northern Jawf province when the heat and noise caught up with them on September 30, 2011. What one

White House official called "a good day for America," an American was killed by his own government in a clandestine military operation.[16] He was never charged with a crime.

Anwar al-Awlaki was described as an individual who possessed the ability to effortlessly shift between countries and cultures. Born in New Mexico in 1971, he lived in the United States until the age of seven, when his father, Nasser, took a prominent post in his native Yemen and moved the family there. Anwar al-Awlaki returned to the United States to attend first university and then graduate school in the early 1990s. During that time he had a son, Abdulrahman, born in Denver in 1995. Abdulrahman was also killed in a drone strike two weeks after his father—the result, authorities claim, of being in the wrong place at the wrong time. Similarly, Abdulrahman's eight-year-old sister, Nawar, was killed in a US-led raid in early 2017. From the mid-1990s onward al-Awlaki served as the imam for several mosques around Colorado, California, and later Virginia. The FBI had begun monitoring al-Awlaki in 1999, suspecting that the charities with which he worked had ties to terrorist organizations. Agents then took note of his recurring solicitation of prostitutes, for which he was arrested several times.[17] These efforts only intensified post-9/11 with the FBI interviewing him three times in the days immediately following the attacks. According to the transcripts, he was questioned about Nawaf al-Hazmi, one of the hijackers whom he recognized from San Diego. The transcripts also show that al-Awlaki publicly condemned the 9/11 attacks; his sermon on the Friday afterward focused on healing, not surprising given his reputation at the time as an imam who attempted to build bridges between communities. It was this reputation that gained him an invitation to an outreach luncheon at the Pentagon in early 2002; as he traveled to the event on public transportation the FBI followed closely behind. He left the United States that same year.

On May 6, 2003, the FBI closed their investigation, concluding that al-Awlaki did not have terrorist ties. Later that year he contacted the FBI in response to media reports stating that he was a "spiritual advisor" to some of the 9/11 hijackers. He wrote, "I am amazed at how absurd the media could be and I hope that the US authorities know better and realize that what was mentioned about me was nothing but lies." Attempts to set up a meeting failed, and before the end of the year emails from FBI agents to al-Awlaki all bounced back. Eventually, the FBI arranged a meeting with him in a Yemeni prison in 2007. He had been placed there a year prior, at the behest of US authorities he would later claim. As of the early 2000s his writing began to support suicide bombing. After he was released from jail he began openly calling for violence against the West, particularly the United States, through *Inspire* and elsewhere.

The media reports that bewildered al-Awlaki often portrayed him as a prototypical other: brown, Arab, and Muslim. Al-Awlaki was described as a "bushy-bearded orator . . . dressed in [a] traditional Yemeni long robe, headscarf and tribal dagger." The invocation of traditional Yemeni culture was prevalent in multiple profiles. Much like Nidal Malik Hasan's "roots," various commentators stressed that al-Awlaki spent his "formative years" in the alternatively rugged, tribal, or medieval country of Yemen, that is, "in the embrace of one of the most traditional societies on earth." His return to America for college was said to have happened only at his father's insistence. Once back he was said to find it difficult to fit in, the apparent result of spending his adolescence idolizing the Mujahideen fighting in Afghanistan and studying the Quran in a society where "women were largely excluded from public life."[18]

Like with many other jihadists, gender relations were prominent in establishing al-Awlaki's outsider status. His wife—a distant cousin—was always covered and never shown to male friends. Some claimed that he was "not able to talk to women at all, even covered women." Anecdotes circulated in media reports. Scott Shane of the *New York Times* made the connection between gender relations and belonging explicit: "I mean, we're talking about Colorado State, right? I mean, there aren't many guys who are running the other way from women on American college campuses." His uneasy relationship with women was also illustrated through his solicitation of prostitutes. Al-Awlaki is thus transformed into a "Yemeni cleric"—gendered hang-ups and all. Despite the fact that he spent half of his life in America, al-Awlaki was depicted as having been "never fully American."[19] Much like labeling him "American-born," in those headlines in which he was referred to as an American citizen, "citizen" acts as a modifier of "American," restricting al-Awlaki to a formal status, one undeserving of sympathy.

The framing of al-Awlaki as other, however, does not capture, I argue, why President Obama was seemingly obsessed with him. With a fervor one advisor compared to that seen in George W. Bush after 9/11, Obama made al-Awlaki his top priority, a position supported by expert and official lines that labeled him the most significant threat to the US homeland. At the same time, however, al-Awlaki was characterized as a "dime-a-dozen cleric" largely unknown to most Middle Easterners who, as the *New York Times* put it, shrugged at his death.[20] Moreover, his status within al-Qaeda was propelled, pundits mused, by the attention he received in US media more than anything else. To understand how a man with few resources attracted so much attention requires a rereading of his repeated positioning as "American-born."

Reducing al-Awlaki's status to American-born was certainly intended to exclude him from the American collective, suggesting that he shed anything American like a worn skin when he left the country. However, placed against the backdrop of the spatial dimension of counterterrorism, American-born should also be read as connoting a threat. Al-Awlaki's firsthand, intimate experience in and of America equipped him with the ability to speak to Americans in a way that no other jihadist could. That is, what was particularly threatening about al-Awlaki was not his otherness. Rather, in a profound sense, it was al-Awlaki's "very American qualities . . . that made him such a dangerous radicalizing force."[21] Just as with *Inspire* magazine there was a fearful recognition of something American in al-Awlaki (which is not the same thing as accepting him as a full American). This recognition went beyond his fluent command of the English language, though this itself garnered much attention.[22] He spoke in an American accent and in a calm and reasonable manner, a far cry from the caricature of Arab and Muslim terrorists in Hollywood movies (here, the uncanny recognition feeds off of long-held stereotypes). Moreover, it was al-Awlaki's "idiomatic" English that was particularly threatening. In his lectures he referenced figures, historical and allegorical, readily identifiable by American audiences, such as Malcolm X and "Joe Sixpack." Once, he used an anecdote about Michael Jackson and his desire to live forever in order to make a point about the inevitability of death. For observers, al-Awlaki displayed more than an elementary familiarity with American culture; that is, he possessed a keen ability to exploit it in efforts to "relate culturally to a Western audience."[23] In a sense, the easily adopted American culture that is often the subject of globalization debates returns home in Frankensteinian form.

Al-Awlaki's reach was powered not only by his cultural lexicon but also by his seemingly expert use of digital media; both assertions depend on a contrast to an unsophisticated, uncultured, and primitive other. Alternatively dubbed "the bin Laden of the Internet," a "YouTube warrior," and an "e-mam," al-Awlaki regularly posted videos to YouTube, one of which was viewed more than a hundred thousand times.[24] He had a Facebook fan page (with almost five thousand followers), a popular blog, and a best-selling lecture series he sold over the Internet. Al-Awlaki's Internet presence and his online video sermons have been thought to be the inspiration for various jihadists, including the Tsarnaev brothers. The removal of these materials is an almost impossible task. His videos and tributes to him remain on YouTube. The site's attempt to remove them in 2010 was described as a mild inconvenience for jihadists or the equivalent of "placing [his videos] just a few inches off prime shelf space."[25] Beyond depictions of martyrdom, his electronic legacy is ensured by a digital Double, one that can be readily copied, distributed, uploaded, and downloaded, endlessly circulating within global communications networks.

Al-Awlaki, who had spent half of his life in the United States and whose first language was English, embodied both his own prediction that jihad would become as American as apple pie as well as official fears of a potential enemy hiding in plain sight—as the story goes, a once moderate preacher who called America his home turned against it. Undoubtedly, the act of killing an American citizen was made easier by racializing al-Awlaki. However, what made targeting him so urgent was his perceived ability to transverse cultural spaces; that is, the uncanny recognition of something American in a face that was so often made other. Media reports highlighted testimonies from former colleagues who positioned al-Awlaki as "just the guy next door."[26] Al-Awlaki was not a lookalike, but a manifestation of the Double by way of accent and cultural proficiency, perpetually reproduced in digital traces and the people he influenced. Al-Awlaki was presented, in his patterns of movement, speech, and Internet use, as a figure in which spatial and identity boundaries of us and other collapse.

. . . Mass Incarceration: Prislam

On May 20, 2009, five men set out to plant car bombs outside of two Riverdale synagogues in the Bronx, New York. The plan was to arm the explosives, drive some sixty miles to the Stewart Air National Guard Base near Newburgh, New York, and detonate the devices remotely while using Stinger missiles to blowup military planes parked at the base. The men who would come to be known as the Newburgh Four, James Cromitie, David Williams IV, Onta Williams, and Laguerre Payen, were not alone in the car. Accompanying them was a man who went by the name Maqsood, ostensibly a wealthy recruiter of Jaish-e-Mohammed, a Pakistani terrorist group. Cromitie had met Maqsood at a mosque in Newburgh the previous year. As soon as the bombs were armed, a mass of police officers dressed in plain clothes descended on the suspects. The scene was one remediated from many disaster-porn terrorist movies with a hundred agents and a bomb squad present. The presence of the latter was a curious sight given that the weapons, all procured through Maqsood, were fakes: the bombs duds and the missiles inoperable. A police helicopter had been filming their entire drive out to Riverdale. The men were caught in an elaborate sting operation. Maqsood, who had lured the men into the plot with promises of money, had recorded their conversations, hundreds of hours, for months. Maqsood was a paid government informant named Shahed Hussain. All four men received twenty-five-year sentences. On August 23, 2013, a three-judge panel at a Manhattan appeals court denied an appeal, two to one, to overturn the convictions. In 2014, the Supreme Court refused to hear the case.

For Karen Greenberg, director of the Center on National Security at Fordham University, the Newburgh case was one of many that indicated "it is no longer possible to think of jihad as a purely foreign phenomenon," seemingly mirroring al-Awlaki's assertion that jihad would become as American as apple pie. However, rather than claiming that Americans have wholeheartedly taken up jihad as al-Awlaki hoped, Greenberg characterizes jihad as having morphed into a repository for a litany of grievances Americans may hold against their own government; some of those she listed as engaged in jihad were not Muslim. For Greenberg, "Jihad has put down roots in America. And, at the same time, it is arguably being shaped by America as well."[27] One can argue that jihad has been shaped by America since at least the late 1970s given the country's involvement in the Afghan-Soviet War. Nevertheless, for many in the security community one space in which homegrown jihad is shaped is the US prison. All four defendants had extensive, though nonviolent, criminal records.

"Prislam" has been the subject of two congressional hearings and a Justice Department report.[28] Coined by Frank Cilluffo, the director of the Homeland Security Policy Institute at George Washington University, Prislam refers to the fear of inmates converting to a version of Islam that justifies violence. While it is estimated that there are about 350,000 Muslim inmates in US prisons, with about 30,000 to 40,000 inmates converting every year, there is little evidence to support anything resembling widespread extremism within the prison population. Perhaps the only documented case, which acts as a stand-in for the potential of further occurrences, is that of Kevin James, who founded Jam'iyyat Ul-Islam Is-Saheeh in California's Folsom Prison. After recruiting three others, they plotted to bomb military bases and synagogues in California in 2005. Their plan was foiled when a cell phone left at the scene of a gas station robbery led police to the apartment of two of the men. There, authorities found evidence of planning and a prepared press release.

The Newburgh Four did not know each other in prison. The group was formed, rather, at the insistence of the government informant who repeatedly badgered James Cromitie to assemble a group of "good Muslims," preferably "guys from the [Newburgh] mosque."[29] Cromitie, who was labeled the group's leader, had been the only "member" for much of the time Hussain worked on him, repeatedly dodging requests to assemble a team. This important detail did not prevent both the media and politicians from tying the case to Prislam, a narrative driven largely by the fact that each man fit the description of the average prison convert: poor and black. The *New York Times* wrote that "the case has in certain circles evoked an old debate about the role prison might play as an incubator of extremist ideas among Muslims." Those circles are often occupied by conservative politicians (though hardly exclusive to them), such as Congressman Peter King, who described the Newburgh Four plot as "a very serious threat that could have cost many, many lives if it had gone through. . . . It would have been a horrible, damaging tragedy. There's a real threat from homegrown terrorists and also from jailhouse converts."[30] King subsequently brought the case up at his 2011 hearing on Prislam, claiming erroneously that Cromitie was radicalized in prison—whether Cromitie was radicalized at all is doubtful. King warned those gathered that Cromitie and company were "not alone."

At trial, the prosecution did not explicitly make the case that the Newburgh plot was an instance of Prislam. Yet, the main tenets of the Prislam narrative were readily employed throughout the trial. Michael P. Downing of the LAPD testified at the 2011 hearing that inmates "by their very nature" are particularly vulnerable to radicalization because of their "isolation, violent tendencies and cultural discontent"; in other words, they have "already stepped outside the norms of societal behavior."[31] Prosecutors portrayed the Newburgh Four exactly in this manner, as men with a "thirst for violence." Cromitie had, in fact, bragged "about violent things he had done and he [claimed] he had used bombs before and led a team of men armed with guns." None of his stories, however, were true, and his defense attorney described him as being a "big talker"—a point that I will show is of deeper significance than simply revealing Cromitie's blowhard personality.[32] In fact, none of the men had a history of violent crime; all had served time for nonviolent drug offences (e.g., Cromitie sold marijuana to an undercover officer and David Williams was once caught with a small amount of cocaine in his pocket).

Commenting on the potential for those who have stepped outside of acceptable societal behavior to transgress civilizational boundaries (from crime to terrorism), Patrick T. Dunleavy, a former deputy inspector general of New York, warned that "putting 60's domestic terrorists in the same prison as convicted Islamic terrorists is not a healthy mix and can produce an unholy alliance."[33] Here Dunleavy was referring to Jamil Abdullah al-Amin, also known as H. Rap Brown, a black activist and honorary member of the Black Panthers.[34] He is a founder of "the Ummah," which federal authorities describe as a "nationwide radical fundamentalist Sunni group consisting mainly of African Americans."[35] Al-Amin is in fact listed in *Inspire* magazine as a political prisoner; however, there is no evidence of contact (another case of *Inspire* reappropriating events for its own propaganda use). Nevertheless, these anxieties materialized in the 2009 case of Luqman Ameen Abdullah, a member of the Ummah. FBI agents in Dearborn, Michigan, shot Abdullah twenty-one times and killed him in what was described as, at best, a sting operation gone wrong and, at worst, a cover-up of a bundled case of entrapment. For Greenberg, Abdullah's case, one in which jihadists took inspiration from "an American icon of black nationalism," illustrated how "jihadism has grown more complicated over the past decade, as it has become, in part, a homegrown US phenomenon."[36]

The Newburgh Four's only connection to any organization was through the informant who posed as a member of Jaish-e-Mohammed. Yet, this was enough to frame their case as an instance of just such an unholy alliance. US prosecutor Adam Hickey stated in his opening remarks that the men were offered an opportunity to do "something for the cause of jihad" and jumped at the chance "without hesitation."[37] In effect, he was suggesting that the men had found an outlet for their bloodlust in jihad. Cromitie undoubtedly said many things that suggested his adherence to a particular anti-American/jihadist narrative. In addition to his repeated anti-Semitic diatribes, in a conversation recorded November 7, 2008, he told Hussain: "Listen, I am an American soldier. Do you hear what I'm saying? Just listen closely. I am an American soldier. I am a soldier right here in America, that the President don't even know about. Do you understand what I'm saying? I'm an American soldier, I am here in America, I am a soldier here, but not for America."[38] Perhaps sealing the four men's fate, and the prosecution made a point to mention this early and often, recordings revealed that the men "prayed for success."[39]

In the Prislam narrative, jihad becomes more complex in that it is shaped in spaces ostensibly meant to contain society's most dangerous. The prison is a thoroughly American space; the United States incarcerates more of its citizens in number and in proportion than any other country. While convicts and inmates are positioned as already-other, the constitutive anxiety of Prislam is that those who are a society's other might morph into civilization's existentially threatening foe. Admittedly, given America's racist history, the distinction between societal and civilizational others is meant to neither be absolute nor connote that the treatment of one might be more severe. Yet, the significance of prison here is how that which is threatening is communicated as not just infiltrating but drawing on American spaces, those authorities claim to control. However, on the margins of society, the Double is invoked here in one's transformation from criminal to traitor. The spaces of policing and of global conflict collapse into one another.

Jihad in America/American Jihad

Following up her 2011 comments on the involvement of Americans in jihad, Janet Napolitano added that because "citizens are often the first to notice signs of potential terrorist activity . . . we need every part of our society to be cognizant of the kinds of threats that exist, and knowledgeable about common sense steps to counter them."[40] In this effort, the See/Say Something campaign aims to, as a video playing continuously on loop at New York's Penn Station boasts, "create thousands of eyes and ears." Americans are thus called to play the role of informer. But, because the potential terrorist may also be a fellow citizen, surveillance thinking positions each person as both a spy and a suspect, an observation Walter Benjamin made in the 1930s: "In times of terror, when everyone is something of a conspirator, everybody will be in the position of having to play detective."[41] Here, the spatial dimension of counterterrorism begins to illustrate its demands on citizenship. More recently, the New York Metro Transit Authority has shifted its use of the See/Say Something campaign and produced videos featuring New Yorkers who have done just that. They have proved themselves by seeing something and saying something, though that "something" is often left in the realm of the subjunctive.[42]

While this function of the campaign has received much attention, there is another dimension to it that has been largely ignored. Namely, the campaign clearly communicates that "seeing something" is no easy task. The Double blends in keeping much out of sight, a line repeated not only in theories of radicalization, but also in the pages of *Inspire*. In one interview, the AQ Chef—the pseudonym for whoever supplies *Inspire* with bomb-making recipes—was asked why he has focused on "the kitchen" in his work (e.g., the now infamous, "How to make a bomb in the kitchen of your mom" in the inaugural issue). He replied:

> Unlike a lab, a kitchen is found in every house. Moreover, if a Mujahid can prepare a bomb from materials used in the kitchen instead of lab materials and use cooking utensils instead of lab apparatus, then we have

a double success and we have overcome the security hurdle. . . . Generally, we are trying as much as possible to move the lone Mujahid from the lab to the pharmacy and from the pharmacy to the kitchen.[43]

In effect, the kitchen allows the enemy to stay out of sight, in a private space more difficult to surveil. The See/Say Something campaign communicates something similar, but to different effect. In a PSA titled "The Drop Off," a white woman exits a cab in front of a commuter station. Her driver, a white man, opens the trunk and arms a bomb, while she enters the building and drops her purse on a bench. In each trigger moment, the camera speed slows and focuses our attention on these actions, indicating a technologically enhanced level of attention and perception that most, if not all, citizens lack.

This has several implications. First, positing that *something* that citizens are supposed to *see* as difficult to spot (beyond the unattended package) works to reinforce the necessity of government surveillance, whether digital or embodied in the informant. The deployment of the latter further suggests that the dual position of spy/suspect is not equally distributed. Some are more suspect than others and less trusted to surveil, illustrated in the NYPD's expansive (but ultimately unsuccessful) attempt to deploy an informant into each of the city's mosques and in the repeated calls for Muslims to show (read: prove) that they are "moderate."[44] Connected to this, the second function is illustrated by a New Jersey Transit pamphlet that urges its riders, "If It Doesn't Feel Right, It Probably Isn't." Beyond fostering a feeling of unease around unattended parcels, the appeal to affect provides what philosopher Judith Butler calls a "license for prejudicial perception" despite official injunctions to the contrary.[45] One need only recall the repeated occurrence on tarmacs in which one's language or dress has led to demands for removal in order for others to *feel right*.

The unequal distribution of trust and suspicion in calls for citizen surveillance requires us to refocus the spatial problematic of counterterrorism. The manner in which the discourse of the Double links space (materialized and hidden) and citizenship provides a frame from which to parse through what is rendered opaque and transparent in the execution of counterterrorism practice. Examining the play of seen and unseen in counterterrorism, from the spaces of executive decision to the prison—the latter conceptualized as neither an incubator of violence nor a storehouse of potential jihadists but in relation to mass incarceration and its effects—the American quality of jihad obtains a starkly different significance. What matters here is not an enemy that speaks our language—at least not beyond its catalytic role—but how features of the American political system in their entanglement in counterterrorism efforts produce articulations of belonging and experiences of citizenship.

Laughing at the Sky: The Open Secret and Belonging

The repercussions of killing al-Awlaki were immediately debated.[46] An American citizen was killed by his government (as much as he disavowed that government) without due process; there was no trial, let alone a charge laid against him. Al-Awlaki had gone from being a propagandist to an operational member of al-Qaeda when he prepared, personally instructed, coordinated, and approved Umar Farouk Abdulmutallab's attempt to set off a bomb he had hidden in his underwear on a Christmas Day Detroit-bound flight in 2009, tantamount to having joined enemy forces. John C. Dehn of the US Military Academy argued that in such cases "Supreme Court precedent firmly supports the idea that the government may properly identify a US citizen as an enemy subject to war measures."[47] Others disagreed. For one legal scholar, al-Awlaki was killed "merely on the assertion that lethal force was necessary to respond to the threat of terrorism."[48] The administration's move was condemned by pundits across the US political spectrum, from the self-proclaimed "warmongering neocon hawk" Jeff Goldberg to the constitutional lawyer Glenn Greenwald, from Libertarian Senator Rand Paul to Democratic Representative Dennis J. Kucinich, who believed "the administration has a crossed a dangerous divide and set a dangerous precedent." Others called the operation an assassination and grossly unconstitutional.[49]

I leave the legitimacy of his killing to legal scholars. What I want to examine here is all that was left partially hidden in the process and the articulations of belonging that emerged. In President Obama's first comments on the killing of al-Awlaki he was able to mention neither the involvement of the CIA nor the Predator drone whose missile found al-Awlaki. That information is classified. The increasing classification of government information is inextricably tied to the gradual expansion of executive power in the United States since the 1970s and its acceleration under the Reagan administration in the 1980s.[50] However, the secrecy displayed in regard to the al-Awlaki case, and by association the drone program, is peculiar in that Americans were well aware of the general contours of the facts Obama omitted. Drone strikes are covered in foreign and American media and have inspired critical art installations. Also, long before al-Awlaki was killed, the public knew he was targeted. Here, "in a mechanism reminiscent of Freudian disavowal, we know perfectly well that the secret is known, but nonetheless we must persist, however ineptly, in guarding it."[51]

The drone program and targeted killing are open secrets, even if the details of both are scantly known. Literary critic D. A. Miller defines that open secret as that which "must always be rigorously maintained in the face of a secret that everybody already knows."[52] In articulating both contemporary threat (as Double) and America's response to it, the politics of boundary maintenance are caught up in the play between known and unknown, transparency and opacity, seen and unseen, us and other. Government communication of secrets follows this general pattern, one in which the boundary between opacity and transparency is strategically managed rather than clearly delineated. In the case of an extrajudicial killing of an American, the power to manage this boundary largely rests in the executive. Vicki Divoll, former legal advisor to the CIA's Counterterrorism Center, observed, "Oddly, under current law, Congress and the courts are involved when presidents eavesdrop on Americans, detain them or harshly interrogate them—but not when they kill them."[53] The al-Awlaki case repeatedly confirmed her views. In throwing out Nasser al-Awlaki's lawsuit challenging his son's placement on a capture or kill list, the presiding judge, John D. Bates, recognized "the somewhat unsettling nature of [his] conclusion—that there are circumstances in which the Executive's unilateral decision to kill a US citizen overseas is . . . judicially unreviewable." He ruled the killing of al-Awlaki a "political question," the purview of the executive. So too was the legal justification for his killing, the infamous "Awlaki memo."[54] In ruling on a lawsuit brought forth by the *New York Times* and the American Civil Liberties Union in 2013, Judge Colleen McMahon—who also presided over the Newburgh Four case—could find no way around the thicket of laws and precedents that effectively allow the executive branch of our government to proclaim as perfectly lawful certain actions that seem on their face incompatible with our Constitution and laws while keeping the reasons for their conclusion a secret. . . . The Alice-in-Wonderland nature of this pronouncement is not lost on me.[55]

Even as the executive slowly relented, it continued to manage what was known and unknown. A month after McMahon's ruling, a sixteen-page white paper was leaked, but gave few specific details. In June 2014, the US Second Circuit Court of Appeals reversed McMahon's decision and ordered the memo released. Retaining a modicum of control, the Department of Justice decided not to appeal the ruling but redacted ten of the memo's forty-one pages.

The public's eventual knowledge of the drone program and al-Awlaki's targeted death was not singularly the result of protracted legal battles. Secrets have their own forms of publicity, and open secrets are made known through a particular mode of communication that involves "rarely [speaking one's] mind, but more often only its screen."[56] In the context at hand, the idea of speaking through a screen can be extrapolated to an executive that never openly admits to a program, memo, and so on; rather, these secrets are discussed, though never with significant detail, through intermediaries such as lawyers, advisors, and leaks to the media, ultimately retaining some amount of deniability. The drone program has largely been communicated in this way. Following al-Awlaki's death, a series of speeches on the topic of drones were given between February and April 2012: the Pentagon's general counsel Jeh Johnson at Yale University, attorney general Eric Holder at Northwestern University, and Obama's top counterterrorism advisor, John Brennan, at the Woodrow Wilson Center. Aspects of the al-Awlaki case, specifically, were communicated through leaks to the media. In 2011 the Awlaki memo was described to Charlie Savage of the *New York Times* "by people who [had] read it" and in 2013, about the same time that Obama decided to share the memo with two legislative committees, a white paper version stripped of all mention of al-Awlaki was leaked to NBC News.[57] Speaking only through a screen, while under the guise of openness—tempered by matters of national security—maintains a distance, actual and symbolic, between the public and the spaces in which one can be ruled an existential threat to one's own country and marked for death.

Yet, the practice of opaquely communicating through screens begs the question of the function of the open secret in the context of national security. What is the purpose of publicizing secrets? How is belonging communicated in an environment characterized by a fluid and shifting play of transparency and opacity? The answer to the first question has been widely discussed. The executive's management of what is known and unknown acts as a public relations campaign, which prevents citizens from fully grasping the context of violence, a strategy likely to garner popular support for government action.[58] Indeed, many cheered the killing of al-Awlaki. Congressman Peter King called the operation "a tribute" to the administration. John McCain was "glad they did it"; Senate Majority Leader Harry Reid was certain that al-Awlaki deserved to die. More generally, recent Pew Research Center opinion polls indicate that a majority of Americans support the use of both drones and intrusive surveillance measures.[59]

The open secret also functions as a "way of imparting knowledge such that it cannot be claimed and acted on."[60] That is, without having the details through which to scrutinize government action, there is no way to effectively challenge the mechanisms of counterterrorism practice. Once the redacted Awlaki memo was released, legal scholars saw a variety of issues: its application of "public authority justification"—which allows, among other things, fire trucks to speed when traveling to an alarm—to killing an American abroad as unconvincing, particularly in its application to the CIA rather than the military; and its dependence on imminence (which does not require evidence of impending action) noting that there is "a big difference between a government official satisfying themselves and the criminal standard of proof."[61] Certainly, these debates cannot begin without access, but the constant battle over access is also problematic. For political philosopher Jodi Dean, the obsession with revelation is a block to democratic participation, directing debate from pressing issues and toward negotiating the boundary of what is accessible and what is not.[62]

To begin to answer the question of belonging, the structure of the open secret must be positioned within the problematic of the Double, in which us and other occupy shared spaces. Rather than simply an omission, aberration, or lack that hinders democratic society, opacity, particularly in its function in the open secret, produces and "correspond[s] to particular knowledges and circulate[s] as part of particular regimes of truth."[63] In the context at hand, the open secret works to reinforce the blurred boundaries of identification seen in the Double. In the open secret's simultaneous acknowledgment and disavowal, both trust and suspicion are communicated; the open secret informs the citizen and keeps information away from the suspect without explicitly delineating a boundary between the two. Here, rather than plainly distinguishing friend from foe in demographic terms or as occupying distinct spaces, the binary between the two—including the "sanctity of the first term"[64] (i.e., citizen)—is recovered in potentials (suspect/spy) that are distributed among the whole population, however unevenly.

How does one signal one's belonging in a space made tense by suspicions of treason, in a cloud of secrecy marked by drones and death? I argue that those who laugh in the face of precarity communicate their belonging, all the while making no demands and, thus, maintain the structure of the open secret. Three examples provide ample illustration. First, at a budget hearing in 2012, Senator Patrick Leahy pressed attorney general Eric Holder regarding the Awlaki memo:

> "I still want to see the Office of Legal Counsel memorandum and I would urge you to keep working on that," Mr. Leahy said to Mr. Holder. "I realize that's a matter of some debate within the administration but. . . ." The senator then paused, smiled and laughed. Mr. Holder responded by nodding and said, chuckling, "That would be true."

Second, during his 2011 speech at Harvard Law School, John Brennan was asked by an audience member plainly, "Does the C.I.A. have a drone program?" As "Mr. Brennan struggled to suppress a smile, he said, 'If the agency did have such a program, I'm sure it would be done with the utmost care, precision . . ' and the next part was garbled by the laughter of the audience." Third, at the 2010 White House Correspondents' Association Dinner, during President Obama's routine, he quipped, "The Jonas Brothers are here tonight. They're out there somewhere. Sasha and Malia are huge fans. But, boys, don't get any ideas. [Laughter.] I have two words for you—Predator drones. [Laughter.] You will never see it coming. [Laughter.] You think I'm joking. [Laughter.]"[65]

Much derided in Western philosophy, laughter has been theorized as a signal of superiority (Hobbes), as the result of an experience of incongruity, that is, when scenarios do not match our expectations (Kant and Schopenhauer), and as a release of excess energy whether of thought or emotion (Freud). In relation to the open secret, laughter retains a semblance of all of these traits in its multiple functions. The first is, as an act of avoidance, procedural. Laughter allows conversations to continue past what would otherwise be an insurmountable impasse, as in the exchange between Leahy and Holder above. One demands information from another, knowing perfectly well that the other cannot disclose that information (regardless of the fact that its existence is already public). Simultaneously an acknowledgment and disavowal, the laughter between Leahy and Holder signals recognition and provides relief in allowing one (Holder) not to utter knowledge of the secret directly and in allowing the government procedural to continue.

Laughter's second function centers on identification and is inextricably linked to the procedural. French philosopher Henri Bergson posited laughter as a collective phenomenon that requires a certain degree of indifference to the potentially serious implications of a given scenario.[66] In the context of national security, particularly in the examples of Brennan's and Obama's speeches, laughter works to signal one's belonging in a group. If one can laugh with the government, that is, show indifference to another's death without needing to know the details surrounding it, then the joke is, in effect, not on them. (Leahy and Holder's conversation could not proceed without this identification.) Laughter marks them as members of the superior group; by laughing they assert that they are not threatened by their government's secrecy. This is a phenomenon not limited to these three instances in the war on terror. Following the January 2015 attack on the *Charlie Hebdo* offices in Paris, various pundits and media outlets chastised those who would not republish the magazine's cartoons, calling them traitors.[67] If you cannot laugh with the group, you are not part of it. It is a dichotomous articulation in a milieu marked by a collapse of boundaries, just one way to mark which side one positions oneself on in the clash of civilizations dyad.

Laughter in this context reveals a process of identification in a milieu marked by blurred boundaries between trust and suspicion, transparency and opacity, one in which us and other are distributed potentials.

This securitizing laughter is directed at someone, without explicitly expressing who that someone is in demographic terms. While some can choose not to laugh, the ability of others is taken away by the trauma wrought by the Predator's missile. The ability to laugh at the sky, like the spy/suspect dichotomy, is not equally distributed. Mimicking the See/Say Something campaign, explicit articulations are abandoned in favor of more fluid practices that mark some as less deserving. Certainly, al-Awlaki and those tied to the markers that made him other/killable—even as it was his status as Double that marked the urgency of his imminent death—would find it difficult to laugh; or those in the spaces hidden by the pixilation of the drone pilot's screen who experience the taunting sound of the drone and the hellfire that comes after (or those who despite being removed from those spaces identify with those therein). In another case, but one within America's borders, the Newburgh Four similarly illustrates that some are less able to laugh than others.

The "Pathetic Newburgh Four": Poor, Black, and Jailed

For the family of the Newburgh Four, the arrest of the men was no laughing matter. On September 16, 2010, an altercation took place in the Lower Manhattan courthouse where the trial of the four men was being held. It was a Thursday and the final session of that week had just let out. As the jury was being led out a family member or friend of one of the defendants spotted them. The individual began to shout. While the exact exchange was not recorded, it was relayed to Judge Colleen McMahon the following Monday. The individual angrily told the jurors that they should know the difference between terrorism and entrapment. If they could *see* Newburgh, New York—the town where the men lived—they would understand the difference.[68] The unidentified individual's comment hints at what remains hidden by the Prislam narrative: the other space affected by mass incarceration, the impoverished/depressed city. Positioning the prison within critical reflections on mass incarceration furnishes an alternative reading of the prison in relation to counterterrorism. Far from dismissing the prison as unimportant, I argue that mass incarceration helps to create the potential for counterterrorism operations to "succeed." To be clear, I am arguing that the confluence of prison and terror remains important, but because of the politics of imprisonment rather than the "nature" of (black) prisoners.

Much of the criticism levied against the government's case focused on the informant, the securitizing Double of counterterrorism. The Newburgh sting was not Shahed Hussain's first operation. A native of Pakistan, he fled the country after being held on kidnapping and murder charges—political-motivated charges, he claimed—and only after his father bribed local officials to secure his release. In 1994 he entered the United States on a fake British passport. Settling in Albany, New York, he worked as an interpreter for the Department of Motor Vehicles. While there, he ran a scheme in which he would feed test answers to individuals for whom he was supposed to be translating. He was caught in an FBI sting operation. Facing deportation and a litany of fraud charges, he agreed to work as an informant. His first operation as Maqsood, a wealthy man with ties to Jaish-e-Mohammed, led to the arrest of a local Albany imam. It was an operation that relied on Hussain's work to set up a loan as money laundering for the terror group. For his work, Hussain received a sentence of time served and a letter from the FBI to help him avoid deportation. For the Newburgh sting, he was compensated.

Much like Mahmoud Omar in Chapter 2, Shahed Hussain was not a passive listening post despite framing his job as that of a listener. Early on in the trial, the prosecution admitted that Hussain was "no wall-flower," but acted as one might expect a terrorist recruiter to act.[69] Upon cross-examination, he admitted as much:

Q: And you were supposed to be passive, correct?
A: Sometimes, yes ma'am, not always.
Q: Not always. And isn't it true that you were the one who initiated conversations many times about jihad; isn't it true?
A: Yes, ma'am.[70]

In his active role, Hussain regularly initiated conversations about jihad, America, or Jews, often with statements as vile as those made by James Cromitie. For example, he once stated that "to eat under the shadow of a Jew, is like eating your own mother's meat."[71] He also did much more. He was the only link the men had to terrorism. The Newburgh Four were not radicalized on the Internet. There was no indication that the Newburgh Four had regular computer access. The smallest digital tasks seemed to impress Cromitie. When Hussain produced a map of their targets via Google Maps, Cromitie exclaimed, "I'm surprised you even got that. That's what's up. You did that on the computer?!"[72] Hussain also suggested, purchased, and/or procured all of the technologies necessary to carry out the plot: digital cameras, burner phones, stinger missiles, and improvised explosive devices. Again, as with the Fort Dix case, the weapons were intended not merely to frighten a jury and the public, but also to connect the men to global jihad through a shared modus operandi.

Hussain shaped the case significantly through his ability to switch the hidden cameras and microphones to which he was attached on and off as he saw fit. Judge McMahon acknowledged the peculiar consequences of this practice in that "the critical [initial] conversations in which Mr. Cromitie ostensibly came up with the idea to do jihad are conveniently not on any tape or video recording."[73] In fact, these statements were the impetus for moving forward with the sting operation. Hussain also acted as an interpreter of what was on and not on those tapes. If Hussain's account of events as recorded in his handler's handwritten notes did not match surveillance recordings, he dismissed these discrepancies as errors made by his handler.[74] Moreover, in the damning prayer for success, the men failed to verbalize their exhortations of jihad despite Hussain's specific instruction to "say it loud so everyone [read: the hidden microphone] could hear." On the stand he resorted to interpreting their motions, "you just do it in your heart you just don't say it loudly. And this—so Mr. Cromitie did do a dua [prayer] in his heart, and so did I. There are no words said in Dua, loudly sir."[75] To further place Cromitie and company in the narrative of jihad, he asserted that Cromitie's purchase of "two Arabic channels" to get news from overseas was a clear indication that "he vied to be in a terrorist organization . . ."—his commentary was cut short by an objection from the defense.[76] Hussain could not confirm the purchase, and it was likely another of Cromitie's lies given that he repeatedly displayed a complete ignorance of international terrorist attacks. For example, during a trip to Philadelphia with Maqsood in 2008, it was clear that he had not heard of the then front-page news of attacks in Mumbai, India. To keep

Cromitie within the narrative of jihad, Hussain bought a newspaper featuring a story on the attacks and gave it to him; that paper was ultimately entered into evidence. Last, and a point I will deal with in detail below, Hussain regularly doled out money to the men and promised much more after the mission.

The entrapment defense has yet to be successful in a post-9/11 terrorism trial. The Newburgh case, because of the egregious behavior of the informant, was expected to draw a line in the sand for what constituted entrapment in informant-led operations. Despite some controversy surrounding it, the definitive test for entrapment is the "subjective test," which focuses on the predisposition of the defendant, that is, whether or not she would carry out a crime given the chance.[77] The Prislam narrative assumes a general predisposition within the prison population that renders inmates more vulnerable to radicalization. It is a predisposition articulated as a violent tendency, which is itself explicitly tied to the politics of 1960s America. Visible here, among other things, is the deeply racist nature of the anxieties concerning violent radicalization in the Prislam narrative. The history of mass incarceration is, thus, crucial for fully grasping how racialized notions of criminality become enmeshed in the machinations of counterterrorism.

The American prison boom from the 1970s onward is well documented, as is the role of racial anxieties therein—blackness long positioned as threatening to white supremacy and order.[78] Almost half a century ago, conceptualizations of the prison as a place of rehabilitation and reform gave way to notions of incapacitation, docility, deterrence, punishment, and enclosure, hiding from the public society's most dangerous. When the United States declared a war on crime, it was at its outset a response to the push for civil rights and steeped in racialized constructions of criminality and victimhood.[79] Whites were portrayed as victims and blacks as receivers of aid who would nevertheless turn to crime. Furthermore, the simultaneous criminalization of urban space—on account of the concentration of African Americans in the country's inner cities—served to increase the proportion and number of blacks in US prisons. African American men are starkly overrepresented in US prisons, "imprisoned at a rate of 6.4 times greater than white men."[80] For communities of color, mass incarceration brought disenfranchisement, poverty, less access to government aid, and lower education—the hindering of the life chances of an entire population in regard to education, employment, life expectancy, health, and so forth.

Mass incarceration puts into motion "a vicious cycle of imprisonment and want, one that both undergirded and ensured civic distress: mass incarceration increased poverty, increased urban poverty led to even more urban incarceration, and so on."[81] That is, two spaces kept from the public's view—the prison and the depressed city—are mutually constitutive, both forms of invisibility and encasement. One's oscillation between the two presents a cyclical movement that is ensured by stigma and a variety of other constraints.[82] Moreover, the cycle also structures societal expectations of predisposition. The movements internal to the mass incarceration phenomenon describe well the life experiences of the Newburgh Four. All four men moved between jail and the impoverished town of Newburgh, New York. James Cromitie, for example, had been in and out of prison since his early teens. In that time he amassed a record of twenty-seven arrests and a total of twelve years served. All four were largely undereducated, held low-paying jobs, and had little access to government aid. The latter point is perhaps most evident in the case of Laguerre Payen, who is schizophrenic. When authorities raided his apartment, they did not find jihadist propaganda or bomb-making manuals. Rather, they found jars of urine; due to his psychological state he had been too afraid to use the shared bathroom at the end of the hall in his building. Just how closely these men's lives are tied to the prison system was poignantly illustrated by the fact that, as the story unfolded, Cromitie's own family could not confirm his religious affiliation. Journalists and police were left to rely on his prison records.[83]

When prosecutors, the media, and politicians invoke Prislam, whether explicitly or implicitly, they invoke the specter of black criminality. The failure of the entrapment defense depends on not only the fear generated by "terrorism" but also that engendered in the racialized stigma of criminality and its accompanying expectations of predisposition (further accompanied by the "fantasy of connectivity"). Here, sociologist Bruce Western's assertion, that "the self-sustaining character of mass imprisonment as an engine of social inequality" ensures that "the penal system will remain as it has become, a significant feature on the new landscape of American poverty and race relations," can be extended to the realm of counterterrorism.[84] It is Hussain's exploitation of systemic inequality that illustrates the American quality of jihad, albeit in a much different way than is presented in the body of al-Awlaki. Just how Hussain operated illustrates how counterterrorism can function through and exacerbate experiences of second-class citizenship.

Hussain's largest task was to establish a relationship first with Cromitie and then with the other men. He did this through exploiting their poverty, developing a relationship of financial dependence. Hussain, as Maqsood, stood out when he arrived at the Newburgh mosque. Rolling up in a variety of luxury cars and dressed in designer clothes, he ostentatiously displayed his apparent wealth. Hussain explained on the stand that posing as a rich man was a necessity so that others would want to talk to him.[85] Hussain and Cromitie met only months after the informant began visiting the mosque, but when Cromitie first spotted him, he was instantly attracted to his wealth. Cromitie introduced himself as Abdul Rahman and commented on Hussain's sandals, which he claimed to recognize as being Afghani because his father was from there. Another of Cromitie's many lies, here his outlandish statements more clearly resemble the attempts of a man trying to ingratiate himself with a wealthy acquaintance. That day, Hussain bought Cromitie a drink. As their relationship continued Hussain paid for every meal, and later, when Cromitie asked, he readily provided money for groceries and Cromitie's $180 monthly rent. Hussain reassured Cromitie, "If you need anything, just call me. If you need money, you come to me. If you need money, I can give you money, you know."[86]

Hussain was not merely a source of petty cash. Rather, he held the promise of a better life for each man. He offered Cromitie a quarter million dollars and a barbershop, playing on the one skill Cromitie had picked up in prison and his only potential way out of the cycle of imprisonment and want in which he was stuck. David Williams was promised enough money to pay for his brother's liver transplant—a fact the prosecution sought, but failed, to have ruled as "irrelevant and prejudicial."[87] Both Onta Williams and a penniless Payen were offered ten thousand dollars.

Here, a different picture of the four men emerges, one in stark contrast to that of a quartet who found in jihad an outlet to satisfy their bloodlust. As Paul Harris of the *Guardian* wrote, "none of the four men fit the usual profile of a terrorist-in-waiting, let alone an active militant.

But they did fit the profile of desperate men who would do anything for money."[88] Here, Cromitie's boastings about his nonexistent violent past and questionable extremist beliefs could be understood as a ploy through which to make him seem credible to Hussain, thus keeping the latter's wallet open. David Williams wrote from prison that "every time James lied to him [Hussain], or said something anti-American or whatever, the informant would give him money. Cromitie knew what the informant wanted to hear and gave it to him so he could get that money." Cromitie's lawyer put it more plainly; he was "singing for his supper."[89] According to Williams the men had intended to con Hussain, taking his money without carrying out any attack.

There is certainly evidence to support the notion that the Cromitie and company were only interested in Hussain's money. For instance, Cromitie baulked at Hussain's requests for months, failing to produce a target, plan, or team. "Well maybe it's not my mission then, maybe my mission hasn't come yet," he once told Hussain.[90] Cromitie's dedication to money rather than martyrdom was starkly displayed in actions large and small. He took the camera Hussain had bought for reconnaissance and sold it for fifty dollars, telling Hussain that it had broken. Also, in the thousands of phone conversations taped by the FBI, not once does Cromitie say anything anti-Semitic or anti-American, except when he is speaking to Hussain. In the lead-up to the night of the plot, a recorded phone call between Cromitie and David Williams reveals that neither mentions jihad, only money.

When Cromitie was not in need he actively avoided Hussain. On February 25, 2009, Hussain was supposed to pick up Cromitie so that they could begin planning (at this point, there had already been several false starts). Cromitie's lawyer narrated what happened next in court:

Now, something very, very remarkable happens at this point of the movie, ladies and gentleman. . . . Cromitie drops out of sight completely. . . . When Hussain shows up the next day at 3:00, James is not home. Or at least he pretends not to be home. . . . And from outside of James' house, Hussain calls James. And James says, well, he is somewhere, but he is not in Newburgh. James says, "I'll call you back at 6:00." At 6:00, Hussain shows up at the house again . . . Cromitie is not there.[91]

Cromitie eventually told Hussain that he was leaving to work in North Carolina. The FBI knew this to be a lie because agents were monitoring his home and phone. Cromitie deleted voicemail after voicemail, up until April 5, 2009, the day Cromitie reestablished contact. He had lost his minimum-wage job at Walmart and was more desperate than ever. Angered at being abandoned—which he reiterated on the witness stand—Hussain relayed to Cromitie that the repeated delays had endangered Hussain's life, insinuating that Jaish-e-Mohammed threatened to behead him.[92] Regardless of whether Cromitie believed that this also meant that his own life was in jeopardy or that his cash flow was at risk, it was only after this warning that a plot began to take shape. Even after this, Cromitie stalled, failing to "arm" the bombs when the men were in Riverdale, forcing Hussain to do it.

While Hussain regularly treated the men to food and gifts, he introduced money into the plot itself only after months of working on Cromitie without any movement. This opened up the operation to charges of entrapment, however mitigated by the stigma of racialized criminality. Hussain was providing an incentive for someone to commit a crime he would otherwise not have. In order to minimize this risk, the informant worked to entangle money and jihad in such a way as to make them inseparable. He referred to the promised sums as "jihad money," repeatedly telling the men that they would be rewarded in two ways: monetarily in this life and with paradise in the next. When pushed about it on the stand he reiterated:

> Q: Now again, jihad money is the same as like regular money in terms of how you might be able to spend it, correct?
> A: On the spending purposes, the *meaning purpose* is very different.[93]

Thus, connecting to global jihad is conceived as a free choice to buy in, regardless of one's social position. For the prosecution there was no consequential difference between accepting money and taking up jihad.

In addition to this characterization, Hussain played down the significance of the money in a variety of ways. First, he claimed that the $250,000 he promised Cromitie was code. The men, at Hussain's insistence, kept a list of code words for weapons and targets. "$250,000" was not on that list. In fact Hussain admitted that he never told Cromitie explicitly that it was code; Hussain simply "thought he would understand."[94] Second, Hussain liked to say something that Cromitie would regularly regurgitate back at him: that the group was acting "for the cause, not just because." Heard throughout the recordings, Hussain repeated ad nauseam that the mission is "not about the money." When Cromitie told Hussain that the others "will do it for the money. . . . they're not even thinking about the cause," he sharply protested. In an exchange on April 23, 2009, when David Williams IV joined the conversation, Hussain told him, "This is not anything to do with money. This has everything to do with Allah." Williams replied, "Right. But they giving us money anyway."[95] Hussain's repeated insistence, the defense argued at trial, was a clear sign that the men's involvement was entirely the result of the money offered rather than jihad. In perhaps his most unnerving moment on the stand, Hussain retorted:

> I have to—in radicalism, in radicalism, money is the last thing anybody could think about. It's all about religion. About the cause. And if somebody—the Agent, Fuller, wanted to know, was they are going to do it for the money, or for the greed, or for the cause. So I have to remind them, every time I met them, are you going to do it for the cause. If it is for the money, we don't want to do it. And I had to keep reminding them, keep reminding them, is it for the cause, or is it for the money. Because the question was Agent Fuller wanted to find out if they—if the mission, or the terrorist attacks, or bombings were done because they wanted to do a prank because of the greed or for the cause. And he wanted to find out. And that's why I was reminding them all the time.[96]

Hussain's strained entanglement of money and jihad is analogous to that of counterterrorism and racialized structures of policing in the United States. During an appeal hearing, the prosecution continued to insist, "Money didn't matter to these guys," to which Judge McMahon quickly replied, "Really? It was painfully obvious that the reason they did it was for the money."[97] Yet, at their sentencing Judge McMahon called the men "thugs for hire," invoking a well-worn trope used to criminalize black men. Her remarks illustrate the self-sustaining nature of mass incarceration: "I imagine that you will be far from here, and quite isolated. . . . I doubt that you will receive any training or rehabilitative treatment of any sort. Your crimes were terrible. Your punishment will indeed be severe. 25 years in the sort of conditions I anticipate you are facing is easily the equivalent of life in other conditions."[98] Placed atop existing structures of policing and imprisonment, counterterrorism here oils the cogs of mass incarceration and vice versa. The success, in the Newburgh case, is starkly dependent on the spaces of imprisonment and want that are kept out of the sight of the public. This is what the unidentified family member meant when she implored the jury to *see* Newburgh. It is only in contextualizing this case against the backdrop of mass incarceration that the American flavor of (counter)jihad comes to the fore. It is only by seeing Newburgh that we can fully grasp the ways in which counterterrorism practice exacerbates already-existing second-class experiences of citizenship.

At his sentencing, Cromitie averred that "I've never been a terrorist and I never will be a terrorist." Similarly, David Williams IV wrote from jail, "Evidence-wise, we had them beat. . . . We got convicted on feelings. They [the prosecutors] started talking about 9/11, and James was saying a lot of stuff that was ill and real stupid, and we got convicted on that. Once you put 'terrorist' in front of anything, it's like being charged with rape or child molestation. Once a jury hears that you're accused of a certain type of crime, you're already guilty."[99] Certainly, Williams is correct that terrorism and the fear it induces perhaps overdetermines how one is seen by a jury of one's peers. But this is not mutually exclusive from the racialized notions of predisposition that decades of mass incarceration have wrought.

Citizenship in an Age of Terror

The war on terror, as the popular narrative goes, began on American soil on September 11, 2001 (even if its beginnings can be traced back decades). The advent of homegrown terrorism marks its uncanny return home, with the adversary communicated as possessing unmistakably American traits—whether al-Awlaki's accent and cultural know-how or the Newburgh Four's entanglement within America's penal system. In the aftermath of 9/11 Americans were called on to support the exportation of violence abroad, and a year later New York's MTA introduced the slogan "If You See Something, Say Something." This call to stand guard has increasingly, with the gaining focus on homegrown terrorism, shifted to the everyday. The latest DHS campaign under the banner of See/Say Something, "Protect Your Everyday," features a firefighter, a teacher, a farmer, a barber, a student, a waitress, and a mom. Together, as a multicultural representational slice of America, they playfully muse about the innocuous unforeseen events that occur every day (e.g., flat tires, traffic delays, etc.). But, they turn stern and warn:

> It's when you experience a moment of uncertainty.
> Something you know shouldn't be there.
> Or someone's behavior that doesn't seem quite right.
> These are the moments to take a pause.
> Because if something doesn't feel right, it's probably not.

The video, which reassures the viewer that it is not about paranoia or fear, but about responsibility, never illustrates this moment of uncertainty; all of the citizens go about their everyday without having to operationalize their responsibility.

As I discussed above, this campaign also buttresses the necessity of government intervention. And recent years have seen initiatives aimed directly at the status of citizenship. In 2011, Senators Joe Lieberman (I-CT) and Scott Brown (R-MA) and Representatives Charlie Dent (R-PA) and Jason Altmire (D-PA) introduced the Enemy Expatriation Act. The act was about a page and sought to amend section 349 of the Immigration and Nationality Act, adding one way in which an American could lose her citizenship: "engaging in, or purposefully and materially supporting, hostilities against the United States" (therein, "hostilities" were defined as "any conflict subject to the laws of war"). Thought to be overly broad and unconstitutional, HR3166/S1698 died; but not for long. While this was seemingly a one-off effort, the potential of Americans traveling to Syria to fight alongside ISIS reinvigorated citizenship-stripping initiatives.

Charles Dent reintroduced the same bill (HR545) on January 27, 2015, which again failed. In December of that year, not to be discouraged, Dent resubmitted the act (HR4186) with an important change. The added actions for which one could lose one's citizenship included "traveling abroad to join, participate in, train with, fight for, conspire with, or otherwise support a foreign terrorist organization designated by the Secretary of State under section 219." At the time of writing, it has been referred to the Committee on the Judiciary for further consideration. This is one of several related efforts. In September 2014, Texas Representative Ted Poe introduced a bill that would revoke the passport of any American for the same reasons (word for word) as Dent's restructured Enemy Expatriation Act. Poe's bill (HR5406) also died, and he also resubmitted twice more (as HR237), in January and July 2015. It passed in the House in a voice vote (no tally was taken) and has moved to the Senate. It allows one to ask for due process, but allows reports to be submitted in classified form.

In January 2015 Representative Steve King of Iowa and Senator Ted Cruz submitted a bill titled the Expatriate Terrorist Act, which in essence combines the Enemy Expatriation Act and the efforts to revoke passports. The approach is broader. Rather than simply tacking on another action by which an American can lose her citizenship at the end of the list found in section 349 of the Immigration and Nationality Act, they not only position the added stipulation in the middle of the list, but aim to add "foreign terrorist organization" to each action listed, such as swearing allegiance to an adversary of the United States. In effect, an American can relinquish his citizenship by "taking oath or making an affirmation or other formal declaration of allegiance to a foreign state," and the bill seeks to extend this to those who have joined ISIS and burned their passports (evidenced by YouTube videos). While one can hardly doubt their intentions, institutionalizing this move grants ISIS a status once reserved for other sovereign states and one that the group is perhaps best denied.

While the proposed bills are unlikely to become law, their recurrence illustrates the anxieties brought about by an adversary in which Americans recognize something of themselves and the spatial collapse of global conflict; this is both a constitutive anxiety and a strategic way of communicating threat to facilitate particular counterterrorism practices. However, what the al-Awlaki and Newburgh Four cases illustrate is the multiple ways in which belonging and citizenship are tied up in counterterrorism. The open secret manages what is known and unknown, producing peculiar ways of voicing one's belonging: through laughter, but a laughter always aimed at someone. The informant's exploitation of systemic inequalities similarly marks that there are those who cannot laugh in the face of death by counterterrorism—in the Foucauldian sense that includes social death (i.e., life imprisonment). Short of the explicit stripping of one's passport, the Double facilitates a plethora of practices that make citizenship precarious. Indeed, the Double positions the citizen as simultaneously suspect and spy, injecting a general sense of precarity into citizenship in the service of counterterrorism. But in counterterrorism's American spaces, its interaction with institutional configurations—secrecy and mass incarceration—the uneven distribution of this dual position is reinforced. Just as the Double as enemy has many manifestations, so too does the effect of positing the citizen as suspect/spy, effects that differ based on one's social position and identity. Some cannot laugh at the use of a hellfire missile to kill an American without charge or due process. Others, rather than being more prone to radicalization as the Prislam narrative assumes, are more susceptible to the consequences of, and targeted by, informant-led operations. All of these effects are the result of counterterrorism's intermingling with American institutional configurations, a relation that deeply affects the shapes of the Double in popular and official discourse.

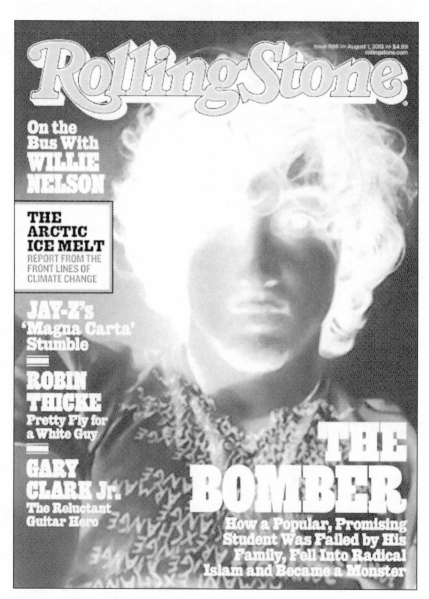

Figure 7. *Rolling Stone*, August 1, 2013.

No Exit

The Double is not a singular phenomenon. It accommodates ever-shifting configurations of difference and likeness; the push-and-pull modality it embodies is both anxiety and remedy. It is a threat that might look, act, or talk "like us" in a variety of registers. And surely, if one scrolls through the profiles of homegrown terrorists (even when limited to those who have been identified and self-identify as jihadists), represented are a variety of faces and histories. Yet, invocations of likeness, much like those of difference, are never self-evident. They are strategic and facilitate particular practices of security. Throughout this book, I have examined the ways and to what effect similarity is injected into how threat is discussed in the context of homegrown terrorism, and what it reveals about identity, media, and belonging in the contemporary United States.

The various manifestations of the Double—along with its temporality and spatiality, embroiled with identity constructs and media technologies—that have been the subject of the book lead back to the case with which the book began. The Boston Marathon bombing could be described as the most striking case of the discourse of the Double. It involves a look-alike, a doppelgänger so apparently familiar (and attractive) that it was thought to have elicited empathy, the most shocking of emotions in the context of terror (though largely dismissed in sexist language, the result of the "more primal and less pretty [impulses] in the female psyche" and diagnosed as "hybristophilia").[1] I purposefully left this case to the conclusion not because it is the most recent chronologically, but for two reasons that structure this conclusion. First, it brings us back to the origin myth of the Double, the Tale of the Two Brothers, and helps to summarize many of the phenomena examined throughout this book: identity, media technologies, and belonging in the context of homegrown terrorism. But its usefulness in this sense depends on not naturalizing the claim that the terrorist threat is "like us." Tsarnaev could surely be said to look the part, but in outlining the discourse of the Double in its historical development across a variety of cases, these claims vis-à-vis Tsarnaev can hardly be said to be spontaneous. That is, neither the bombing itself nor the appearance of "Jahar" on the cover of a popular magazine were catalysts of a discourse in which terrorists are made sense of through narratives of likeness and familiarity. Placing the case one might deem "most obvious" at the end not only acts as a crescendo but has allowed me to develop a theory of the Double in a way that does not rely on seemingly self-evident notions of likeness that only reinforce problematic identity constructs. To be clear, denaturalizing likeness does not in turn depend on essentialist notions of difference. Instead, I have been aiming to illustrate how invocations of likeness, which are part and parcel of contemporary US security discourse, are as much the result of a complex process as are the enemy images that pivot on reductive articulations of difference. Even the most familiar can be made other. Those, like al-Awlaki, that were readily made other were also depicted to be "like us." And, it is at this intersection, the work of making familiar and making other, where I locate the second reason for ending with this case. To address a question that moves throughout the book: is the image of the Double an enemy image?

The Brothers Tsarnaev

Throughout the book I have argued that the figure of the Double represents both the anxieties surrounding homegrown terrorism as well as the securitization that comes with them; it demarcates a plane of security in which boundaries of identification are pushed and pulled. Much like in other cases, the revelation that a friend committed an act so violent as to be called terrorism was met with disbelief, shock, and terror: "I can't feel that my friend, the Jahar I knew, is a terrorist. . . . That Jahar isn't, to me," relayed one of his closest friends.[2] In their lament is the idea that the bomber was someone else, a Hyde to their Jekyll, a shadow they never saw. Even his older brother, Tamerlan, who was more readily made other in media reports—via his accent, conservatism, and open faith—"seemed so nice."[3] The reaction to the Boston Marathon bombing illustrates well the anxieties surrounding the Double. How is one to tell apart a good-looking popular kid who had been excited about gaining

American citizenship and the one who scribbled "Fuck America" in his own blood as he lay dying during his run from police? Or, to paraphrase his former wrestling coach, how is one to separate the good kid from the monster?[4] Fyodor Dostoyevsky's *The Double*, in which a lowly civil servant meets his copy, one that has all of the qualities that he lacks, illustrates the conundrum well: "If the two of them had been placed next to each other, no one, absolutely no one, would have been able to say who was the real Mr. Golyadkin and who the imitation, who the old and who the new, who the original and who the copy."[5] In the novel, Dostoyevsky provides only suffixes (Sr. and Jr.) and they retain the same name. Similarly, the Jahar his friend knew and the one staring back at America on newsstands cannot be adequately separated. The enemy cannot be named, placed, or identified. But, as I have shown throughout the book, this is a formulation of threat that security works with rather than simply against. Blurred boundaries underwrite the placement of novel spaces in the purview of counterterrorism, the use of informants, and mass surveillance.

In response to the controversy spurned by the placement of Dzhokhar Tsarnaev on its cover, in a pose and light many found too glamorous, *Rolling Stone* enlisted Matt Taibbi to explain it to the American public.[6] Taibbi, a Bostonian, positioned the cover and its accompanying story, Janet Reitman's "Jahar's World," as an effort to understand contemporary terrorism:

> The jarringly non-threatening image of Tsarnaev is exactly the point of the whole story. If any of those who are up in arms about this cover had read Janet's piece, they would see that the lesson of this story is that there are no warning signs for terrorism, that even nice, polite, sweet-looking young kids can end up packing pressure-cookers full of shrapnel and tossing them into crowds of strangers. Thus the cover picture is not intended to glamorize Tsarnaev. Just the opposite, I believe it's supposed to frighten. It's Tsarnaev's very normalcy and niceness that is the most monstrous and terrifying thing about him.

Here, despite the insinuation that the cover and story challenged dominant notions concerning terrorism, Taibbi is echoing the sentiments of attorney general Eric Holder and Janet Napolitano in their assertions that the homegrown terrorist lacks a typical profile. While there is certainly some value in stories that provide details of an individual's history in cases of violence, here the intention remains to frighten. Here, the invocations of likeness only reinforce the now commonplace security discourses that I have examined in this book.

Beyond the general contours of the anxieties and strategies of security the Double embodies, the Tsarnaev case also showcases its other aspects: the ways in which identity constructs and media technologies are implicated in structuring the Double; and the repercussions of this discourse and its practices for notions of belonging. The brothers Tsarnaev illustrate well the ways that identity constructs, both individual and collective, are invoked in the context of homegrown terrorism. Individual Americans (and residents) are positioned as suspect and susceptible. The Double often manifests in a psychological split and has long been associated with conditions such as schizophrenia; Dostoyevsky's tale is often interpreted in this way. For example, in the cases of Wade Michael Page and Nidal Malik Hasan, the mental states of both men were discussed at length; the potential of depression and a form of transferred PTSD, respectively. Of course, these had different inflections and were connected to other constructs in various degrees. Nevertheless, the psychological state of the brothers was also the subject of intense speculation. Tamerlan Tsarnaev, it was reported, confided in his mother that he felt there were "two people living in him," and reports framed his transformation into a killer as one that involved an increasingly aggressive "internal rambling that only he could hear," one that eventually began to issue orders.[7] Even as Dzhokhar's pressures and stresses were more explicitly connected to familial strife in media reports, he was said to have experienced "terrifying nightmares about murder and destruction."[8]

The mental state of each brother was connected to crises of social and collective identity. Media accounts stressed that the brothers struggled to "define themselves or where they belonged" and that their actions were potentially driven by a desire to resolve these tensions.[9] Much like with Hasan and al-Awlaki, the duo's "roots" became a subject of interest. The brothers were described as "reared by both Chechnya and America."[10] The former was thought to be stronger in Tamerlan, who emigrated at a later age and never shed his accent. Moreover, his lack of American friends and white wife who converted and wore the hijab (at his behest, it was said) were taken as signs that he never truly assimilated. Yet, as a boxer with aspirations to represent the United States in the Olympics, his friends called him "Tim." A rule change in the US Tournament of Champions (an Olympic qualifying event) disqualified permanent residents from competition, effectively ending his boxing career. For Tamerlan, this experience, among others, reduced his green card to a reminder "[that he was] not really an American."[11] His crisis of belonging was only further compounded during a 2012 trip to Dagestan (a republic within Russia, neighboring Chechnya). There, having grown a beard and given up drinking, Tamerlan showed up to prayer at a mosque known to be frequented by radicals. He greased his hair with olive oil and lined his eyes with dark makeup, "apparently in an effort to copy contemporary jihadist fashion," only to be chided as "too American."[12]

Described as attractive, happy, and charismatic, Dzhokhar was thought the better adjusted (read: assimilated) of the two, even tweeting his excitement at becoming a US citizen. Initially, it was thought that this pot-smoking popular kid who used his barbed wit to talk himself out of many precarious situations must have been brainwashed by his older brother. However, the more reporters and officials dug into the younger brother's life, the more the elder's influence was placed in doubt: "Up to his arrest, he drank and smoked marijuana—more marijuana than most high school or college students, friends said—despite . . . Tamerlan's clear disapproval."[13] Dzhokhar's story in the media became one of displacement and alienation. His parents divorced in 2011, with both eventually moving to Russia; his friends were going off to different colleges and he would eventually be on the verge of flunking out. The younger Tsarnaev's tie to his "roots" was described as more purposeful and reactionary. Feeling more isolated, he began to exert a strong interest in Chechnya despite never having lived there. He contacted an expert on the region, University of Massachusetts–Dartmouth Islamic studies professor Brian Glyn Williams, who agreed to help Dzhokhar in his genealogical pursuit. Williams was struck by "how little he actually knew. . . . He didn't know anything about Chechnya, and he wanted to know *everything*." Thus, while Tamerlan was framed as never shedding his roots, Dzhokhar was thought to have actively sought them out, revealing a "deeply fractured" teenager.[14]

As a threat that cannot be adequately named, the Double circulates. I have shown how connectivity is conceptualized in security discourses, positioning citizens as suspect and susceptible. More problematic, security officials operationally exploit connectivity vis-à-vis conspiracy charges in and through the informant to implicate, entrap, and convict Americans. Connectivity and social media were central in making sense of the transformation of the Tsarnaevs. One official commented, "I would not be surprised if they [the Tsarnaevs] had another life over social media."[15] Tamerlan maintained a YouTube channel he created after returning to the United States from his 2012 trip to Dagestan. Therein, he had two videos listed under "terrorism." He also followed an obscure Russian jihadist, Gadzhimurad Dolgatov, online. Dzhokhar's online activity was stressed as one indicating a cultural as well as psychological shift. He "abandoned his American Facebook for the Russian version Vkontakte," wrote Reitman in her *Rolling Stone* profile.[16] Dzhokhar also maintained two separate Twitter accounts. One broadcast the slacker image that his friends knew. The other showed a wannabe jihadist. The maintenance of these dual identities was the work of a teenager the *New York Times* called a "master of concealment."[17]

The brothers also downloaded jihadist propaganda particularly, the sermons of Anwar al-Awlaki, who has been linked to a dozen incidents both before and after his death in 2011. Most consequentially, the brothers apparently fashioned their bombs from instructions found in al-Qaeda's *Inspire*. In fact, if one closely examines the New America Foundation's statistics on homegrown jihadist incidents, the Boston Marathon bombing is the only case in which individuals successfully constructed an improvised explosive device through the utilization of Internet materials alone, that is, without any hands-on training or guidance. Based on interviews with explosive experts, Michael Kenney argues that online manuals, while providing abstract technical knowledge (*techne*), cannot provide the necessary *mētis* or situational knowledge necessary to handle the volatile mixtures needed to build a bomb. In short, someone trying to construct a bomb from just an online manual is likely to hurt or kill himself before he can harm anyone else. Indeed, parsing through New America's data, one notices that in more than half of the jihadist plots that involve explosives, those explosives are fake and provided by paid government informants (much like the Fort Dix and

Newburgh plots). The others have all traveled abroad to receive training, have failed to successfully construct an explosive, or have been caught in the process of acquiring the necessary components.[18] The deadliest homegrown terrorist jihadists (as well as "non-jihadists," to use New America's dichotomy) involve profoundly American weapons, access to which is constitutionally protected. The Boston Marathon bombing seems to be the one exception, though doubts remain due to the sophistication of the devices and their well-timed execution (which has also fueled conspiracy theories about Dzhokhar's innocence). Upon further examination, there was no evidence of testing found in Tamerlan's apartment. For example, there was no circuit tester that experts deem necessary in ensuring that the components will work.[19]

However, it was not only the brothers' travel to and virtual projection into foreign spaces that accounted for their transformation. Models of radicalization were deployed in understanding the Tsarnaevs. Tom Neer of the Soufan Group—a counterterrorism think tank—was quoted in Reitman's piece:

> There is no single precipitating event or stressor. . . . Instead, what you see with most of these people [i.e., homegrown terrorists] is a gradual process of feeling alienated or listless or not connected. But what they all have in common is a whole constellation of things that aren't working right.[20]

This constellation includes innumerable experiences, any of which can act as triggers (economic hardship, experiences of prejudice, psychological issues, familial pressure, etc.). In Neer's comments the connectivity that is epistemologically inseparable from the Double manifests itself in disconnection on a personal and local level, repeating a well-worn anxiety concerning connectivity and alienation. Indeed, blame was spread out: their turbulent home life; the women in their lives, particularly their mother; a mysterious uncle named Misha; their Chechen heritage; social media; Tamerlan's battered brain (a result of his boxing career) and chronic unemployment; their faith; and failed attempts at realizing the American dream.

Some commentators mused that, despite their consumption of jihadist literature, the story of the brothers Tsarnaev "in the end . . . is not a story about Chechnya or radical Islam or the insurgency in the

North Caucasus" but also about something fundamentally American.[21] That is, radicalization is not equivalent to unidirectional infiltration. For example, Tamerlan's descent into conspiracy theories was not only the stuff of jihadist chatrooms. His fascination with 9/11 "truther" conspiracies was equally fueled through American sources, such as Alex Jones's Infowars and the film *Zeitgeist*.[22] Moreover, his failures (in providing for his family) that were thought to weigh heavily on him were explained not simply by his Chechen roots and traditions but also by the difficulties and systemic barriers for immigrants in achieving the American dream. Last, it was reported that Tamerlan had been questioned by federal agents—the defense suggesting that he had been asked to be an informant, though they were unable to obtain corroborating evidence—suggesting the role played by counterterrorism in fomenting the animosity it is charged with preventing; the "auto-immunological" dimensions of counterterrorism.[23]

The Tsarnaev case also illustrates the repercussions of the Double for thinking through citizenship and belonging. I have highlighted both exceptional and administrative ways in which terrorism has been dealt with in (and through the suspension of) the law. Neither approach, as I have shown, is without its implications for notions of belonging and experiences of citizenship. Which approach is more appropriate or effective remains a point of debate among America's political elite. For example, former US ambassador to the United Nations John Bolton criticized the Obama administration over what he refers to as the "criminal-law paradigm" in fighting terrorism, claiming that it signals defeat in the war on terror.[24] Supporting this line of thinking, some (including Senator Lindsey Graham) called for Dzhokhar Tsarnaev to be labeled an "unlawful enemy combatant"—similar to the labeling of al-Awlaki as a "specially designated global terrorist"—and denied Miranda rights.[25] Others called for him to be processed through the criminal justice system. Dzhokhar was read his Miranda rights, pled "not guilty," was tried, and was found guilty. He has been sentenced to death.

It is not only those who are directly charged with terrorism whose allegiance is questioned and, thus, their place within the collective made more precarious. In a strategic environment marked by the open secret and in which citizens are positioned, however unequally, as suspect and spy, there is no bounded positionality that saves one from suspicion;

there is, as the French collective Tiqqun states, "only proof."[26] What is the "If You See Something, Say Something" campaign if not a demand for citizens to prove their allegiance, even as the campaign suggests the impossibility of "seeing" clearly. Burdens of proof, much like the dual suspect/spy position, are not equally distributed, and the fallout of the Boston Marathon bombing provides an incisive example of the various inflections of this inequality. After the Boston Marathon bombing, news outlets asked what Katherine Russell, Tamerlan's widow, knew about the plot.[27] How had she failed to notice her husband's planning and plotting? At best, a case of a citizen asleep at her post, or worse, a sign that she was involved. In either case, her burden of proof was built upon normative gender constructs of the "good wife." "I don't know how she could not have known. I know when my husband farts in the basement," one *Huffington Post* reader wrote.[28] This statement captures precisely the extent of the detail citizens are expected to notice as well as the extent of their expected vigilance—those affects and intuitions one can access only through close contact and that might escape digital surveillance. Inadequately fulfilling her duty, Russell failed to provide proof that she was "still one of us." I include "still" because her burden of proof was undoubtedly compounded by her conversion and religious dress.[29]

The Boston Marathon bombing illustrates well the relationship between identity, media, and belonging with which this book is concerned. Various identity constructs are communicated in and through media, at times delineated, at times confused, overlapping, or superimposed onto one another. The loss of boundaries of identification is simultaneously positioned as affected and/or structured by media. This phenomenon, however, is not simply fought against. That is, counterterrorism is not simply concerned with reestablishing clear boundaries, but works in and through the relations embodied in the Double. Subsequently, these efforts produce novel articulations of belonging and reinforce and exploit already existing unequal experiences of citizenship. This book is as much about counterterrorism as it is about homegrown terrorism. The increasing articulations of homegrown terrorists as "like us" or "once a regular guy" are not simply a reflection of the inability to identify the enemy in contemporary distributed conflict. Rather, they are strategic invocations. Likeness on the plane of identification is as much a work of construction as difference. It is at this juncture, at the intersection of constructions of difference and likeness that I return to a question that permeates the entire book. That of whether or not the Double constitutes an enemy image.

The Terrorist Has Been Absorbed

Is the Double an enemy image? In considering the question I take my cue from a piece written in perhaps the most unlikely of sources, the *New York Times Style Magazine* (the September 15, 2013, Men's Fashion edition). In his piece, "Let Us Now Praise Infamous Men," American writer Joshua Ferris bemoans the "impoverishment of the image." He argues that the new media environment, marked by the democratization of communication and info-glut, severs the once uncontested link between the hero and the icon. As a result, the "heroic male icon" that inspired, defined, and unified a nation is lost (his gendering of the hero construct is not inconsequential, part and parcel of the nostalgic and conservative tone of his article). The apotheosis of the contemporary crisis of American identity—as reflected in the continuing war on terror (if by another name), economic hardship, the feared death of the American dream, an ineffective Congress, etc.—he argues is found "on the cover of the *Rolling Stone*," as the old song goes.[30] The figure of the terrorist, Ferris contends, which had remained outside of mass culture since the latter's dawn, is now a fixture in the popular American imagination. The placement of Tsarnaev's visage within a space of cultural affirmation, "the terrorist as icon," can mean only one thing: "the terrorist has been absorbed."

The writer's contentions could be dismissed as naïve and ahistorical, ignoring the magazine's tradition of investigative journalism as well as the other controversial figures that have been featured on its cover (e.g., Charles Manson). Nevertheless, he was not alone in his critique, and it provides the base from which to understand what kind of image the Double generates. If the Double marks the loss of the icon, what does this mean for the enemy image? A good point from which to build is precisely the loss of the identifiable enemy. As the minutes after 9/11—if one wagers to mark its end—turned into hours, days, and weeks, George W. Bush sang a number of variations on a theme that would come to characterize contemporary enmity (or its loss): "you are either with us or against us in the war on terror."[31] At times he altered the wording of the second half of the pairing to "with the terrorists." In any event, in his statements there is no "them," either literally ("against us") or at least in any legitimate sense ("with the terrorists"). Jacques Derrida posited, in his immediate thoughts on the attacks, that Bush's inability to identify the enemy against which he declared war indeed marked the dissolution of the political enemy in the Schmittean sense—indeed what I have been referring to in this book as an enemy, would be a "foe" for Schmitt.[32] Already in the wake of the Cold War (and its spectral rebirth) Derrida argued that the disappearance of the identifiable enemy, because of its constitutive role in defining "us," indeed implies the loss of the friend. But the Schmittean enemy is the political structuring enemy, and its loss, as Žižek reminds us, has simultaneously reinvigorated the binary logic of the enemy image. The enemy and the enemy image are certainly connected but belong to different registers. For Carlo Galli, the resurgence, if not intensification, of what he calls hyper-representations of enemy others is a symptom of "Global War," a futile attempt to remake boundless conflict in an obsolete mold. However, Tsarnaev's image and the instances of doubling examined throughout this book more generally do not fit this template. Rather, the Double marks the superimposition of the loss of political boundaries onto the plane of representation.

If the political enemy depends on clear political/state borders, by analogy an enemy image requires similar boundaries but on the level of representation be they racial, religious, classed, and so on. In the Double these binaries are blurred. This suggests that the loss of the icon and the disappearance of the enemy image are one and the same. The Double is, thus, clearly not an enemy image. Rather, it is better to think about the Double as an attempt to narrativize and visualize *threat* (one that is always-already veiled), a risk beyond the calculable, distinct from the enemy and enemy image; it is not simply the representation of Calli's "phantom enemy" (the most uncanny and absolute of enemies because it marks the indistinction between friend and enemy) but the injection of its (lack of) structure into practices of representation through marking difference, likeness, and their conflation. As such, the function of the Double image is not that of the enemy image; it is, in effect, the enemy image's negative inverse or its double exposure. It disrupts rather than unifies, lurks rather than looms. Threat is more dispersed than the enemy, fundamentally circulating, non-present, and beyond the measure of risk. While radicalization models posit a slew of possible triggers and factors, these are not subject to measurement in the same way as other risks (e.g., carbon emission levels for global warming). Rather, they are intended to open up spaces for surveillance (by government, by neighbor, by self). I will return to this functionality of the Double below, but at this juncture I want to detour into a cautionary point. The Double may not be an enemy image, but this claim is not intended to imply that the enemy image is lost in any absolute sense.

Hyper-representations of the (lost) enemy continue to populate official and cultural discourses concerning terrorism. Invocations of this binary enemy image surface throughout this book, and in some instances it is invoked as a haunting, a shadow cast over others that do not fit the profile. This is evident in the debate concerning Tsarnaev. In his defense of *Rolling Stone*, Matt Taibbi juxtaposes the Tsarnaev image to those of bin Laden on the covers of *Time* and *Newsweek*. In the latter, bin Laden's eyes are painted over with a streak of white, accompanied by the headline "Mission Accomplished" and an ominous subtitle, "But are we any safer?" For Taibbi, the answer is clearly "no" due to the fact that a clearly bounded enemy image has morphed into one of a veiled threat—"you can't see him coming." This temporal juxtaposition is instructive. Even with bin Laden's death, the other is not gone, but remains *not underneath but within* the mask of a handsome young American. Here, the terrorist has been absorbed, mixed into a veneer of agreeability and familiarity. In a landscape that lacks a politically identifiable enemy, the enemy image is made equally phantom in the context of homegrown terrorism.

The enemy image relegated, however momentarily to the background, can rematerialize. The appearance of the Double can spurn attempts at hyper-representation. In other words, the Double can arouse an urge to kill. Instructive here is De Quincey's "Milton versus Southey and Landor," admittedly transposed to the present context:

> Nature does not repeat herself. . . . Any of us would be jealous of his own duplicate; and if I had a doppelganger who went about personating

me, copying me, and pirating me . . . I might (if the Court of Chancery would not grant me an injunction against him) be so far carried away by jealousy as to attempt the crime of murder upon his carcass; and no great matter as regards HIM. But it would be a sad thing for me to find myself hanged; and for what, I beseech you? for murdering a sham, that was either nobody at all, or oneself repeated once too often.[33]

To appreciate fully the implications of the arousal of the Double vis-à-vis homegrown terrorism, killing must be understood, as it has been throughout the book, as more than murder. Following Michel Foucault, "When I say 'killing,' I obviously do not mean simply murder as such, but also every form of indirect murder: the fact of exposing someone to death, increasing risk of death for some people, or, quite simply, political death, expulsion, rejection and so on."[34] The doubles in this book have been killed in a variety of ways: extrajudicial killing, the death penalty, and life imprisonment. As in al-Awlaki's case, his positioning as a prototypical other surely made killing him easier—as did the positions of the Duka brothers (undocumented) and the Newburgh Four (African Americans with criminal records)—but it was his positioning as Double, as familiar that made his death so urgent. This very relation is manifest in the Tsarnaev case. He first appeared to the American public as a familiar face. And, following Foucault, to expose him to death or make his death more palatable there were a series of attempts to revert his image to that of a clearly bounded other, to materialize the spectral enemy that lies within the face of the Double.

This tendency is visible in the various alternative covers produced in response to *Rolling Stone*. Some, critiquing the glamorization of a violent individual, photoshopped Tsarnaev's face onto other sexualized bodies: a seminude Janet Jackson featured on a 1993 *Rolling Stone* issue and a chiseled body flaunted on the cover of *Men's Health*, for example. Some suggested that the magazine would have been wise to feature victims and showcase their perseverance. In the controversy, a Massachusetts State Police photographer leaked photos of Tsarnaev emerging from the boat in which he was hiding, hands bloodied and raised, the red dot of a sniper's scope squarely on his forehead. The photographer wanted to show "the true face of terror."[35] The effort that received the most attention, however, was that of the conservative magazine *The Week*. Its May 3, 2013 cover featured the brothers drawn, their complexions made markedly darker, reduced to a racialized and more bounded enemy image.

The exaggerated features on *The Week*'s cover fall well within Galli's futile hyper-representations (much like the "misidentifications" that occurred early in the manhunt). But these do not exist in isolation, nor are they reactions to an apparently natural doppelgänger. While the Double certainly functions in security discourse to uncover an other within, it does not stop at an other, but endlessly opens up the collective to more interrogation. To transpose Freud, the Double also "leads back to what is . . . long familiar."[36] I have argued that the relational trajectories between Double and other, as figures of representation, modulate between parallel, perpendicular, oblique, and acute movements. They intertwine, merge, and separate in complex ways, creating a productive tension of deferral and closure, disruption and suture. Against Tsarnaev's likeness, a reduction to other secured his death; for al-Awlaki, assertions of his likeness hastened his demise.

The movement between other and Double is plainly visible in more recent visual depictions of the Americans who have taken up arms for ISIS or the Islamic State. Shannon Conley, a nineteen-year-old white woman from Colorado, was arrested at Denver's International Airport as she was about to board a plane for Turkey, en route to Syria. She was sentenced to four years in prison. Elton Simpson, a twenty-nine-year-old African American who resided in Arizona, was killed outside of the Curtis Culwell Center. Inside the center, the American Freedom Defense Initiative, a hate group also known as Stop Islamization of America, was holding the First Annual Muhammad Art Exhibit and Contest. Simpson and Nadir Soofi approached the center guns in tow but were shot and killed by a police officer before they were able to enter the facility. Media reports of both incidents featured uncanny juxtapositions. An image from Conley's school yearbook, short hair and smile, was placed beside her in a courtroom, donning military camouflage and a hijab. Simpson's high school picture, on a basketball court and clean-shaven, was positioned against one of him wearing a scraggily beard and a white skullcap. In these double visions the other is extracted from the image of the Double. But, this is not a unidirectional movement, but a refraction that moves back onto the "before" image. While reinforcing xenophobic articulations of hostility, the tension also requires another look back, a search for "what else?"

In an age of "Global War" the phantom enemy signifies "a humanity that opens itself up to its own inhumanity, to its own ontological un-doing."[37] The Double is the functionalization of this disruption in the register of representation and of communicating threat. In reference to the cases of young Americans of a variety of backgrounds joining ISIS, Peter Bergen and David Sterman write without irony, "The first line of defense against terrorism: Mom and Dad."[38] This runs parallel to Foucault's argument regarding the dangerous individual, the move-ment and transposition of the rare and the monstrous into the "common everyday figure of the degenerate, of the pervert, of the constitutionally unbalanced, of the immature, etc."[39] But, it is an ever-widening fissure. It is the intensification of a process sparked by the loss of the political enemy; the disappearance/inter-pixelization of the enemy image in the Double and the oscillation that results from futile attempts to extract an enemy image from it penetrates the most intimate spaces of collective life. Of course, the sacrificial killing this engenders is much like the dual position begat by the Double. We might all be potentially an enemy or suspect, but this suspicion is unequally experienced and felt, even if it can be projected, transposed, and superimposed.

This leaves us in a precarious balancing act. Surely, violence mate-rializes in ways that go beyond political borders and their identifiable enemies—even if this violence is inseparable from institutional assem-blages native to the American legal system. But on the plane of rep-resentation, the at times well-intentioned if naïve deployment of the Double in narrative form (he looks like us, he seemed so normal, he was just a normal guy) proves vexing.[40] First, it takes our attention away from the continued reach and effect of markers of difference in hyper-representations of terror. These demand a continued and vigilant dis-ruption. However, in addition to questioning constructions of reductive difference, the Double forces us to reconsider the mirrors of likeness. Markers of difference used in formulating an enemy image, as Schmitt points out, are never factual. Even in situations of conventional enmity in which two clearly delineated political groupings are involved in com-bat, the enemy image remains a purposeful and selective construction. In this book, I have shown that similarity and likeness in the register of the image of threat are equally nonfactual. But this claim does not and cannot depend on an assertion of natural, self-evident, or essential difference. Practically, it simply points to the fact that the Double depends on selective and purposeful articulations of likeness and familiarity: one's looks, accent, residence, occupation, and so on. More generally, however, the Double points to the limits of disruption in and through identity as a strategy to disturb the machinations of the increasingly mundane war on terror. The discourse of the Double reappropriates the disruption of the enemy image in the service of security, but in a way that does not abandon the enemy image in any absolute sense; the result is a cyclical movement between rupture and closure. In instrumentalizing Lec's aphorism, the disjunctural quality of "seeing" my own monstrosity becomes part and parcel of security, rather than a maneuver to begin to think otherwise.

In Galli's gray global twilight

> . . . if there is a lunatic in the house, what can one know, of course I don't want to exaggerate, but there's no question of peace any more until this is cleared up, even in one's own home one is at the mercy of . . . I say, at the mercy of . . .[41]

Epilogue

Much has changed in the time since this book was finalized. Such is the nature of writing about such an endlessly modulating conflict that this epilogue will likely require updating by the time it reaches print.

This book is set, so to speak, in Obama's America. The discourse of homegrown terrorism and its accompanying figure, the Double, congealed early on in his tenure. Both are a reflection and product of the so-called postracial moment with which his term coincided. During that time government officials and the news media described an adversary that grew out from within, one that seemingly complicated orthodox war on terror optics. This shift, of course, did little in the way of reducing Islamophobia or the persistence of the "other" in security discourse. Nevertheless, it is a moment in which the familiar and unfamiliar were presented not as embodied in the pairing of friend/enemy but as scrambled within threat itself.

During the 2016 US presidential election, Donald Trump, who ran a multifront race-baiting campaign, promised a return to ostensibly simpler times. In his trademark schoolyard self-touting style he claimed to be the anti-PC candidate who was willing to "name the enemy." "Islam hates us," he asserted, promising a "total and complete shutdown" of Muslim immigration to the United States. Couched in the liberal tendency to separate "good" from "bad" in clashes within rather than clashes between, the Double perhaps came and went with the Obama presidency.

Yet, on May 21, 2017, Trump gave a speech in Riyadh, Saudi Arabia, that contained passages that could have easily scrolled across President Obama's teleprompter: "This is not a battle between different faiths, different sects, or different civilizations. This is a battle between barbaric criminals who seek to obliterate human life, and decent people of all religions who seek to protect it. This is a battle between Good and Evil."[1] The notion of the Double is perhaps not yet ready to leave the scene of security. The other-Double relation is a shifting one, in which emphases and relations change. For someone who follows reality TV logic there is no contradiction in his varying statements, only messages that play well to certain audiences. In his speech there is much to unpack and also much that will unfold over time. Thus, I can make only some preliminarily observations.

Trump himself touted his remarks in Riyadh as his "Islam speech." Two opinion contributors for the *New York Times*, Mustafa Aykol and Wajahat Ali, were quick to point out that the speech wasn't really about Islam.[2] What Trump did discuss at length was terrorism; the significance of the conflation cannot be understated. Despite the fact that Trump only said "Islamic terrorism" once—apparently going off script, a telling slip—and despite the fact that the section advocating for a "total and complete shutdown" of Muslim immigration has been taken off of his campaign web page, the brown-Arab-Muslim-other, along with other racial formations, are clearly central to his worldview. His campaign and early tenure—marked by policies steeped in racism—have certainly emboldened white supremacists who now appear in public with torches but without the hoods that once covered their faces. In the wake of such rising violence, he has not made (and most certainly will not make) a similar (Christian) speech within America's borders calling on white Americans to weed out the radicalized among them (though this criticism is not exclusive to Trump). For example, it took Trump three days to address the May 26, 2017, deaths of two men who intervened in an altercation in which a white supremacist was subjecting two women to anti-Muslim epithets. When he did, he used the official POTUS Twitter account rather than his personal one, the latter being the one his base follows.[3] Just one day prior, the Fourth Circuit Court of Appeals upheld a lower court's decision to block Trump's second "Muslim ban."

At the same time as shouldering the responsibility of curbing terrorism on Arabs and Muslims (as much as Saudi Arabia merits that responsibility), Trump in his speech also strained to group all god-fearing people together against terrorists. Terrorists "do not worship god, [but] . . . worship death," he professed, reminiscent of Cold War efforts to mobilize Americans against a godless evil empire. His national security advisor, Lt. Gen. H. R. McMaster—who has pushed Trump to drop "radical Islamic terror" from his lexicon—reiterated this stance, while claiming Trump was "learning": "I think it's important that whatever we call it, we recognize that these are not religious people and, in fact, these enemies of all civilizations, what they want to do is to cloak their criminal behavior under this false idea of some kind of religious war."[4] In this effort, Trump's trip marked the establishment of a joint US-Saudi Global Center for Combating Extremist Ideology, however ironic and superficial this partnership might be. At the same time, some US media have framed Saudi Arabia's own problems with ISIS through the discourse of the Double: "ISIS Turns Saudis Against the Kingdom, and Families Against Their Own," reads one *New York Times* headline.[5] Whether this is a frame that structures discourses about terrorism within the country itself is a question I cannot answer here. Nevertheless, framing victory in the battle against terrorism as a goal "that transcends every other" and one that requires a purge brings its own violence. The marked emphasis in the middle of his speech, all caps to ensure he would not go off script, makes this clear:

> Drive. Them. Out.
> DRIVE THEM OUT of your places of worship.
> DRIVE THEM OUT of your communities.
> DRIVE THEM OUT of your holy land, and
> DRIVE THEM OUT OF THIS EARTH.

This ostensible effort for peace is also marked by a $110 billion sale of military arms. No longer a battle for "hearts and minds," for Trump and his business partners, it is a battle for "hearts and souls"—a shift whose significance will only unfold over time.

Early in Trump's America the other-Double relation has certainly reconfigured, the Double taking second chair. The future of US security discourse and how particular figures of threat will be deployed and operationalized by a white supremacist administration are perhaps not difficult to gauge. Ultimately, for the Trump era, however long it lasts, this book serves as a cautionary tale. Trump himself provides an all-too-neat package in which to place the country's ills. Certainly the violence that has accompanied Trump's election, fomented by the words and deeds of Trump himself and those closest to him, is terrifying and abhorrent. Yet, it is perhaps too easy to forget that which has been the subject of much of this book: that Obama-era approaches to counterterrorism, couched in the discourse of the Double, come with their own violent baggage. Thus, in a moment in which we are already seeing a misguided fondness for George W. Bush, it is essential that efforts to counter Trump's racist policies not be marked by a deceptive nostalgia for a lighter and gentler war on terror.

ACKNOWLEDGMENTS

To begin, or in this case end a book by unloading some of the responsibility for its oversights is one of the academy's strangest traditions. Its only redeeming quality is that it simultaneously prevents an author from taking full credit for an often years-long project, with so many twists, turns, trap doors, and (seemingly) dead ends that no single person could navigate alone.

I am indebted to my mentor Barbie Zelizer. Without her keen mind, attention, and insistence, much of the prose would be far less comprehensible. I am thankful for her ongoing support, guidance, and example of critical scholarship.

I was lucky enough to have an interdisciplinary committee of advisors. To John Jackson, Marwan Kraidy, Anne Norton, and Rogers Smith I am grateful for the input, conversations, and interactions that have helped to shape this book and my thought more generally. The generosity and support of Michael X. Delli Carpini and the entire Annenberg School were invaluable. I am also indebted to the programs that have further supported my research and writing: Rogers Smith's Democracy, Citizenship, and Constitutionalism Program and the George Gerbner Postdoctoral Fellowship.

To my former neighbors in the west hall at Annenberg, Sharrona Pearl and Jessa Lingl, the open office doors, advice, and support have not gone unappreciated. And a special thanks to my first Annenberg family: Loi Sessions-Goulet, Alison Perelman, Jeff Gottfried, Adrienne Shaw, Brooke Duffy, Heidi Khaled, Michael Serazio, Matt Lapierre, Nora Draper, Christopher Ali. I would also like to express my gratitude to my colleagues at the University at Albany, SUNY, particularly Nico Bencherki.

Thank you to Alicia Nadkarni and the NYU Press series editors, Jonathan Gray, Aswin Punathambekar, and Nina Huntemann, for their help in navigating the world of academic publishing.

I am profoundly indebted to my parents, Hanna and Roman Szpunar. A courageous pair that took their kids on "vacation" in the early eighties only to come home to another country. Their ethic, effort, volume, and persistence continue to shape my approach to any undertaking. My brother, Karol (Karl), has been a constant source of support, friendship, and, more recently, collaboration. My sister, Monika, continues to set an example that I can only futilely imitate.

To my wife Jen. To ease any anxiety about now living with a me that is not attached to this project, I can only promise to continue to be as pleasant as I have been throughout this process, particularly after a dusk-to-dawn writing shift. Without your love, support, encouragement, and patience, I could not have finished this book.

NOTES

ENTRANCE

1 Taibbi, "Explaining the Rolling Stone Cover"; Žižek, "Are We in a War?"; Derrida, *Politics of Friendship*; Schmitt, *Concept of the Political*.

2 On the function of the other in this regard, see Hall, "Question of Cultural Identity"; Said, *Orientalism*; Žižek, *Sublime Object of Ideology*. On the other in the war on terror, see Alsultany, *Arabs and Muslims in the Media*; Kumar, "Framing Islam"; Semati, "Islamophobia, Culture and Race in the Age of Empire."

3 Quoted in Madison, "Attorney General Eric Holder."

4 Napolitano, "Nine years after 9/11."

5 Galli, "On War and on the Enemy."

6 Bhabha, *Location of Culture*. This point can be put another way, transposing Arjun Appadurai's thesis on small numbers. The Double constitutes the smallest of numbers (<1) that prevents the externalization of a collective's inability to achieve wholeness. Indeed, "small numbers can unsettle big issues." Appadurai, *Fear of Small Numbers*, 73.

7 Lec, *Myśli Nieuczesane*, 44. The translation used in the epigraph is my own.

8 Rapoport, "Four Waves of Rebel Terror and September 11."

9 Schmid, *Routledge Handbook of Terrorism Research*, 102.

10 Schmid and Jongman, *Political Terrorism*, 66.

11 See "Condition of Kansas"; "Discouraging to 'Fanatics'"; "Terrorism in Louisiana." For another early example of racist violence discussed as terrorism, see "Robeson Asks U.S. to Probe 'Terrorism.'" This *Washington Post* headline is telling. First, placing terrorism in scare quotes is a practice not readily seen today, marking the emergence of terrorism as an episteme over the past half century. Second, the use of scare quotes in the context of racist violence speaks to the unequal usage of the term vis-à-vis the racial identity of the victims of violence.

12 I use the concept of the refrain because it most effectively addresses a process of territorial movement (of de- and reterritorialization), an oscillation between articulation and flight that accounts for not only how knowledge and practice concerning terrorism are organized (*articulated* and repeated) but also how new spaces, utterances, and actors are enclosed within this particular epistemic lens that marks the possibilities of de-organization (*flight*). It simultaneously traces out a territory that does not preexist and produces "stems and filaments that seem to be roots . . . [and can also be put] to strange new uses." Deleuze and Guattari, *Thousand Plateaus*, 311, 15. On how the refrain holds together fuzzy aggregates, see

Murphie, "Sound at the End"; on the refrain's three aspects of injection, inscription, and interception vis-à-vis organization, see Sørensen, "Immaculate Defecation."

13 Stampnitzky, *Disciplining Terror*; Kumar, *Islamophobia and the Politics of Empire*.

14 US Congress, Senate, Committee for Internal Security, *Terrorism*; US Congress, Senate, Committee for Internal Security, "Terrorism: A Staff Study." This is a complex history in itself. While Nixon originally attempted to revive the list, he was met with congressional resistance due in large part to the belief that the list was not of much use in dealing with the emerging threat of terrorism. See Goldstein, *American Blacklist*. It should also be noted that there were initiatives centered on terrorism before 1974, such as the short-lived Cabinet Committee on Terrorism formed in 1972. However, there is agreement that terrorism did not "hit the stands" until 1974 (H. H. A. Cooper, former staff director of the National Advisory Committee Task Force on Disorders and Terrorism, quoted in Stampnitzky, *Disciplining Terror*, 90).

15 Alexander, Baum, and Danziger, "Terrorism."

16 Jackson, "Argument for Terrorism."

17 Merari, "Classification of Terrorist Groups."

18 The first act to have terrorism in the title was the 1984 Act to Combat International Terrorism, which primarily focused on authorizing rewards for foreign nationals who provided the US government with information.

19 FBI, "FBI Analysis of Terrorist Incidents."

20 On this question of state terrorism, see Sproat, "Can the State Be Terrorist?" The recent murder of nine AME church members in Charleston, South Carolina, on June 17, 2015, has been hotly contested, with many voices calling for the incident, perpetrated by Dylann Roof, to be publicly deemed an act of terrorism. Similarly, the endemic killing of black men by police forces across the United States has received similar traction. More recently, commentators have been stating that the first US antiterrorism laws were directed at the KKK. The reference is to the Third Force Act of 1871. The term "terrorism" was not used in this act, but it has been interpreted as such in the contemporary moment. See Craven, "Dylann Roof Wasn't Charged with Terrorism Because He's White."

21 DHS, "Domestic Terrorism."

22 Schmitt, *Theory of the Partisan*. For Schmitt, "limits" do not connote the brutality of violence. All forms of hostility—conventional (between nation states), real (between a nation-state and a subnational group), and absolute (between ideological actors)—can be equally brutal. Rather, "limits" demarcate the boundaries used to define the actors themselves as well as the timeframe of open conflict. It is in this limitless space-time that Galli's phantom enemy materializes.

23 Badiou, *Infinite Thought*, 126.

24 Razack, *Casting Out*.

25 Said, *Orientalism*; Said, *Covering Islam*. On culture talk, see Mamdani, *Good Muslim, Bad Muslim*. On respectable racism, see Alsultany, *Arabs and Muslims in the Media*.

26 Naber, *Arab America*. This formulation, of course, does not apply equally to all Muslim-American communities, particularly those made up of largely African Americans.

27 One signpost being the hearings held by Republican Peter King on the radicalization of the Muslim American community from 2011 onward. See Kundnani, *Muslims Are Coming!*; Naber, "Arab Americans and U.S. Racial Formations"; Volpp, "Citizen and the Terrorist."

28 See "H.R. 1777 (100th)." This particular statement is problematic for two reasons. First, and most obvious, is the politics of naming terrorists. Second, it obfuscates the complex assemblages out of which violence erupts.

29 FBI, "FBI Analysis of Terrorist Incidents," 90.

30 Kumar, *Islamophobia and the Politics of Empire*, 121.

31 Mamdani, *Good Muslim, Bad Muslim*, 177. For a different angle on the connection between Cold War anxieties and those concerning global terrorism, see Stohl and Stohl, "Networks of Terror," 95–96.

32 Huntington, "Clash of Civilizations?"; Lewis, "Roots of Muslim Rage."

33 Semati, "Terrorists, Moslems, Fundamentalists"; Semati, "Islamophobia, Culture and Race in the Age of Empire." The terrorism-related legislation that emerged in the wake of the Oklahoma City bombing and other domestic and international events, such as President Clinton's Antiterrorism and Effective Death Penalty Act, focused on (in coded language) "alien terrorists," allowing for their deportation via secret evidence. See Kumar, *Islamophobia and the Politics of Empire*, 141.

34 Laqueur, *New Terrorism*.

35 Galli, "On War and on the Enemy," 216–17.

36 Though claims of an absolute state of exception are tempered by several Supreme Court decisions: *Boumediene v. Bush*, 553 US 723 (2008); *Hamdan v. Rumsfeld*, 548 US 557 (2006); *Hamdi v. Rumsfeld*, 542 US 507 (2004).

37 While these violent practices have received much attention, through the work of Italian philosopher Giorgio Agamben and those building off of his notion that the "camp is the biopolitical paradigm of the modern," they are hardly the entire picture. German social theorist Thomas Lemke critiques Agamben for his overwrought focus on "a formal and repressive conception of the state," which limits sovereignty to state agencies and does not allow for differentiations of experience. One would add that it does not allow for differentiation of state practice. Moreover, Louise Amoore expertly illustrates how Agamben's "zone of indistinction" is teeming with life. Agamben, *Homo Sacer*; Agamben, *State of Exception*; Amoore, *Politics of Possibility*; Lemke, "Zone of Indistinction."

38 US Sentencing Commission, "2012 Federal Sentencing Guidelines Manual," www .ussc.gov.

39 In the United States, individuals can be stripped of their citizenship only if it can be proved that they committed fraud *during* the naturalization process. In addition, citizens can relinquish their citizenship. See *Perez v. Brownwell*, 356 US 44 (1958); *Nishikawa v. Dulles*, 356 US 129 (1958); *Afroyim v. Rush*, 387 US 253 (1967); and *Vance v. Terrazas*, 444 US 252 (1980). International laws on statelessness would also make any such practice illegal (though as Canada's Bill C-24 shows, this can be sidestepped by limiting this practice to those who have another nationality, whether or not they were born in Canada).

40 Ditrych, "From Discourse to *Dispositif.*"

41 One of the main tensions in the war on terror exists in the use of "noncombatants" in defining terrorism. Groups, such as al-Qaeda, claim that those who elected governments involved in conflicts in the Muslim are in fact not noncombatants (a similar notion was promoted by Israeli hard-liners in justifying operations against Gaza after the election of Hamas in 2006). In his work on bare life, Giorgio Agamben suggests that this distinction is obliterated by the operations and governmentality of the West. This is also suggested by the declaration of America as part of the battlefield in the war on terror (National Defense Authorization Act, 2012), and the disparity between civilian and noncivilian casualties in US drone strikes. Thus, the notion of noncombatants, the protection of whom is a fundamental driver of the war on terror, all but disappears in those efforts. This, of course, is not an absolute formation—in the way Agamben suggests—and there are gradations of innocence and suspicion, which I discuss later.

42 The notion of incorporeal transformation refers to the manner in which the body passes from one experiential state to another, as when a judge announces a guilty verdict. See Deleuze and Guattari, *Thousand Plateaus*, xvi, 76–82.

43 Foucault, "About the Concept of the 'Dangerous Individual.'"

44 This is not to suggest that some perpetrators' actions cannot be understood through a psychological account, only that the approach of radicalization ignores how the assemblages to which an individual may become attached have formed.

45 Patel, *Rethinking Radicalization*; Kundnani, *Muslims Are Coming!*

46 Studies that do not exclusively focus on jihadists include Bjelopera, *Domestic Terrorist Threat*; Krueger and Malečková, "Education, Poverty and Terrorism"; McCauley and Moskalenko, "Mechanisms of Political Radicalization"; Moghaddam, "Staircase to Terrorism."

47 Foucault, "About the Concept of the 'Dangerous Individual,'" 17.

48 Freud, "'Uncanny,'" 224.

49 The Double is prominent in the work of Jean Paul (who coined the term "doppelgänger"), E. T. A. Hoffmann, Shelley, Dostoyevsky, Stevenson, Poe, Melville, and Wilde, to name but a few. See Coates, *Double and the Other*; Crawley, "Doubles"; Hallam, "Double as Incomplete Self."

50 See Tymms, *Doubles in Literary Psychology*. The Double also continues to be the subject of film. Most recently, Dostoyevsky's novella and Saramago's novel, both

titled (in their English translations) *The Double*, have undergone cinematic adaptation.

51   See Ascroft, "Lacan's Desire and Dostoevsky's Double"; Lizama, "Body of Information"; Plank, "Différance"; Herdman, *Double in Nineteenth-Century Fiction*; Vardoulakis, *Doppelgänger*; Webber, *Doppelgänger*.

52   Guerard, "Concepts of the Double."

53   Freud, "'Uncanny'"; Rank, *Double*; Fleming, "Doppelgänger/Doppeltgänger."

54   Poe, "William Wilson," 561.

55   The name we are given is William Wilson, which, the narrator states, is similar to his own common name, but is a pseudonym.

56   Jean Paul, who coined the term, defines doppelgänger as follows: "So people who see themselves are called." See Hallam, "Double as Incomplete Self." The doppelgänger has, however, come to refer to the figure one sees, rather than the one who sees it. Moreover, Fleming notes that this definition is originally tied to the word "doppeltgänger," while "doppelgänger" refers to two meal courses served simultaneously. Regardless, the term is here used in its popular connotation, of a look-alike figure that appears to an individual, whose own constitution (and singularity) it puts in doubt. See Fleming, "Doppelgänger/Doppeltgänger."

57   Webber, *Doppelgänger*, 60.

58   See specifically Dryden, *Modern Gothic and Literary Doubles*; Coates, *Double and the Other*.

59   Coates, *Double and the Other*, 3.

60   Hallam, "Double as Incomplete Self," 17.

61   Rank, *Beyond Psychology*.

62   Fleming, "Doppelgänger/Doppeltgänger."

63   Borges, *Book of Imaginary Beings*; Ng, "Introduction"; Rosenfield, "Shadow Within."

64   Guerard, "Concepts of the Double"; Herdman, *Double in Nineteenth-Century Fiction*; Webber, *Doppelgänger*. Often, splitting and duplication occur simultaneously: in Robert Louis Stevenson's *Strange Case of Dr. Jekyll and Mr. Hyde*, a single man is split in two (good-natured Jekyll and sinister Hyde); in Dostoyevsky's *The Double*, Mr. Golyadkin meets his exact copy, who happens to possess all the traits that he lacks.

65   Dostoyevsky puts this phenomenon another way: "If the two of them had been placed next to each other, no one, absolutely no one, would have been able to say who was the real Mr. Golyadkin and who the imitation, who the old and who the new, who the original and who the copy." Dostoyevsky's *The Double*, quoted in Rank, *Double*, 30.

66   Webber, *Doppelgänger*, 7.

67   Schmitt, *Theory of the Partisan*, 73.

68   Neighbor of Daniel Boyd, quoted in "Nicest Terrorist I Ever Met." Boyd, a North Carolina man, pled guilty to conspiracy to provide material support to terrorists in 2011.

69 Chow, *Age of the World Target*, 59.

70 Foucault, *Security, Territory, Population*, 45.

71 Ibid., 63.

72 Ibid., 20, 37. Herein lies another distinction between other and Double. The other is spatially oriented while the Double is temporally oriented, particularly toward the future.

73 Ibid., 45.

74 Massumi, "Potential Politics and the Primacy of Preemption."

75 Aaronson, *Terror Factory*; Apuzzo and Goldman, *Enemies Within*; Ali Musawi, *Cheering for Osama*.

76 Chow, *Age of the World Target*, 48.

77 Foucault, *Security, Territory, Population*, 363.

78 Gomez, "Robert Doggart."

79 Brown, *Walled States, Waning Sovereignty*.

CHAPTER 1. IDENTITY AND INCIDENCE

1 Schmid, *Routledge Handbook of Terrorism Research*, 86. In Schmid's definition it is evident that the politics of vilification remain: terrorists, according to him, are without "moral restraint."

2 Even the pithiest definitions have been put into the service of political interests. For example, the co-optation and reduction of the widely accepted notion of terrorism as a "communicative act" certainly underwrote Margaret Thatcher's infamous characterization of the (mass) media as "terrorism's oxygen." The dubious science used to support an overly deterministic formulation of the "contagion thesis" (via a hypodermic needle model of communication) set off a long and overdrawn debate over how, and even if, the media ought to cover political violence; the thesis continues to have purchase in the digital age. To say that a phenomenon involves the media is not saying very much, particularly when much of our lives are mediated. Schmid and de Graaf, *Violence as Communication*; Picard, "News Coverage as the Contagion of Terrorism"; Archetti, "Terrorism, Communication and New Media."

3 Jacques Derrida, interviewed in Borradori, *Philosophy in a Time of Terror*.

4 Massumi, "Potential Politics and the Primacy of Preemption."

5 François Ewald, quoted in Beck, "Living in the World Risk Society," 335. Contra Beck, I do not distinguish between environmental risk and the risk wrought by terrorism (which he bases in intentionality). Contemporary terrorism, particularly seen in its historical development outlined in the Entrance, has the characteristics that Beck reserves for environmental crisis: unintentional—though "unforeseen" is a preferable term—consequences of human activity.

6 Described in detail in Curry, *If a Tree Falls*; Desphande and Ernst, "Countering Eco-terrorism"; National Lawyers Guild, "Operation Backfire."

7 He was originally released in December 2012, but after penning an article for the *Huffington Post*, he was retaken into custody for supposedly violating a stipulation

of his release by publishing. This regulation was deemed unconstitutional and he was again released.

8 While the use of the term spiked in 2001, this occurred prior to the attack on the Twin Towers. See Wagner, "Reframing Ecotage as Ecoterrorism." The term itself first appeared in the *New York Times* in regard to the tactics of Saddam Hussein. Safire, "Don't Throw Away Victory." For an account of its formulation, see Smith, "Ecoterrorism?"

9 Badolato, "Environmental Terrorism."

10 Mainstream organizations such as People for the Ethical Treatment of Animals (PETA) and the Humane Society of the United States are, at times, vilified through spurious associations to these groups; ironically, radical environmentalists often refer these two as "industry friends." See Animal Liberation Front, "Manifesto for Radical Abolitionism."

11 Testimony of Carson Carroll of the ATF in US Congress, Senate, Committee on Environment and Public Works, *Eco-terrorism Specifically Examining the Earth Liberation Front and the Animal Liberation Front* (hereafter *Examining ELF and ALF*), 13–14.

12 US Congress, Senate, Subcommittee on Forests and Forest Health of the Committee on Resources, *Ecoterrorism and Lawlessness on the National Forests* (hereafter *Ecoterrorism and Lawlessness*), 50.

13 *Examining ELF and ALF*, 8. For testimonies, see Testimony of Michelle Basso in US Congress, Senate, Subcommittee on Crime, Terrorism, and Homeland Security of the Committee on the Judiciary, *Animal Enterprise Terrorism Act*, 13–14, and Statement of Skip Boruchin in US Congress, Senate, Committee on Environment and Public Works, *Eco-terrorism Specifically Examining Stop Huntingdon Animal Cruelty* (hereafter *Examining SHAC*), 18.

14 Senator Frank Lautenberg (D-NJ) in *Examining ELF and ALF*, 5. On care, see Animal Liberation Front, "ALF Credo."

15 Curry, *If a Tree Falls*.

16 Statement of Frank Riggs in which he compares environmentalists to antiabortionists who kill doctors. US Congress, Senate, Subcommittee on Crime of the Committee on the Judiciary, *Acts of Ecoterrorism by Radical Environmental Organizations* (hereafter *Acts of Ecoterrorism*), 10.

17 Statement of Nick Nichols, CEO of Nichols-Dezenhall Communications Management Group, in *Ecoterrorism and Lawlessness*, 130–33.

18 "Green Monsters"; Drabelle, "Extremism in the Defense of Trees."

19 The radical environmental movement has long been criticized for the "whiteness" of their rhetoric and politics. For example, ignoring the political causes of and the populations that are disproportionately affected by AIDS and famine, in the early to mid-1980s prominent figures within the movement stated that environmentalists should celebrate the advent of AIDS as well as opposed famine relief to Ethiopia as both would produce the population decline necessary for a sustainable and balanced ecosystem. See Scarce, *Eco-warriors* and Lee, *Earth First!*

20 Animal Liberation Front, "Manifesto for Radical Abolitionism"; Gruen, Singer, and Hine, *Animal Liberation*.

21 Scarce, *Eco-warriors*, 32, xv. Moreover, others claim that their actions originate themselves in the West; they are the result of the contemporary American system. A co-founder of Earth First!, Howie Wolke writes, "We played by the rules. . . . We were moderate, reasonable, professional. We had data, statistics, maps, graphs. And we got fucked. . . . That's what led to Earth First! more than anything else." Quoted in Scarce, *Eco-warriors*, 24.

22 Quotes in order: Statement of Nick Nichols, *Ecoterrorism and Lawlessness*, 133 (for examples of this in academic literature, see Leader and Probst, "Earth Liberation Front and Environmental Terrorism," and Vanderheiden, "Eco-terrorism or Justified Resistance?"); Testimony of Mark L. Bibi, Counsel for Huntingdon Life Sciences, in *Examining SHAC*, 15; *Ecoterrorism and Lawlessness*, 19.

23 Testimony of Hapreet Singh Saini in US Congress, Senate, Subcommittee on the Constitution, Civil Rights, and Human Rights, Committee of the Judiciary, *Hate Crimes and the Threat of Domestic Extremism* (hereafter *Hate Crimes and Domestic Extremism*).

24 Weinstein, "Sikh Temple Shooter's Racist Tattoos, Deciphered."

25 Yaccino, Schwirtz, and Santora, "Gunman Kills 6 at Sikh Temple in Wisconsin."

26 Simi and Futrell, *American Swastika*, 15.

27 Heidi Beirich, personal communication, March 13, 2013.

28 Beirich and Potok, "USA," 256. The claim that there is a significant change in the nature of the racist right circa 1995 is overstated. As the case study highlights, there are still concerns over other bogeyman who have infiltrated America in lieu of the Communists such as the brown-Arab-Muslim-other. Surely, globalization has altered the racist right's restorationist effort, but most assertions that the government must be toppled are still supported by what Beirich and Potok refer to as an "Edenic past." Only now the government has been corrupted to the point that it cannot be "restored" without a revolutionary agenda.

29 See Eichenwald, "Right-Wing Extremists." On the gutting of the DHS, see Ackerman, "DHS Crushed This Analyst" and Smith, "Homeland Security Department."

30 Quoted in Beirich and Potok, "USA," 256.

31 David Duke quoted in Beirich and Potok, "USA," 258.

32 Stolberg, "Obama Offers Sympathy."

33 Reader comment no. 43 in Mackey, "Mass Shooting at Fort Hood."

34 Adjudicating one's religious devotion is not a topic I intend to take up; I am simply restating the arguments of others.

35 Reader comment no. 168 in Johnston and Shane, "U.S. Knew of Suspect's Tie to Radical Cleric."

36 William H. Webster Commission, "Final Report," 6.

37 Reader comment no. 257 in Mackey, "Mass Shooting at Fort Hood"; Reader comment no. 33 in Mackey, "Updates on the Shootings at Fort Hood."

38 Gaffney, "Siren Call of Shariah." It should be noted that the author of this article, who served as Ted Cruz's national security advisor in the 2016 Republican primaries, has espoused all of these views publicly. While he writes for the *Washington Times*, which is at best a marginal newspaper in the United States, this line of articulation reflects the considerable amount of paranoia in the United States over the specter of sharia: Tennessee and Louisiana have enacted legislation banning it, Mississippi and Utah have tried and failed, and another eleven states are considering similar measures. See Murphy, "Map."

39 Reader comment no. 231 in Johnston and Shane, "U.S. Knew of Suspect's Tie to Radical Cleric"; Reader comments no. 193 and no. 65 in Mackey, "Mass Shooting at Fort Hood."

40 Reader comment no. 102 in Mackey, "Mass Shooting at Fort Hood," quoted in Moss, "Muslims at Fort Voice Outrage and Ask Questions."

41 A popular assertion in the mainstream press as well. See, e.g., Yaccino, Schwirtz, and Santora, "Gunman Kills 6 at Sikh Temple in Wisconsin."

42 Posts made by users "Breitling" and "Pat88," August 5, 2012.

43 Herbert, "Stress Beyond Belief."

44 Brooks, "Rush to Therapy."

45 Reader comment no. 20 in Friedman, "America vs. the Narrative."

46 Barcott, "From Tree-Hugger to Terrorist."

47 A supporter of Chelsea D. Gerlach, a member of "the Family," at her trial, quoted in Yardley, "Radical Environmentalist Gets 9-Year Term."

48 E.g., Michael, *Lone Wolf Terror*.

49 According to the forums on www.crew38.com, the relationship between the Hammerskin Nation and Stormfront, for example, is fragile and varied. A thread titled "Stormfront?" on the Hammerskins forum asks members what they think of Stormfront. The responses vary from contempt to affinity.

50 Post by user "Poacher," August 5, 2012.

51 Post by user "beerrunner13," August 20, 2011.

52 "Topic A." She mentions "Jordanian" because Hasan was mistakenly (or wishfully) thought to have been born in Jordan.

53 Beck, "Living in the World Risk Society," 330.

54 *Ecoterrorism and Lawlessness*, 80, emphasis added.

55 While the term "doppelgänger" is often defined as a look-alike, Jean Paul's original connotation is the "double-goer" or "one who goes twice." Fleming, "Doppelgänger/Doppeltgänger."

56 Genosko and Thompson, "Tense Theory," 130.

57 Barcott, "From Tree-Hugger to Terrorist"; Leader and Probst, "Earth Liberation Front and Environmental Terrorism"; Testimony of John Lewis in *Examining ELF and ALF*.

58 "Boy Who Cried 'Elf.'"

59 See www.originalelf.com/earthlib.htm.

60 Animal Liberation Front, "ALF Credo."

61 See Testimony of Congressman Greg Walden in *Ecoterrorism and Lawlessness*; Testimony of John Lewis in *Examining ELF and ALF*, 15; Testimony of Porter Wharton III of Vail Resorts in *Ecoterrorism and Lawlessness*, 54.

62 Quoted in Chase, *Harvard and the Unabomber*, 94.

63 "Boy Who Cried 'ELF.'" The article does not provide citations or evidence for these claims.

64 Smith, "Ecoterrorism?"; *Ecoterrorism and Lawlessness*, 33.

65 *Ecoterrorism and Lawlessness*, 2.

66 Testimony of Senator James Inhofe in *Examining ELF and ALF*, 8.

67 *Acts of Ecoterrorism*, 15.

68 FBI, "White Supremacist Recruitment"; Beirich and Potok, "USA."

69 "Chorus of Protest Grows"; Thompson, "Apology to Veterans."

70 Dao and Kovaleski, "Hatecore Music."

71 Weinstein, "Sikh Temple Shooter's Racist Tattoos, Deciphered."

72 Laris, Somashekhar, and Leonnig, "Gunman in Wisconsin."

73 William Pierce of the National Alliance (and the author of *The Turner Diaries*) founded Resistance Records in an attempt to have "millions of young, white Americans and Europeans . . . make resistance music their music of choice, instead of the Negroid filth churned out by MTV." Quoted in Simi and Futrell, *American Swastika*, 80.

74 One need only think of the Columbine High School massacre in 1999 in which the music of Marilyn Manson was thought by some to have led the two perpetrators to commit their crimes as well as the 1990 court case of *James Vance v. Judas Priest* in which the music of a British heavy metal band was blamed for the suicide of two US teens.

75 Senator Durbin in *Hate Crimes and Domestic Extremism*.

76 Dao and Kovaleski, "Hatecore Music"; Goode and Kovaleski, "Wisconsin Killer Fed"; Lee, "Inside the Creepy World of 'Hate Music.'"

77 See www.hammerskins.net.

78 Post by user "Ballistic," August 5, 2012, emphasis added.

79 Leyden, "I Used to Be a Skinhead."

80 Quoted in *Fox News Sunday*.

81 Krauthammer, "Medicalizing Mass Murder."

82 Reader comments no. 24 and no. 59 in "Horror at Fort Hood"; "Topic A."

83 Much of the correspondence is available in William H. Webster Commission, "Final Report."

84 Quoted in Raghavan, "Cleric Says He Was Confidant to Hasan."

85 On al-Awlaki's relationship to al-Hazmi, see Berger, "Anwar al-Awlaki's Links to the September 11 Hijackers."

86 Quotes in Samuels, "New Mastermind of Jihad"; see also Lia, *Architect of Global Jihad*.

87 Quoted in al-Qaeda in the Arabian Peninsula, *Inspire* 5 (Spring 2011): 29.

88 Quoted in Lia, *Architect of Global Jihad*, 383.

89 This includes converts, who become part of the community through their violence. Thus, in effect, how much they "believe" or "follow" al-Qaeda's system likely
matters little. Dead men cannot challenge one's reading of their intent, nor can
they sully their assumed devotion.

90 Al-Qaeda in the Arabian Peninsula, *Inspire* 1 (Summer 2010): 57.

91 For a critique of radicalization, see Kundnani, *Muslims Are Coming!*, esp. 115–52.
For an analysis of various approaches to radicalization, see Patel, *Rethinking Radicalization*.

92 Ironically, the successes of anticipatory politics, those cases in which the state prevents terrorism—often characterized as entrapment due to the use of informants
who goad individuals into action and intrusive surveillance—also fail both in the
fact that these only highlight and create the enigmatic threats that lurk among
Americans and in their infringement on civil liberties.

93 Michael, *Lone Wolf Terror*. Admittedly the strategy had been used long before
Beam coined it; he himself traces it to a 1962 article by Colonel Ulius Louis
Amoss, who described it as a strategy to be used in case of Communist invasion.
US Congress, Senate, Committee for Internal Security, "Terrorism: A Staff Study";
al-Suri quoted in Lia, *Architect of Global Jihad*.

94 From an ALF primer reprinted in Best and Nocella, *Terrorists or Freedom Fighters?*, quoted in Heim, "Wisconsin Shooter Embraced 'Hate Rock'"; Abu Mus'ab
al-Suri quoted in Brahimi, "'Changing' Face of Al-Qaeda."

95 Statement of Frank Riggs in *Acts of Ecoterrorism*, 8; *Ecoterrorism and Lawlessness*,
15, 19, 83.

96 Simi and Futrell, *American Swastika*, 4; Goode and Kovaleski, "Wisconsin Killer
Fed."

97 Quoted in Newman and Brick, "Neighbor Says Hasan Gave Belongings Away."

98 Galloway and Thacker, *Exploit*, 11, emphasis added.

99 *Examining ELF and ALF*, 17.

CHAPTER 2. INFORMANTS AND OTHER MEDIA

1 The defendants included Benjamin J. Davis, Jr., Eugene Dennis, John Gates, Gil
Green, Gus Hall, Irving Potash, Jack Stachel, Robert G. Thompson, John William-
son, Henry Wilson, and Carl Winter. There were originally twelve defendants, but
William Z. Foster, the CPUSA national secretary, took ill and was not tried.

2 Roosevelt, "Memo to Moscow"; "Letters," Communist Party of the United States,
TAM 132 (box 7, folder 7), 1949, Tamiment Library/Robert F. Wagner Labor Archives, New York University.

3 Kocieniewski, "6 Men Arrested."

4 See Galloway and Thacker, *Exploit*; Hu, *Prehistory of the Cloud*.

5 Cited in Hu, *Prehistory of the Cloud*, 6. What follows is not intended to completely
dismiss the usefulness of the network diagram in understanding violence (as in
Klausen's project). Rather, it is intended to examine some of the repercussions of
its deployment vis-à-vis the law.

6   The netwar conception was itself part of the broader developments in the use of the network metaphor across disciplines in the 1990s; see Stohl and Stohl, "Networks of Terror."

7   Dilling, *Red Network*.

8   Internal Security Act, subsection 2(9), http://tucnak.fsv.cuni.cz.

9   Jacobs, "Cartography's Favourite Map Monster."

10 Sampson, *Virality*; Latour, "On Actor-Network Theory"; Latour, *Reassembling the Social*.

11 Erickson, "Network as Metaphor." As early as the 1980s Wilhelm Baldamus stated that the concept is interesting only in that examining how "a metaphor with hardly any explanatory power to start with can maintain its popularity for long periods with no tangible reason" (912–13). In the context of terrorism, communication scholars Cynthia and Michael Stohl vividly show the pitfalls of the ways in which the US administration has conceptualized terrorism as a network. See Stohl and Stohl, "Networks of Terror."

12 Bloom, "Historical Overview of Informants."

13 Massumi, "Potential Politics and the Primacy of Preemption."

14 "Who Won?"

15 Lerner, "Ideas as Criminals."

16 For example, Freeman, "Communist Trial."

17 Testimonies of George K. Hunton, director of the Catholic Interracial Council of New York and Rabbi Benjamin Schultz in HUAC, *Infiltration of Minority Groups*, 448, 440.

18 Budenz, *This Is My Story*.

19 *United States v. Foster et al.*, 81 F. Supp. 280 (SDNY 1948), Stenographer's Notes, vols. 3–5, National Archives and Records Administration–Northeast Region, New York, March 23–April 12, 1949, vol. 4, 2066.

20 "Little Commissar," 24.

21 Belknap, *Cold War Political Justice*, 21.

22 Hardt and Negri, "Sovereignty."

23 This notebook is cited in "Affidavit of Benjamin J. Davis, Jr.," Communist Party of the United States, TAM 132 (box 7, folder 24), 1949, Tamiment Library.

24 "Presence of Evil," 23; Armed Forces Information Film, no. 5 (1960), www.youtube.com/watch?v=y1UHQ795K8k; Chamberlain, "Communist Trial."

25 HUAC, *Infiltration of Minority Groups*, 468.

26 "Evolution or Revolution," 26.

27 Nixon, "Plea for an Anti-Communist Faith," in Bentley, *Thirty Years of Treason*, 570.

28 "Little Commissar."

29 Quoted in Faiola and Russakoff, "Terrorists Next Door?," quoted in Ripley, "Fort Dix Conspiracy."

30 Each man also had a different status in the United States. Shnewer is a naturalized citizen, the Dukas are undocumented, and Tatar is a legal resident.

31 Of course they frame this as a reality. And indeed it is perhaps indisputable that the network structures the efforts of activists, terrorists, and governments alike. However, not all networks are equal, and their mapping requires effort.

32 Chamberlain, "Communist Trial."

33 Yang, "Terrorist Search Engine."

34 Apuzzo and Goldman, *Enemies Within*.

35 Granovetter, "Strength of Weak Ties," 1366, 1375.

36 Latour, "On Actor-Network Theory," 370.

37 Berger, "Metronome of Apocalyptic Time."

38 *US v. Foster et al.*, Stenographer's Notes, vol. 3, 1405; vol. 4, 2209.

39 Ibid., vol. 3, 1404, 1715.

40 Philbrick, *I Led 3 Lives*, 71; *US v. Foster et al.*, Stenographer's Notes, vol. 5, 2655.

41 *US v. Foster et al.*, Stenographer's Notes, vol. 4, 2393.

42 Ibid., vol. 4, 2187–89; vol. 5, 2979–80.

43 Porter, "U.S. Reds Ordered to Revolt in 1945"; Porter, "Budenz Describes a U.S. 'Politburo.'"

44 Philbrick, *I Led 3 Lives*, 65.

45 "Brief on Constitutional Issues," Communist Party of the United States, TAM 132 (box 7, folder 27), 1949, Tamiment Library; Porter, "Communists Plan to 'Colonize' Key Industries Told at Trial."

46 Testimonies of Professor Davis and Granville Hicks in HUAC, *Communist Methods of Infiltration—Education*, 7, 99.

47 *US v. Foster et al.*, Stenographer's Notes, vol. 5, 3001.

48 Alsultany, *Arabs and Muslims in the Media*.

49 *United States v. Mohamad Ibrahim Shnewer, Dritan Duka, Eljvir Duka, Shain Duka, and Serdar Tatar*, Court Transcripts, Criminal No. 07-CR-00459 (RBK), 2008, 3200.

50 Hussain and Ghalayini, "Christie's Conspiracy."

51 *US v. Shnewer et al.*, Court Transcripts, 4344.

52 Hussain and Ghalayini, "Christie's Conspiracy."

53 *US v. Shnewer et al.*, Court Transcripts, 3282–83.

54 Ibid., 4027.

55 Ibid., 5599.

56 Arquilla and Ronfeldt, *Advent of Netwar*, 10.

57 HUAC, *Infiltration of Minority Groups*, 454. Paul Robeson, a popular African American entertainer, had his travel to the Soviet Union used in this way to place him within the international Communist network. His statement that if America were to go to war with the Soviet Union African Americans would not fight in it was the supposed impetus for the hearings on Communist infiltration of minority groups.

58 *US v. Foster et al.*, Stenographer's Notes, vol. 5, 2628.

59 Ibid., vol. 3, 1830.

60 "Brief on Constitutional Issues," 24.

61 *US v. Foster et al.*, Stenographer's Notes, vol. 4, 2497.

62 Ibid., vol. 5, 2706.

63 "Brief on Constitutional Issues."

64 For a counterargument to this, see "Defense Closing Statement," Communist Party of the United States, TAM 132 (box 11, folder 9), 1949, Tamiment Library.

65 "Prosecution Closing Argument," Communist Party of the United States, TAM 132 (box 11, folder 10), 1949, Tamiment Library.

66 See Testimony of Alvin Stokes in HUAC, *Infiltration of Minority Groups*.

67 On the stand, Budenz equated recommending a text with advocacy, calling the former the "Communist method." *US v. Foster et al.*, Stenographer's Notes, vol. 4, 2311–12.

68 *US v. Shnewer et al.*, Court Transcripts, 6443; Hussain and Ghalayini, "Christie's Conspiracy." The six constants are (1) jihad will continue until Judgment Day, (2) jihad does not rely on a leader, (3) jihad is not tied to a particular land, (4) jihad does not depend on a specific battle, (5) victory in jihad is not equivalent to military victory, and (6) defeat in jihad is not equivalent to military defeat.

69 *US v. Shnewer et al.*, Court Transcripts, 5830.

70 Ibid., 5912.

71 Ibid., 6486–87.

72 Ibid., 5914.

73 Ibid., 5943.

74 Ibid., 1571.

75 Ibid., 3561.

76 Ibid., 2950.

77 One is left to wonder how Budenz, who had read various Communist texts before joining the party, had not been infected—he claimed he had not "studied" the books. See *US v. Foster et al.*, Stenographer's Notes, vol. 4, 2115–17. Philbrick, on the other hand, described himself as "natively so unreceptive to their doctrines that it was only by swallowing my gorge that I was able to convince them they should take me in the first place." Philbrick, *I Led 3 Lives*, 64.

78 Testimony of Joshua D. White in HUAC, *Infiltration of Minority Groups*, 2838, emphasis added.

79 "Brief on Constitutional Issues."

80 *US v. Foster et al.*, Stenographer's Notes, vol. 3, 1675, quoted in "Due Process in a Political Trial," Communist Party of the United States, TAM 132 (box 7, folder 29), 1949, Tamiment Library.

81 "Prosecution Closing Argument."

82 *US v. Foster et al.*, Stenographer's Notes, vol. 4, 1919.

83 Budenz, *This Is My Story*, 233.

84 *US v. Foster et al.*, Stenographer's Notes, vol. 3, 1809.

85 Ibid., vol. 4, 2164, emphasis added.

86 Ibid., vol. 5, 3178–88.

87 Ibid., vol. 4, 2224.
88 "Brief on Constitutional Issues."
89 *US v. Shnewer et al.*, Court Transcripts, 5834.
90 Friedman, "America vs. the Narrative."
91 *US v. Shnewer et al.*, Court Transcripts, 2273.
92 Ibid., 4213–14.
93 Ibid., 4127.
94 Ibid., 2993.
95 Ibid., 6490, 6369.
96 Ibid., 5852.
97 Ibid., 1517–18.
98 Quoted in ibid., 4011.
99 Ibid., 5923–24.
100 Ibid., 6525.
101 Ibid., 1520.
102 Ibid., 5937–38.
103 Ibid., 5835.
104 Hussain, "Judge Upholds Life Sentences."
105 HUAC, *Communist Methods of Infiltration—Education*, 9.
106 "Little Commissar."
107 "Conviction of Communists."
108 Philbrick, *I Led 3 Lives*, 78.
109 Siesseger, "Conspiracy Theory," 1182.
110 Chun, *Control and Freedom*, 3.
111 Van Dijck, *Culture of Connectivity*.
112 *US v. Shnewer et al.*, Court Transcripts, 3561.
113 Hu, *Prehistory of the Cloud*, xxvii.

CHAPTER 3. OPACITY AND TRANSPARENCY IN COUNTERTERRORISM

1 Parks, "Drones, Vertical Mediation, and the Targeted Class." See also Chow, *Age of the World Target*.
2 Marshall, *Class, Citizenship, and Social Development*.
3 Smith, *Civic Ideals*, 2. The denial of rights along these lines often happens in spite of formal equality. See also Sassen, *Territory, Authority, Rights*. Smith, *Stories of Peoplehood*; Anderson, *Imagined Communities*.
4 Al-Qaeda in the Arabian Peninsula, *Inspire* 3 (November 2010): 20; *Inspire* 9 (May 2012): 23, 30; *Inspire* 10 (March 2013): 50; *Inspire* 12 (March 2014): 14; *Inspire* 14 (September 2015): 70.
5 Al-Qaeda in the Arabian Peninsula, *Inspire* 11 (May 2013): 3.
6 Department of Homeland Security, *If You See Something, Say Something* [Video file], www.youtube.com/watch?v=6jAV1dbGPB4.
7 Al-Qaeda in the Arabian Peninsula, *Inspire* 4 (January 2011): 24; *Inspire* 2 (October 2010): 63.

8   For example, "Suleiman al-Halaby, 18th Century Lone Mujahid Assassin," *Inspire* 14 (September 2015): 30–31; al-Qaeda in the Arabian Peninsula, *Inspire* 13 (December 2014): 50.

9   Miller and Samuels, "Glossy Approach to Inciting Terrorism."

10 Ibid.

11 Brahimi, "Inspiring Extremism."

12 Al-Qaeda in the Arabian Peninsula, *Inspire* 1 (January 2010): 8–10. On poverty, see *Inspire* 1 (January 2010): 18; on racism, see *Inspire* 10 (March 2013): 29, and *Inspire* 14 (September 2015): 19.

13 Quoted in Millstone, "Anwar al-Awlaki Hails Rise of 'Western Jihad.'"

14 Quotes in order: Franklin, "Do Suicide Bombers Cancel Their Subscriptions?" (if Neumann is mistaken, it is all the more indicative of the phenomenon of the Double as the writers of *Inspire* can be misidentified as American); Napolitano, "Progress toward a More Secure and Resilient Nation"; Shane and Mekhennet, "Imam's Path."

15 Dreyfuss, "My Fellow Americans," 250.

16 Quoted in Ignatius, "Killing of Anwar Al-Aulaqi."

17 As with other terrorists, the media focused on his deviant and/or starved sexuality. Al-Awlaki not only visited prostitutes but mostly talked with them according to FBI surveillance transcripts.

18 Holmes, "Why Hasn't Yemen Hunted Down Anwar al-Awlaki?"; Symmes, "Anwar al-Awlaki"; Shane and Mekhennet, "Imam's Path."

19 Christopher Heffelfinger and Scott Shane in Boucek, "Rise of Anwar al-Awlaki."

20 Klaidman, *Kill or Capture*; Raghavan, "Anwar al-Aulaqi"; Shadid and Kirkpatrick, "As the West Celebrates."

21 Shane, "Judging a Long, Deadly Reach."

22 Ghosh, "How Dangerous is the Cleric Anwar al-Awlaki?"; Raghavan, "Anwar al-Aulaqi."

23 Heffelfinger, "Anwar Al-'Awlaqi." See also Holmes, "Why Hasn't Yemen Hunted Down Anwar al-Awlaki?"; Stanglin, "Al-Awlaki's Diatribes"; Shadid and Kirkpatrick, "As the West Celebrates"; Shane and Mekhennet, "Imam's Path."

24 *Al-Arabiya*, cited in Ghosh, "How Dangerous Is the Cleric Anwar al-Awlaki?"; Engelhardt, "Redefining the Language of War."

25 Rawnsley, "YouTube Yanks Jihadi Videos"; Shane, "Judging a Long, Deadly Reach."

26 Madhani, "Cleric al-Awlaki."

27 Greenberg, "Homegrown."

28 US Congress, Senate, Subcommittee on Terrorism, Technology, and Homeland Security, *Terrorism: Radical Islamic Influence of Chaplaincy*; US Congress, Senate, Committee on Homeland Security, *Threat of Muslim-American Radicalization in U.S. Prisons* (hereafter *Threat of Muslim-American Radicalization*); Hamm, "Prisoner Radicalization."

29 Government Exhibit 119-E1. All government exhibits have been retrieved from www.investigativeproject.org. The website is run by Steve Emerson, a key figure on the American paranoid right. He pushes a variety of conspiracy theories including that the Muslim Brotherhood has infiltrated all levels of the US government.

30 Wakin, "Imams Reject Talk"; Baker and Hernandez, "4 Accused of Bombing Plot."

31 Testimony of Michael P. Downing, Los Angeles Police Counterterrorism Officer, in *Threat of Muslim-American Radicalization*, 221, 232.

32 *United States v. James Cromitie, David Williams, Onta Williams, and Laguerre Payen*, Court Transcripts, Criminal No. 09-CR-00558, 2010, 38, 44–49.

33 *Threat of Muslim-American Radicalization*, 215.

34 Dunleavy is not referring to the Nation of Islam, despite its presence in US prisons. By the 1960s, the Nation of Islam boasted a membership of 65,000 to 100,000. This group had a largely apolitical separatist stance, but did file various lawsuits to claim rights for the incarcerated. The Nation of Islam historically provided a base of racial solidarity and collectivity for black prisoners, one whose focus on black superiority formed a threatening alternative imagined community antithetical to mainstream American white culture. It is discussed in the hearings concerning prison radicalization and is listed therein as a racist organization. However, the fears that this group may breed recruits for al-Qaeda are unlikely as the Nation of Islam has long been considered heretical by other Muslim sects and organizations. For example, an American prison convert, Kevin James, who founded a group called Jam'iyyat Ul-Islam Is-Saheeh (JIS) while in prison, has listed members of the Nation of Islam as legitimate targets of violence (though he himself was once a member). See *Threat of Muslim-American Radicalization*, 218; Gottschalk, *Prison and the Gallows*.

35 Quoted in Gray, "Why Was a Controversial Imam Shot 20 Times?" In his statement, Dunleavy emphasizes that an issue of *Inspire* magazine refers to al-Amin as a "political prisoner and faithful mujahid" (in *Threat of Muslim-American Radicalization*, 212).

36 Greenberg, "Homegrown." On this incident, see also Gray, "Why Was a Controversial Imam Shot 20 Times?" and White, "Luqman Ameen Abdullah."

37 *US v. Cromitie et al.*, Court Transcripts, 16.

38 Government Exhibit 105A-E3.

39 *US v. Cromitie et al.*, Court Transcripts, 3.

40 Napolitano, "Progress toward a More Secure and Resilient Nation."

41 Walter Benjamin, quoted in Vaughan-Williams, "Borderwork beyond Inside/Outside?," 70; see also Andrejevic, *iSpy*, 43; Sassen, *Territory, Authority, Rights*, 284.

42 Chung, "MTA Updates Famous 'See Something, Say Something' Campaign."

43 Al-Qaeda in the Arabian Peninsula, *Inspire* 13 (December 2014): 19.

44 All this despite evidence that the Muslim American community has been much more involved in terrorism prevention than others. See Schanzer, Kurzman, and Moosa, "Anti-terror Lessons of Muslim-Americans."

45 Butler, *Precarious Life*, 77.

46 Al-Awlaki was not the only American killed by a drone. Adam Gadahn (née Pearlman), a California native with Jewish roots who was raised Protestant, joined al-Qaeda and became an advisor to bin Laden. In 2006, he was indicted by a federal grand jury for treason; the indictment was largely based on the testimony of an FBI field agent. That day, Deputy Attorney General Paul J. McNulty warned, "Betrayal of our country will bring severe consequences." In January 2015, Gadahn was killed in Pakistan, though the administration claimed he was not directly targeted. See Eggen and DeYoung, "US Supporter of Al-Qaeda," and White House, "Statement by the Press Secretary."

47 Dehn and Heller, "Debate," 181. Here Dehn and Heller cite the 1863 *Prize Cases*, in which residents of Confederate states claimed that they, by the Constitution, were to be treated as "loyal citizens" until proved otherwise. The Court found that US citizenship did not exempt any individual enemy from actions allowed by the laws of war. Dehn and Heller further claim that this was maintained in *Hamdi v. Rumsfeld* (2004), *Ex Parte Quirin* (as to petitioner Haupt, 1942), *Juragua Iron Co Ltd v. US* (1909).

48 McKelvey, "Due Process Rights," 1356.

49 See statements in Baumann, "Jeff Goldberg Agrees"; Goodman, "Awlaki Killing Incites Criticism"; Wilson, "No Safe Haven Anywhere"; Kendall, "Guy Fawkes's Dangerous Remedy"; Qadhi, "Illegal and Counterproductive Assassination"; Shane, "Judging a Long, Deadly Reach."

50 Sassen, *Territory, Authority, Rights*.

51 Miller, "Secret Subjects, Open Secrets," 27.

52 Ibid., 19.

53 Divoll, "Who Says You Can Kill Americans, Mr. President?"

54 *Nasser al-Awlaki v. Obama, Gates & Panetta* (10–1469 JDB, 2010), https://ecf.dcd .uscourts.gov.

55 Quoted in Liptak, "Secrecy of Memo on Drone Killing Is Upheld."

56 Miller, "Secret Subjects, Open Secrets," 24.

57 Savage, "Secret U.S. Memo"; "Justice Department Memo Reveals Legal Case."

58 Masco, "'Sensitive but Unclassified.'"

59 King quoted in Landler, "Obama Hailed after Awlaki Killing"; McCain quoted in Whitlock, "After Yemen Attack"; Reid quoted in Serwer, "Bipartisan Approval for Targeted Killing." Opinion polls in Drake, "Most Americans Believe"; Pew Research Center for the People and the Press, "Majority Views NSA Phone Tracking."

60 François, *Open Secrets*, 1.

61 Ross, "Legal Experts Dissect."

62 Dean, *Publicity's Secret*.

63 Sedgwick, *Epistemology of the Closet*, 8.

64 Miller, "Secret Subjects, Open Secrets," 27.

65 Quoted in Savage, "Not-Quite Confirmation of a Memo Approving Killing"; Brisbane, "Secrets of Government Killing"; video available at www.youtube.com /watch?v=WWKG6ZmgAX4.

66   Bergson, *Laughter*.

67   See, for example, Griswold, "(Ever-Growing) List of Cowards."

68   *US v. Cromitie et al.*, Court Transcripts, 1567–70.

69   Ibid., 28.

70   Ibid., 1397.

71   Ibid., 1610.

72   Government Exhibit 119-E1.

73   Judge McMahon in *US v. Cromitie et al.*, 2011.

74   *US v. Cromitie et al.*, Court Transcripts, 1602–3.

75   Ibid., 1908.

76   Ibid., 740.

77   Sherman, "'Person Otherwise Innocent.'"

78   Alexander, *New Jim Crow*; Wacquant, *Punishing the Poor*; Western, *Punishment and Inequality in America*; Thompson, "Why Mass Incarceration Matters"; Berger, *Captive Nation*.

79   Western, *Punishment and Inequality in America*, 192. The crime rate itself cannot account for the rise of mass incarceration as "new methods of counting crime"—which included the criminalization of urban spaces—distorted the size of the increase, nor can mass incarceration take credit for the subsequent drop in crime rates, accounting for only 10 percent of the drop by one study's measure.

80   Berger, *Captive Nation*, 18.

81   Thompson, "Why Mass Incarceration Matters," 716.

82   Wacquant, *Punishing the Poor*, 204–5. The ghetto is an important phenomenon for Wacquant. Even whites who accepted integration found ways to "keep distance" through the concentration of blacks in ghettos. So central was this separation that many liberal whites who supported Martin Luther King Jr. had turned on him when "he confronted the issue of the ghetto in the northern metropolis."

83   In fact, Cromitie's sister almost scoffed at the idea that he had converted: "They do a little time in jail and they don't eat pork no more." Quoted in Chan and Schweber, "Updates in Terror Plot."

84   Western, *Punishment and Inequality in America*, 198.

85   *US v. Cromitie et al.*, Court Transcripts, 1545.

86   Quoted in ibid., 46.

87   Ibid., 79–81.

88   Harris, "Newburgh Four."

89   Quoted in Rayman, "Were the Newburgh 4 Really Out to Blow Up Synagogues?";
US v. Cromitie et al., Court Transcripts, 45.

90   Government Exhibit 112–E3.

91   *US v. Cromitie et al.*, Court Transcripts, 54–55.

92   Ibid., 1827–31; Government Exhibit 116-E1.

93   *US v. Cromitie et al.*, Court Transcripts, 1869.

94   Ibid., 1795–1801, 1880–81.

95   Quoted in Fahim, "Agent Wanted Backup Charge."

96 *US v. Cromitie et al.*, Court Transcripts, 1900.

97 Judge McMahon quoted in Moynihan, "Entrapment Argued."

98 Judge McMahon quoted in Weiser, "3 Men Get 25 Years."

99 Cromitie quoted in Weiser, "3 Men Get 25 Years"; Williams in Rayman, "Were the Newburgh 4 Really Out to Blow Up Synagogues?"

NO EXIT

1 Allen, "Dzhokhar Tsarnaev and His Fangirls"; Le Tellier, "Dzhokhar Tsarnaev and His Disgusting Fangirls"; Bruenig, "Dzhokhar Tsarnaev's Female Supporters Are Not 'Fangirls.'"

2 A friend, quoted in Reitman, "Jahar's World," 48.

3 Remnick, "Culprits."

4 Dzhokhar's wrestling coach, quoted in Reitman, "Jahar's World," 48.

5 Fyodor Dostoyevsky's *The Double*, quoted in Rank, *Double*, 30.

6 Taibbi, "Explaining the Rolling Stone Cover."

7 Reitman, "Jahar's World," 53; Jacobs, Filipov, and Wen, "Fall of the House of Tsarnaev."

8 Wines and Lovett, "Dark Side, Carefully Masked."

9 Reitman, "Jahar's World," 54, 53, 55. After the bombing there were tributes to the brothers in *Inspire* magazine, another reappropriation of disparate events by al-Qaeda in the Arabian Peninsula.

10 Ioffe, "Boston Bombing Suspects."

11 Reitman, "Jahar's World," 55.

12 Cullison, "Family Terror."

13 Wines and Lovett, "Dark Side, Carefully Masked."

14 Reitman, "Jahar's World," 55, 52, emphasis original.

15 Quoted in Remnick, "Culprits."

16 Dewey, "Obscure Russian Jihadist"; Harding and Dodd, "Tamerlan Tsarnaev's YouTube Account"; Reitman, "Jahar's World," 55. The contact with Russia was so troubling that a congressional party was sent there to investigate.

17 Wines and Lovett, "Dark Side, Carefully Masked."

18 On the limits of online bomb-making instructions, see Kenney, "Beyond the Internet." At the time of writing there were twenty-eight such cases: seventeen involved informants, six involved hands-on training abroad, and the remaining five all failed, save the Tsarnaevs. Data retrieved from "Terrorism in America after 9/11."

19 Field and Almasy, "Did the Tsarnaev Brothers Have Help?"

20 Quoted in Reitman, "Jahar's World," 57.

21 Ioffe, "Boston Bombing Suspects."

22 Cullison, "Family Terror."

23 Debrix and Barder, *Beyond Biopolitics*; Jacques Derrida in Borradori, *Philosophy in a Time of Terror*.

24 Bolton, "Barack Obama Declares Defeat."

25 Reilly, "Dzhokhar Tsarnaev Will Not Be Treated as Enemy Combatant"; Ungar, "Senator Lindsey Graham Says Suspend the Constitution."

26 Tiqqun, *Introduction to Civil War*. An interesting example of this type of practice is that of naturalization through military service. Noncitizens prove their allegiance by risking their lives and, in return, gain citizenship.

27 For example, Pearson, McPike, and Cooper, "What Did Suspected Bomber's Widow Know?"

28 Comment in "Katherine Russell Not Involved in Boston Bombing."

29 The women in Dzhokhar's life received a similar amount of attention. *Newsweek*'s October 24, 2014, cover featured a black-and-white drawing of Dzhokhar Tsarnaev accompanied by his sisters Ailina and Bella. The caption read "Twisted Sisters," suggesting that the women pushed for "jihad."

30 Shel Silverstein, "Cover of the Rolling Stone," recorded by Dr. Hook & the Medicine Show on *Sloppy Seconds* (San Francisco, CA: Columbia Records, 1972). The band made it on the cover the following year.

31 "You Are Either with Us or against Us."

32 In Borradori, *Philosophy in a Time of Terror*; Derrida, *Politics of Friendship*. Others who have addressed this theme include Galloway and Thacker, *Exploit*; Masco, *Theater of Operations*.

33 De Quincey, "Milton versus Southey and Landor," 202.

34 Foucault, *Society Must Be Defended*, 256.

35 Quoted in Pearson, "Trooper Who Leaked Boston Bomber Pictures."

36 Freud, "'Uncanny,'" 219.

37 Debrix and Barder, *Beyond Biopolitics*, 109. Here they are building on Carlo Galli's notion of "Global War."

38 Bergen and Sterman, "First Line of Defense."

39 Foucault, "About the Concept of the 'Dangerous Individual,'" 17.

40 Attempts to humanize those labeled terrorist need to be assessed critically. In addition to being appropriated into security discourse, as I have outlined in this book, there is certainly a racial component concerning who can and who cannot be humanized. That is, Tsarnaev "looks the part" while others certainly do not. Even in the case of Tsarnaev there are limits. Journalist Masha Gessen received much criticism for being too empathetic toward the brothers in her book about them. See Gessen, *The Brothers*.

41 Gombrowicz, *Cosmos*, 89.

EPILOGUE

1 Full text is available online at www.thehill.com. Note that all emphases and caps are from the original.

2 Akyol and Ali, "This Wasn't a Speech about Islam."

3 Dockray, "President Trump Finally Calls Portland Attack 'Unacceptable.'"

4 Quoted in Rossoll, "McMaster Hints."

5 Hubbard, "ISIS Turns Saudis."

BIBLIOGRAPHY

Aaronson, Trevor. *The Terror Factory: Inside the FBI's Manufactured War on Terrorism.* Brooklyn, NY: Ig Publishing, 2014.

Ackerman, Spencer. "DHS Crushed This Analyst for Warning about Far-Right Terror." *Wired*, August 7, 2012. www.wired.com.

Agamben, Giorgio. *Homo Sacer: Sovereign Power and Bare Life.* Translated by Daniel Heller-Roazen. Stanford, CA: Stanford University Press, 1998.

———. *State of Exception.* Translated by Kevin Attell. Chicago: University of Chicago Press, 2005.

Akyol, Mustafa, and Wajahat Ali. "This Wasn't a Speech about Islam." *New York Times*, May 21, 2017. www.nytimes.com.

Alexander, Michelle. *The New Jim Crow: Mass Incarceration in the Age of Colorblindness.* New York: New Press, 2010.

Alexander, Yonah, Phil Baum, and Raphael Danziger. "Terrorism: Future Threats and Responses." *Terrorism* 7, no. 4 (1985): 367–410. doi:10.1080/1057610850 8435587.

Ali Musawi, Mohammed. *Cheering for Osama: How Jihadists Use Internet Discussion Forums.* London: Quilliam, 2010. www.quilliaminternational.com.

Allen, Charlotte. "Dzhokhar Tsarnaev and His Fangirls." *Los Angeles Times*, May 22, 2013. www.latimes.com.

Alsultany, Evelyn. *Arabs and Muslims in the Media: Race and Representation after 9/11.* New York: New York University Press, 2012.

Amoore, Louise. *The Politics of Possibility: Risk and Security beyond Probability.* Durham, NC: Duke University Press, 2013.

Anderson, Benedict. *Imagined Communities: Reflections on the Origin and Spread of Nationalism.* New York: Verso, 1983.

Andrejevic, Mark. *iSpy: Surveillance and Power in the Interactive Era.* Lawrence: University Press of Kansas, 2007.

Animal Liberation Front. "ALF Credo." N.d. www.animalliberationfront.com.

———. "Manifesto for Radical Abolitionism: Total Liberation by Any Means Necessary." N.d. www.animalliberationfront.com.

Appadurai, Arjun. *Fear of Small Numbers: An Essay on the Geography of Anger.* Durham, NC: Duke University Press, 2006.

Apuzzo, Matt, and Adam Goldman. *Enemies Within: Inside the NYPD's Secret Spying Unit and Bin Laden's Final Plot against America.* New York: Touchstone, 2013.

Archetti, Cristina. "Terrorism, Communication and New Media: Explaining Radical-ization in the Digital Age." *Perspectives on Terrorism* 9, no. 1 (2015). www.terroris manalysts.com.

Arquilla, John, and David Ronfeldt. *The Advent of Netwar*. Santa Monica, CA: RAND, 1996.

Ascroft, Edward. "Lacan's Desire and Dostoevsky's Double: The Problematics of Psy-choanalytic Discourse in a Fictional Psychosis." *Dostoevsky Journal* 6 (2005): 1–20.

Badiou, Alain. *Infinite Thought*. London: Bloomsbury Academic, 2005.

Badolato, Edward V. "Environmental Terrorism: A Case Study." *Studies in Conflict & Terrorism* 14, no. 4 (1991): 237–39.

Baker, Al, and Javier C. Hernandez. "4 Accused of Bombing Plot at Bronx Synagogues." *New York Times*, May 21, 2009, A1.

Barcott, Bruce. "From Tree-Hugger to Terrorist." *New York Times*, April 7, 2002. www .nytimes.com.

Baumann, Nick. "Jeff Goldberg Agrees with . . . Glenn Greenwald? About Anwar al-Awlaki?" *Mother Jones*, November 16, 2010. www.motherjones.com.

Beck, Ulrich. "Living in the World Risk Society." *Economy and Society* 35, no. 3 (2006): 329–45. doi:10.1080/03085140600844902.

Beirich, Heidi, and Mark Potok. "USA: Hate Groups, Radical-Right Violence, on the Rise." *Policing* 3, no. 3 (2009): 255–63. doi:10.1093/police/pap020.

Belknap, Michal R. *Cold War Political Justice: The Smith Act, the Communist Party, and American Civil Liberties*. Westport, CT: Praeger, 1977.

Bentley, Eric. *Thirty Years of Treason: Excerpts from Hearings before the House Commit-tee on Un-American Activities 1938–1968*. New York: Viking, 1971.

Bergen, Peter, and David Sterman. "First Line of Defense against Terrorism: Mom and Dad." *CNN*, October 29, 2014. www.cnn.com.

Berger, Dan. *Captive Nation: Black Prison Organizing in the Civil Rights Era*. Chapel Hill: University of North Carolina Press, 2014.

Berger, J. M. "Anwar al-Awlaki's Links to the September 11 Hijackers." *Atlantic*, Septem-ber 9, 2011. www.theatlantic.com.

———. "The Metronome of Apocalyptic Time: Social Media as Carrier Wave for Mille-narian Contagion." *Perspectives on Terrorism* 9, no. 4 (2015). www.terrorismanalysts .com.

Bergson, Henri Louis. *Laughter—An Essay on the Meaning of the Comic*. Translated by Cloudesley Brereton and Fred Rothwell. New York: Macmillan, 1917.

Best, Steven, and Anthony J. Nocella. *Terrorists or Freedom Fighters? Reflections on the Liberation of Animals*. New York: Lantern Books, 2004.

Bhabha, Homi K. *The Location of Culture*. London: Routledge, 2004.

Bjelopera, Jerome P. *The Domestic Terrorist Threat: Background and Issues for Congress*. Washington, DC: Congressional Research Service, 2012. http://digital.library.unt .edu.

Bloom, Robert M. "A Historical Overview of Informants." *Legal Studies Research Paper Series (Boston College Law School)* 64 (2005). https://papers.ssrn.com.

Bolton, John. "John Bolton: Barack Obama Declares Defeat in Global War on Terror." *Daily Beast*, January 30, 2017. www.thedailybeast.com.

Borges, Jorge Luis. *The Book of Imaginary Beings*. Translated by Andrew Hurley. New York: Penguin, 2006.

Borradori, Giovanna. *Philosophy in a Time of Terror: Dialogues with Jurgen Habermas and Jacques Derrida*. Chicago: University of Chicago Press, 2003.

Boucek, Christopher. "The Rise of Anwar al-Awlaki." Washington, DC: Carnegie Endowment for International Peace, June 1, 2010. http://carnegieendow ment.org.

"The Boy Who Cried 'ELF.'" *Wall Street Journal*, February 14, 2001. www.wsj.com.

Brahimi, Alia. "The 'Changing' Face of Al-Qaeda." *Al-Jazeera*, July 5, 2011. www .aljazeera.com.

———. "Inspiring Extremism." *Majalla Magazine*, March 27, 2013. http://eng.majalla .com.

Brisbane, Arthur S. "The Secrets of Government Killing." *New York Times*, October 9, 2011, SR12.

Brooks, David. "The Rush to Therapy." *New York Times*, November 9, 2009. www .nytimes.com.

Brown, Wendy. *Walled States, Waning Sovereignty*. New York: Zone Books, 2014.

Bruenig, Elizabeth Stoker. "Dzhokhar Tsarnaev's Female Supporters Are Not 'Fangirls.'" *Atlantic*, July 12, 2013. www.theatlantic.com.

Budenz, Louis F. *This Is My Story*. New York: McGraw-Hill, 1949.

Butler, Judith. *Precarious Life: The Powers of Mourning and Violence*. New York: Verso, 2004.

Chamberlain, William Henry. "The Communist Trial." *Wall Street Journal*, October 20, 1949.

Chan, Sewell, and Nate Schweber. "Updates in Terror Plot." *New York Times*, May 21, 2009. https://cityroom.blogs.nytimes.com.

Chase, Alston. *Harvard and the Unabomber: The Education of an American Terrorist*. New York: Norton, 2003.

"Chorus of Protest Grows over Report Warning of Right Wing Radicalization." *Fox News*, April 15, 2009. www.foxnews.com.

Chow, Rey. *The Age of the World Target: Self-Referentiality in War, Theory, and Comparative Work*. Durham, NC: Duke University Press, 2006.

Chun, Wendy Hui Kyong. *Control and Freedom: Power and Paranoia in the Age of Fiber Optics*. Cambridge, MA: MIT Press, 2006.

Chung, Jen. "MTA Updates Famous 'See Something, Say Something' Campaign with Real NYers Who Saw Something, Said Something." *Gothamist*, March 3, 2016. http://gothamist.com.

Coates, Paul. *The Double and the Other: Identity as Ideology in Post-romantic Fiction*. New York: Palgrave Macmillan, 1988.

"The Condition of Kansas." *New York Times*, August 13, 1856. www.nytimes.com.

"Conviction of Communists [Op-Ed]." *Portland (ME) Press-Herald*, October 16, 1949.

Craven, Julia. "Dylann Roof Wasn't Charged with Terrorism Because He's White." *Huffington Post*, July 24, 2015. www.huffingtonpost.com.

Crawley, Alfred E. "Doubles." In *Encyclopedia of Religion and Ethics IV*, edited by James Hastings, 853–60. New York: Charles Scribner's Sons, 1908.

Cullison, Alan. "A Family Terror: The Tsarnaevs and the Boston Bombing." *Wall Street Journal*, December 14, 2013. www.wsj.com.

Curry, Michael, director. *If a Tree Falls: A Story of the Earth Liberation Front*. USA: Oscilloscope, 2011.

Dao, James, and Serge F. Kovaleski. "Hatecore Music Is Called White Supremacist Recruiting Tool." *New York Times*, August 8, 2012, A10.

Dean, Jodi. *Publicity's Secret: How Technoculture Capitalizes on Democracy*. Ithaca, NY: Cornell University Press, 2002.

Debrix, Francois, and Alexander D. Barder. *Beyond Biopolitics: Theory, Violence, and Horror in World Politics*. New York: Routledge, 2012.

Dehn, John C., and Kevin Jon Heller. "Debate: Targeted Killing: The Case of Anwar Al-Aulaqi." *University of Pennsylvania Law Review PENNumbra* 159 (2011): 175–201.

Deleuze, Gilles, and Felix Guattari. *A Thousand Plateaus: Capitalism and Schizophrenia*. Translated by Brian Massumi. Minneapolis: University of Minnesota Press, 1987.

Department of Homeland Security. "Domestic Terrorism and Homegrown Violent Extremism Lexicon." November 10, 2011. www.dhs.gov.

De Quincey, Thomas. "Milton versus Southey and Landor." In *The Notebook of an Opium-Eater, and Miscellaneous Essays*, 193–216. Boston: J.R. Osgood, 1873.

Derrida, Jacques. *The Politics of Friendship*. Translated by George Collins. London: Verso, 2006.

Desphande, Nick, and Howard Ernst. "Countering Eco-terrorism in the United States: The Case of Operation Backfire." College Park, MD: National Consortium for the Study of Terrorism and Responses to Terrorism, 2012. www.start.umd.edu.

Dewey, Caitlin. "The Obscure Russian Jihadist Whom Tamerlan Tsarnaev Followed Online." *Washington Post*, April 24, 2013. www.washingtonpost.com.

Dilling, Elizabeth Kirkpatrick. *The Red Network: A Who's Who and Handbook of Radicalism for Patriots*. Chicago: Published by the Author, 1934.

"Discouraging to 'Fanatics.'" *New York Times*, October 5, 1857. www.nytimes.com.

Ditrych, Ondrej. "From Discourse to *Dispositif*: States and Terrorism between Marseille and 9/11." *Security Dialogue* 44, no. 3 (2013): 223–40. doi:10.1177/0967010613484076.

Divoll, Vicki. "Who Says You Can Kill Americans, Mr. President?" *New York Times*, January 16, 2013. www.nytimes.com.

Dockray, Heather. "President Trump Finally Calls Portland Attack 'Unacceptable'—But Slyly Avoids His Base," May 29, 2017. www.mashable.com.

Donnelly, Michael. "Criminalizing Dissent." *Counterpunch*, May 24, 2006. www.counterpunch.org.

Drabelle, Dennis. "Extremism in the Defense of Trees." *Washington Post*, March 24, 1991. www.washingtonpost.com.

Drake, Bruce. "Most Americans Believe Government Surveillance Program Helped Prevent Terrorist Attacks." Pew Research Center, 2013. www.pewresearch.org.

Dreyfuss, Mike. "My Fellow Americans, We Are Going to Kill You: The Legality of Targeting and Killing U.S. Citizens Abroad." *Vanderbilt Law Review* 56 (2012): 249–92.

Dryden, Linda. *The Modern Gothic and Literary Doubles: Stevenson, Wilde and Wells.* New York: Palgrave Macmillan, 2003.

Edgerton, David. *The Shock of the Old: Technology and Global History since 1900.* Oxford: Oxford University Press, 2007.

Eggen, Dan, and Karen DeYoung. "U.S. Supporter of Al-Qaeda Is Indicted on Treason Charge." *Washington Post*, October 12, 2006. www.washingtonpost.com.

Eichenwald, Kurt. "Right-Wing Extremists Are a Bigger Threat to America Than ISIS." *Newsweek*, February 4, 2016. www.newsweek.com.

Engelhardt, Tom. "Redefining the Language of War: Nine Words with New Meanings." *Mother Jones*, June 23, 2011. www.motherjones.com.

Erickson, Mark. "Network as Metaphor." *International Journal of Criminology and Sociological Theory* 5, no. 2 (2012): 912–21.

"Evolution or Revolution." *Time*, April 4, 1949, 26.

Fahim, Kareem. "Agent Wanted Backup Charge in Synagogue Bomb Case." *New York Times*, August 27, 2010, A16.

Faiola, Anthony, and Dale Russakoff. "The Terrorists Next Door?" *Washington Post*, May 10, 2007. www.washingtonpost.com.

Federal Bureau of Investigation. "FBI Analysis of Terrorist Incidents in the United States—1982." *Terrorism* 7, no. 1 (1984): 87–117. doi:10.1080/10576108408435564.

———. "White Supremacist Recruitment of Military Personnel after 9/11." July 7, 2008. www.splcenter.org.

Ferris, Joshua. "Let Us Now Praise Infamous Men." *New York Times Style Magazine*, September 15, 2013.

Field, Alexandra, and Steve Almasy. "Did the Tsarnaev Brothers Have Help Making the Boston Marathon Bombs?" *CNN*, March 5, 2015. www.cnn.com.

Fleming, Paul. "Doppelgänger/Doppeltgänger." *Cabinet*, 14 (Summer 2004). www.cabinetmagazine.org.

Foucault, Michel. "About the Concept of the 'Dangerous Individual' in 19th-Century Legal Psychiatry." Translated by Alain Baudot and Jane Couchman. *International Journal of Law and Psychiatry* 1, no. 1 (1978): 1–18.

———. *Security, Territory, Population: Lectures at the Collège de France 1977—1978.* Edited by Michel Senellart. Translated by Graham Burchell. New York: Picador, 2009.

———. *Society Must Be Defended: Lectures at the Collège de France, 1975–1976.* Translated by David Macey. New York: Picador, 2003.

Fox News Sunday. Fox News, November 8, 2009. www.foxnews.com.

François, Anne-Lise. *Open Secrets: The Literature of Uncounted Experience.* Stanford, CA: Stanford University Press, 2008.

Franklin, O. "Do Suicide Bombers Cancel Their Subscriptions? Uncovering Inspire, Al-Qaeda's Jihadist Magazine." *British GQ*, April 24, 2013.

Freeman, F. L. "Communist Trial [Letter to the Editor]." *Washington Post*, February 9, 1949.

Freud, Sigmund. "The 'Uncanny.'" In *The Standard Edition of the Complete Psychological Works of Sigmund Freud, XVII (1917–1919): An Infantile Neurosis and Other Works*, 217–56. New York: Norton, 1919.

Friedman, Thomas L. "America vs. the Narrative." *New York Times*, November 28, 2009. www.nytimes.com.

Gaffney, Frank J., Jr. "The Siren Call of Shariah." *Washington Times*, November 10, 2009. www.washingtontimes.com.

Galli, Carlo. "On War and on the Enemy." Translated by Amanda Minervini and Adam Sitze. *CR: The New Centennial Review* 9, no. 2 (2010): 195–219. doi:10.1353/ncr.0.0070.

Galloway, Alexander R., and Eugene Thacker. *The Exploit: A Theory of Networks*. Minneapolis: University of Minnesota Press, 2007.

Genosko, Gary, and Scott Thompson. "Tense Theory: The Temporalities of Surveillance." In *Theorizing Surveillance: The Panopticon and Beyond*, edited by Gary Genosko and David Lyon, 123–38. Cullompton, Devon: Willan, 2006.

Gessen, Masha. *The Brothers: The Road to an American Tragedy*. New York: Riverhead Books, 2015.

Ghosh, Bobby. "How Dangerous Is the Cleric Anwar al-Awlaki?" *Time*, January 13, 2010. www.time.com.

Goldstein, Robert Justin. *American Blacklist: The Attorney General's List of Subversive Organizations*. Lawrence: University Press of Kansas, 2008.

Gombrowicz, Witold. *Cosmos: A Novel*. Translated by Danuta Borchardt. New York: Grove Press, 2011.

Gomez, Dayana Morales. "Robert Doggart, Man Who Allegedly Plotted to Kill Muslims, Indicted on Federal Charges." *Huffington Post*, July 7, 2015. www.huffington post.com.

Goode, Erica, and Serge F. Kovaleski. "Wisconsin Killer Fed and Was Fueled by Hate-Driven Music." *New York Times*, August 6, 2012. www.nytimes.com.

Goodman, J. David. "Awlaki Killing Incites Criticism on Left and Libertarian Right." *New York Times*, September 30, 2011. https://thelede.blogs.nytimes.com.

Gottschalk, Marie. *The Prison and the Gallows: The Politics of Mass Incarceration in America*. Cambridge: Cambridge University Press, 2006.

Granovetter, Mark S. "The Strength of Weak Ties." *American Journal of Sociology* 78, no. 6 (1973): 1360–80.

Gray, Steven. "Why Was a Controversial Imam Shot 20 Times?" *Time*, February 1, 2010. www.time.com.

"Green Monsters [Op-Ed]." *Washington Post*, June 13, 1992.

Greenberg, Karen J. "Homegrown: The Rise of American Jihad." *New Republic*, May 21, 2010. www.newrepublic.com.

Griswold, Alex. "The (Ever-Growing) List of Cowards Refusing to Publish the Mohammad Cartoons." *Daily Caller*, January 7, 2015. http://dailycaller.com.

Gruen, Lori, Peter Singer, and David Hine. *Animal Liberation: A Graphic Guide*. London: Camden Press, 1987.

Guerard, Albert J. "Concepts of the Double." In *Stories of the Double*, edited by Albert J. Guerard, 1–14. Philadelphia: J. B. Lippincott, 1967.

Hall, Stuart. "The Question of Cultural Identity." In *Modernity: An Introduction to Modern Societies*, edited by Stuart Hall, David Held, Don Hubert, and Kenneth Thompson, 595–634. Malden, MA: Wiley-Blackwell, 1996.

Hallam, Clifford. "The Double as Incomplete Self: Toward a Definition of Doppelgänger." In *Fearful Symmetry: Doubles and Doubling in Literature and Film*, edited by Eugene J. Crook, 1–31. Tallahassee: University Press of Florida, 1982.

Hamm, Mark S. "Prisoner Radicalization: Assessing the Threat in U.S. Correctional Institutions." *National Institute of Justice Journal* 261 (October 27, 2008). www.nij.gov.

Harding, Luke, and Vikram Dodd. "Tamerlan Tsarnaev's YouTube Account Shows Jihadist Radicalisation in Pictures." *Guardian*, April 22, 2013. www.theguardian.com.

Hardt, Michael, and Antonio Negri. "Sovereignty." In *Reflections on Empire*, edited by Antonio Negri, 49–59. Cambridge: Polity, 2008.

Harris, Paul. "Newburgh Four: Poor, Black, and Jailed under FBI 'Entrapment' Tactics." *Guardian*, December 12, 2011. www.theguardian.com.

Heffelfinger, Christopher. "Anwar Al-'Awlaqi: Profile of a Jihadi Radicalizer | Combating Terrorism Center at West Point." *Combating Terrorism Center Sentinel* 3, no. 3 (2010): 1–4.

Heim, Joe. "Wisconsin Shooter Embraced 'Hate Rock.'" *Washington Post*, August 8, 2012. www.washingtonpost.com.

Herbert, Bob. "Stress Beyond Belief." *New York Times*, November 6, 2009. www.nytimes.com.

Herdman, J. *The Double in Nineteenth-Century Fiction*. New York: St. Martin's Press, 1991.

Holmes, Oliver. "Why Hasn't Yemen Hunted Down Anwar al-Awlaki?" *Time*, November 9, 2010.

"The Horror at Fort Hood." *New York Times*, November 6, 2009. www.nytimes.com.

"H.R. 1777 (100th): Foreign Relations Authorization Act, Fiscal Years 1988 and 1989." GovTrack, n.d. www.govtrack.us.

Hu, Tung-Hui. *A Prehistory of the Cloud*. Cambridge, MA: MIT Press, 2015.

Hubbard, Ben. "ISIS Turns Saudis against the Kingdom, and Families against Their Own," *New York Times*, March 31, 2016. www.nytimes.com.

Huntington, Samuel P. "The Clash of Civilizations?" *Foreign Affairs*, June 1, 1993.

Hussain, Murtaza. "Judge Upholds Life Sentences in Fort Dix Plot, but Advocates Say Fight Will Go On." *Intercept*, June 3, 2016. https://theintercept.com.

Hussain, Murtaza, and Razan Ghalayini. "Christie's Conspiracy: The Real Story behind the Fort Dix Five Terror Plot." *Intercept*, June 25, 2015. https://theintercept.com.

Ignatius, David. "The Killing of Anwar Al-Aulaqi: The White House's Drone Attack Policy." *Washington Post*, September 30, 2011. www.washingtonpost.com.

Ioffe, Julia. "The Boston Bombing Suspects Were Reared in Both Chechnya and America." *New Republic*, April 19, 2013. www.newrepublic.com.

Jackson, Richard. "An Argument for Terrorism." *Perspectives on Terrorism* 2, no. 2 (2008): 25–32.

Jacobs, Frank. "Cartography's Favourite Map Monster: The Land Octopus." *Big Think*, July 4, 2011. http://bigthink.com.

Jacobs, Sally, David Filipov, and Patricia Wen. "The Fall of the House of Tsarnaev." *Boston Globe*, December 15, 2013. www.bostonglobe.com.

Johnston, David, and Scott Shane. "U.S. Knew of Suspect's Tie to Radical Cleric, Authorities Say." *New York Times*, November 9, 2009. www.nytimes.com.

"Justice Department Memo Reveals Legal Case for Drone Strikes on Americans." *NBC News*, February 4, 2013. http://investigations.nbcnews.com.

"Katherine Russell Not Involved in Boston Bombing, Dzhokhar Tsarnaev Allegedly Says." *Huffington Post*, May 8, 2013. www.huffingtonpost.com.

Kendall, Emily C. "Guy Fawkes's Dangerous Remedy: The Unconstitutionality of Government-Ordered Assassination against U.S. Citizens and Its Implications for Due Process in America." *John Marshall Law Review* 45 (2012): 1121–50.

Kenney, Michael. "Beyond the Internet: Mētis, Techne, and the Limitations of Online Artifacts for Islamist Terrorists." *Terrorism and Political Violence* 22, no. 2 (2010): 177–97.

Klaidman, Daniel. *Kill or Capture: The War on Terror and the Soul of the Obama Presidency*. Boston: Houghton Mifflin Harcourt, 2012.

Kocieniewski, David. "6 Men Arrested in a Terror Plot against Fort Dix." *New York Times*, May 9, 2007, A1.

Krauthammer, Charles. "Medicalizing Mass Murder." *Washington Post*, November 13, 2009. www.washingtonpost.com.

Krueger, Alan B., and Jitka Malečková. "Education, Poverty and Terrorism: Is There a Causal Connection?" *Journal of Economic Perspectives* 17, no. 4 (2003): 119–44.

Kumar, Deepa. "Framing Islam: The Resurgence of Orientalism during the Bush II Era." *Journal of Communication Inquiry* 34, no. 3 (2010): 254–77. doi:10.1177/0196859910363174.

———. *Islamophobia and the Politics of Empire: The Cultural Logic of Empire*. Chicago: Haymarket Books, 2012.

Kundnani, Arun. *The Muslims Are Coming! Islamophobia, Extremism, and the Domestic War on Terror*. New York: Verso, 2015.

Landler, Mark. "Obama Hailed after Awlaki Killing, but for How Long?" *New York Times*, September 30, 2011. https://thecaucus.blogs.nytimes.com.

Laqueur, Walter. *The New Terrorism: Fanaticism and the Arms of Mass Destruction*. Oxford: Oxford University Press, 1999.

Laris, Michael, Sandhya Somashekhar, and Carol D. Leonnig. "Gunman in Wisconsin Was Deeply Involved in White-Supremacist Music Scene." *Washington Post*, August 7, 2012. www.washingtonpost.com.

Latour, Bruno. "On Actor-Network Theory: A Few Clarifications." *Soziale Welt* 47, no. 4 (1996): 369–81.

———. *Reassembling the Social: An Introduction to Actor-Network-Theory.* Oxford: Oxford University Press, 2005.

Leader, Stefan H., and Peter Probst. "The Earth Liberation Front and Environmental Terrorism." *Terrorism and Political Violence* 15, no. 4 (2003): 37–58. doi:10.1080/09546550390449872.

Lec, Stanisław Jerzy. *Myśli Nieuczesane.* Kraków, Poland: Wydawnictwo Literackie, 1957/1968.

Lee, Chris. "Inside the Creepy World of 'Hate Music.'" *Daily Beast*, January 30, 2017. www.thedailybeast.com.

Lee, Martha. *Earth First! Environmental Apocalypse.* Syracuse, NY: Syracuse University Press, 1995.

Lemke, Thomas. "'A Zone of Indistinction'—A Critique of Giorgio Agamben's Concept of Biopolitics." N.d. www.thomaslemkeweb.de.

Lerner, Max. "Ideas as Criminals [Op-Ed]." *New York Post*, October 17, 1949.

Le Tellier, Alexandra. "Dzhokhar Tsarnaev and His Disgusting Fangirls." *Los Angeles Times*, July 10, 2013. www.latimes.com.

Lewis, Bernard. "The Roots of Muslim Rage." *Atlantic Monthly*, September 1990.

Leyden, T. J. "I Used to Be a Skinhead [Op-Ed]." *Washington Post*, August 12, 2012. www.washingtonpost.com.

Lia, Brynjar. *Architect of Global Jihad: The Life of Al-Qaeda Strategist Abu Mus'ab Al-Suri.* Oxford: Oxford University Press, 2008.

Liptak, Adam. "Secrecy of Memo on Drone Killing Is Upheld." *New York Times*, January 3, 2013, A17.

"The Little Commissar." *Time*, April 25, 1949, 24.

Lizama, Natalia. "A Body of Information: Posthumanism, the Digital Doppelgänger and Don DeLillo's White Noise." In *The Poetics of Shadows: The Double in Literature and Philosophy*, edited by Andrew Hock Soon Ng, 162–75. Stuttgart: ibidem-Verlag, 2008.

Lyon, David. *Surveillance Society: Monitoring Everyday Life.* Philadelphia: Open University Press, 2001.

Mackey, Robert. "Mass Shooting at Fort Hood." *New York Times*, November 5, 2009. https://thelede.blogs.nytimes.com.

———. "Updates on the Shootings at Fort Hood." *New York Times*, November 6, 2009. https://thelede.blogs.nytimes.com.

Madhani, Aamer. "Cleric al-Awlaki Dubbed 'bin Laden of the Internet.'" *USA Today*, August 24, 2010. www.usatoday.com.

Madison, Lucy. "Attorney General Eric Holder: Threat of Homegrown Terrorism 'Keeps Me Up at Night.'" *CBS News*, December 21, 2010. www.cbsnews.com.

Mamdani, Mahmood. *Good Muslim, Bad Muslim: America, the Cold War, and the Roots of Terror.* New York: Harmony, 2005.

Markon, Jerry. "Judge Slashes Sentences of 2 in 'Va. Jihad.'" *Washington Post*, February 25, 2006. www.washingtonpost.com.

Marshall, Thomas Humphrey. *Class, Citizenship, and Social Development*. Chicago: University of Chicago Press, 1973.

Masco, Joseph. "'Sensitive but Unclassified': Secrecy and the Counterterrorist State." *Public Culture* 22, no. 3 (2010): 433–63. doi:10.1215/08992363-2010-004.

———. *The Theater of Operations: National Security Affect from the Cold War to the War on Terror*. Durham, NC: Duke University Press, 2014.

Massumi, Brian. "Potential Politics and the Primacy of Preemption." *Theory & Event* 10, no. 2 (2007). doi:10.1353/tae.2007.0066.

McCauley, Clark, and Sophia Moskalenko. "Mechanisms of Political Radicalization: Pathways toward Terrorism." *Terrorism and Political Violence* 20, no. 3 (2008): 415–33. doi:10.1080/09546550802073367.

McKelvey, Benjamin. "Due Process Rights and the Targeted Killing of Suspected Terrorists: The Unconstitutional Scope of Executive Killing Power." *Vanderbilt Journal of Transnational Law* 44 (2011): 1353–84.

Merari, Ariel. "A Classification of Terrorist Groups." *Terrorism* 1, nos. 3–4 (1978): 331–46. doi:10.1080/10576107808435418.

Michael, George. *Lone Wolf Terror and the Rise of Leaderless Resistance*. Nashville, TN: Vanderbilt University Press, 2012.

Miller, D. A. "Secret Subjects, Open Secrets." *Dickens Studies Annual* 14 (1985): 17–38.

Miller, Judith, and David Samuels. "A Glossy Approach to Inciting Terrorism." *Wall Street Journal*, November 27, 2010. www.wsj.com.

Millstone, Ken. "Anwar al-Awlaki Hails Rise of 'Western Jihad.'" *CBS News*, March 22, 2010. www.cbsnews.com.

Moghaddam, Fathali M. "The Staircase to Terrorism: A Psychological Exploration." *American Psychologist* 60, no. 2 (2005): 161–69. doi:10.1037/0003-066X.60.2.161.

Morreall, John. "A New Theory of Laughter." *Philosophical Studies* 42, no. 2 (1982): 243–54.

Moss, Michael. "Muslims at Fort Voice Outrage and Ask Questions." *New York Times*, November 7, 2009, A17.

Moynihan, Colin. "Entrapment Argued in Bomb-Plot Appeal." *New York Times*, March 25, 2011, A24.

Murphie, Andrew. "Sound at the End of the World as We Know It." In *Deleuze and Guattari: Critical Assessments of Leading Philosophers*, edited by Gary Genosko, 255–80. New York: Routledge, 2001.

Murphy, Tim. "Map: Has Your State Banned Sharia?" *Mother Jones*, February 11, 2011. www.motherjones.com.

Naber, Nadine. *Arab America: Gender, Cultural Politics, and Activism*. New York: New York University Press, 2012.

———. "Arab Americans and U.S. Racial Formations." In *Race and Arab Americans before and after 9/11: From Invisible Citizens to Visible Subjects*, edited by Nadine Naber and Amaney Jamal, 229–75. Syracuse, NY: Syracuse University Press, 2008.

Nacos, Brigitte L. *Terrorism and the Media.* New York: Columbia University Press, 1994.

———. *Mass-Mediated Terrorism: The Central Role of Media in Terrorism and Counterterrorism.* London: Rowman & Littlefield, 2002.

———. *Terrorism and Counterterrorism: Understanding Threats and Responses in the Post-9/11 World.* New York: Penguin, 2005.

Napolitano, Janet. "Nine Years after 9/11: Confronting the Terrorist Threat to the Homeland." US Department of Homeland Security, September 22, 2010. www.dhs.gov.

———. "Progress toward a More Secure and Resilient Nation." *Homeland Security Affairs* 7 (2011). www.hsaj.org.

National Lawyers Guild. "Operation Backfire: A Survival Guide for Environmental and Animal Rights Activists." N.d. www.nlg.org.

Negri, Antonio, ed. *Reflections on Empire.* Malden, MA: Polity, 2008.

Newman, Maria, and Michael Brick. "Neighbor Says Hasan Gave Belongings Away before Attack." *New York Times,* November 6, 2009. www.nytimes.com.

Ng, Andrew Hock Soon. "Introduction: Reading the Double." In *The Poetics of Shadows: The Double in Literature and Philosophy,* edited by Andrew Hock Soon Ng, 1–16. Stuttgart: ibidem-Verlag, 2008.

"The Nicest Terrorist I Ever Met." *CBS News,* July 30, 2009. www.cbsnews.com.

Parks, Lisa. "Drones, Vertical Mediation, and the Targeted Class." *Feminist Studies* 42, no. 1 (2016): 227–35. doi:10.15767/feministstudies.42.1.227.

Patel, Faiza. *Rethinking Radicalization.* New York: New York University, Brennan Center for Justice, 2011.

Pearson, Michael. "Trooper Who Leaked Boston Bomber Pictures Retires with 'No Regrets.'" *CNN,* November 7, 2013. www.cnn.com.

Pearson, Michael, Erin McPike, and Aaron Cooper. "What Did Suspected Bomber's Widow Know?" *CNN,* May 3, 2013. www.cnn.com.

Pew Research Center for the People and the Press. "Majority Views NSA Phone Tracking as Acceptable Anti-terror Tactic." 2013. www.people-press.org.

Philbrick, Herbert Arthur. *I Led 3 Lives: Citizen, "Communist," Counterspy.* New York: McGraw-Hill, 1952.

Picard, Robert G. "News Coverage as the Contagion of Terrorism: Dangerous Charges Backed by Dubious Science." *Political Communication* 3, no. 4 (1986): 385–400. doi:10.1080/10584609.1986.9962800.

Plank, William G. "Différance: Hypostatization of the Dialectic Synthesis." In *Fearful Symmetry: Doubles and Doubling in Literature and Film,* edited by Eugene J. Crook, 163–71. Tallahassee: University Press of Florida, 1982.

Poe, Edgar Allan. "William Wilson." In *Edgar Allan Poe: Complete Tales and Poems,* 555–68. Edison, NJ: Castle Books, 1985.

Porter, Russell. "Budenz Describes a U.S. 'Politburo.'" *New York Times,* March 31, 1949.

———. "Communists Plan to 'Colonize' Key Industries Told at Trial." *New York Times,* April 8, 1949.

———. "U.S. Reds Ordered to Revolt in 1945, Budenz Tells Court." *New York Times*, March 25, 1949.

"The Presence of Evil." *Time*, October 24, 1949, 23.

Qadhi, Yasir. "An Illegal and Counterproductive Assassination." *New York Times*, October 1, 2011. www.nytimes.com.

Raghavan, Sudarsan. "Anwar Al-Aulaqi, U.S.-Born Cleric Linked to Al-Qaeda, Killed in Yemen." *Washington Post*, October 1, 2011. www.washingtonpost.com.

———. "Cleric Says He Was Confidant to Hasan." *Washington Post*, November 16, 2009. www.washingtonpost.com.

Rank, Otto. *Beyond Psychology*. Mineola, NY: Dover, 1958.

———. *The Double: A Psychoanalytic Study*. Chapel Hill: University of North Carolina Press, 1971.

Rapoport, David C. "The Four Waves of Rebel Terror and September 11." *Anthropoetics* 8, no. 1 (2002): 1–17.

Rawnsley, Adam. "YouTube Yanks Jihadi Videos; Terror Wannabes Mildly Inconvenienced." *Wired*, November 3, 2010. www.wired.com.

Rayman, Graham. "Were the Newburgh 4 Really Out to Blow Up Synagogues? A Defendant Finally Speaks Out." *Village Voice*, March 2, 2011. www.villagevoice.com.

Razack, Sherene. *Casting Out: The Eviction of Muslims from Western Law and Politics*. Toronto: University of Toronto Press, 2008.

Reilly, Ryan J. "Dzhokhar Tsarnaev Will Not Be Treated as Enemy Combatant: White House." *Huffington Post*, April 22, 2013. www.huffingtonpost.com.

Reitman, Janet. "Jahar's World." *Rolling Stone*, July 2013, 46–57.

Remnick, David. "The Culprits." *New Yorker*, April 29, 2013.

Ripley, Amanda. "The Fort Dix Conspiracy." *Time*, December 6, 2007. www.time.com.

"Robeson Asks U.S. to Probe 'Terrorism.'" *Washington Post*, August 29, 1949.

Roosevelt, Eleanor. "Memo to Moscow." *Washington Times*, October 24, 1949.

Rosenfield, Claire. "The Shadow Within: The Conscious and Unconscious Use of the Double." In *Stories of the Double*, edited by Albert J. Guerard, 311–31. Philadelphia: J. B. Lippincott, 1967.

Ross, Alice K. "Legal Experts Dissect the US Government's Secret Drone Memo: A Round-Up." Bureau of Investigative Journalism, June 25, 2014. www.thebureauinvestigates.com.

Rossoll, Nicki. "McMaster Hints at Break from Trump Campaign Rhetoric on 'Radical Islamic Terror.'" *ABC News*, May 20, 2017. www.abcnews.go.com.

Safire, William. "Essay: Don't Throw Away Victory." *New York Times*, January 31, 1991. www.nytimes.com.

Said, Edward W. *Orientalism*. New York: Vintage, 1979.

Sampson, Tony D. *Virality: Contagion Theory in the Age of Networks*. Minneapolis: University of Minnesota Press, 2012.

Samuels, David. "The New Mastermind of Jihad." *Wall Street Journal*, April 7, 2012. www.wsj.com.

Sassen, Saskia. *Territory, Authority, Rights: From Medieval to Global Assemblages.* Princeton, NJ: Princeton University Press, 2006.

Savage, Charlie. "A Not-Quite Confirmation of a Memo Approving Killing." *New York Times*, March 9, 2012, A16.

———. "Secret U.S. Memo Made Legal Case to Kill a Citizen." *New York Times*, October 9, 2011, A1.

Scarce, Rik. *Eco-warriors: Understanding the Radical Environmental Movement.* Chicago: Noble Press, 1990.

Schanzer, David, Charles Kurzman, and Ebrahim Moosa. "Anti-terror Lessons of Muslim-Americans." National Institute of Justice, January 6, 2010. https://fds.duke .edu.

Schmid, Alex P., ed. *The Routledge Handbook of Terrorism Research.* New York: Routledge, 2013.

Schmid, Alex P., and Janny de Graaf. *Violence as Communication: Insurgent Terrorism and the Western News Media.* Beverly Hills, CA: Sage, 1982.

Schmid, Alex P., and A. J. Jongman. *Political Terrorism: A Research Guide to Concepts, Theories, Data Bases, and Literature.* Amsterdam: North-Holland, 1984.

Schmitt, Carl. *The Concept of the Political.* Translated by George Schwab. Chicago: University of Chicago Press, 2005.

———. *Theory of the Partisan: Intermediate Commentary on the Concept of the Political.* Translated by G. L. Ulmen. New York: Telos Press, 2007.

Sedgwick, Eve Kosofsky. *Epistemology of the Closet.* Berkeley: University of California Press, 1990.

Semati, Mehdi. "Islamophobia, Culture and Race in the Age of Empire." *Cultural Studies* 24, no. 2 (2010): 256–75. doi:10.1080/09502380903541696.

———. "Terrorists, Moslems, Fundamentalists and Other Bad Objects in the Midst of 'Us.'" *Journal of International Communication* 4, no. 1 (1997): 30–49. doi:10.1080/132 16597.1997.9751843.

Serwer, Adam. "Bipartisan Approval for Targeted Killing of Suspected Terrorists." *Mother Jones*, March 14, 2012. www.motherjones.com.

Shadid, Anthony, and David D. Kirkpatrick. "As the West Celebrates Awlaki's Death, the Mideast Shrugs." *New York Times*, October 2, 2011, A1.

Shane, Scott. "Awlaki Killing Is Awash in Open Secrets." *New York Times*, October 5, 2011, A18.

———. "Judging a Long, Deadly Reach." *New York Times*, October 1, 2011, A1.

Shane, Scott, and Souad Mekhennet. "Imam's Path from Condemning Terror to Preaching Jihad." *New York Times*, May 8, 2010. www.nytimes.com.

Sherman, Jon. "'A Person Otherwise Innocent': Policing Entrapment in Preventative, Undercover Counterterrorism Investigations." *University of Pennsylvania Journal of Constitutional Law* 11 (2008): 1475–1510.

Siesseger, Marie E. "Conspiracy Theory: The Use of the Conspiracy Doctrine in Times of National Crisis." *William & Mary Law Review* 46, no. 3 (2004): 1177–1218.

Simi, Pete, and Robert Futrell. *American Swastika: Inside the White Power Movement's Hidden Spaces of Hate*. Lanham, MD: Rowman & Littlefield, 2010.

Smith, R. Jeffrey. "Homeland Security Department Curtails Home-Grown Terror Analysis." *Washington Post*, June 2, 2011. www.washingtonpost.com.

Smith, Rebecca K. "Ecoterrorism? A Critical Analysis of the Vilification of Radical Environmental Activists as Terrorists." *Environmental Law* 38 (2008): 537–76.

Smith, Rogers M. *Civic Ideals: Conflicting Visions of Citizenship in U.S. History*. New Haven, CT: Yale University Press, 1997.

———. *Stories of Peoplehood: The Politics and Morals of Political Membership*. Cambridge: Cambridge University Press, 2003.

Sørensen, Bent Meier. "Immaculate Defecation: Gilles Deleuze and Félix Guattari in Organization Theory." *Sociological Review* 53, no. 1 (2005): 120–33.

Sproat, Peter Alan. "Can the State Be Terrorist?" *Terrorism* 14, no. 1 (1991): 19–29. doi:10.1080/10576109108435854.

Stampnitzky, Lisa. *Disciplining Terror: How Experts Invented "Terrorism."* Cambridge: Cambridge University Press, 2014.

Stanglin, Douglas. "Al-Awlaki's Diatribes Came in an American Accent." *USA Today*, September 30, 2011. www.usatoday.com.

Stohl, Cynthia, and Michael Stohl. "Networks of Terror: Theoretical Assumptions and Pragmatic Consequences." *Communication Theory* 17, no. 2 (2007): 93–124.

Stolberg, Sheryl Gay. "Obama Offers Sympathy and Urges No 'Jump to Conclusions.'" *New York Times*, November 8, 2009. www.nytimes.com.

Symmes, Patrick. "Anwar al-Awlaki: The Next Bin Laden." *GQ*, June 21, 2011. www.gq.com.

Taibbi, Matt. "Explaining the Rolling Stone Cover, by a Boston Native." *Rolling Stone*, July 19, 2013. www.rollingstone.com.

"Terrorism in America after 9/11." *New America*, n.d. www.newamerica.org.

"Terrorism in Louisiana." *New York Times*, October 19, 1859. www.nytimes.com.

Thompson, Ginger. "An Apology to Veterans over Intelligence Report." *New York Times*, April 17, 2009. www.nytimes.com.

Thompson, Heather Ann. "Why Mass Incarceration Matters: Rethinking Crisis, Decline, and Transformation in Postwar American History." *Journal of American History* 97, no. 3 (2010): 703–34.

Tiqqun. *Introduction to Civil War*. Translated by Alexander R. Galloway and Jason E. Smith. Los Angeles: Semiotext(e), 2010.

"Topic A [Letters to the Editor]." *Washington Post*, November 8, 2009. www.washingtonpost.com.

Tymms, Ralph. *Doubles in Literary Psychology*. Cambridge: Bowes & Bowes, 1977.

Ungar, Rick. "Senator Lindsey Graham Says Suspend the Constitution for Boston Marathon Suspect and Designate Him an Enemy Combatant." *Forbes*, April 19, 2013. www.forbes.com.

US Congress, House Un-American Activities Committee. *Hearings Regarding Communist Infiltration of Minority Groups* [Hearings]. July 13, 14, and 18, 1949, and September 1, 1950.

US Congress, House Un-American Activities Committee. *Communist Methods of Infiltration—Education* [Hearings]. February 25–27, March 12, 13, 17, and 18, 1953.

US Congress, Senate, Committee on Environment and Public Works. *Eco-terrorism Specifically Examining the Earth Liberation Front and the Animal Liberation Front* [Hearing]. May 18, 2005.

US Congress, Senate, Committee on Environment and Public Works. *Eco-terrorism Specifically Examining Stop Huntingdon Animal Cruelty* [Hearing]. October 26, 2005.

US Congress, Senate, Committee on Homeland Security. *The Threat of Muslim-American Radicalization in U.S. Prisons* [Hearing]. June 15, 2011.

US Congress, Senate, Committee for Internal Security. *Terrorism* [Hearings]. February 27 and 28, March 21, 22, and 26, 1974.

US Congress, Senate, Committee for Internal Security. "Terrorism: A Staff Study." Washington, DC: Government Printing Office, 1974.

US Congress, Senate, Subcommittee on the Constitution, Civil Rights, and Human Rights, Committee of the Judiciary. *Hate Crimes and the Threat of Domestic Extremism* [Hearing]. September 19, 2012.

US Congress, Senate, Subcommittee on Crime of the Committee on the Judiciary. *Acts of Ecoterrorism by Radical Environmental Organizations* [Hearing]. June 9, 1998.

US Congress, Senate, Subcommittee on Crime, Terrorism, and Homeland Security of the Committee on the Judiciary. *Animal Enterprise Terrorism Act* [Hearing]. May 23, 2006.

US Congress, Senate, Subcommittee on Forests and Forest Health of the Committee on Resources. *Ecoterrorism and Lawlessness on the National Forests* [Hearing]. February 12, 2002.

US Congress, Senate, Subcommittee on Terrorism, Technology, and Homeland Security. *Terrorism: Radical Islamic Influence on Chaplaincy of the U.S. Military and Prisons* [Hearing]. October 14, 2003.

US Sentencing Commission. "2012 Federal Sentencing Guidelines Manual." www.ussc.gov.

Vanderheiden, S. "Eco-terrorism or Justified Resistance? Radical Environmentalism and the 'War on Terror.'" *Politics & Society* 33, no. 3 (2005): 425–47. doi:10.1177/0032329205278462.

van Dijck, Jose. *The Culture of Connectivity: A Critical History of Social Media.* Oxford: Oxford University Press, 2013.

Vardoulakis, Dimitris. *The Doppelgänger: Literature's Philosophy.* New York: Fordham University Press, 2010.

Vaughan-Williams, Nick. "Borderwork beyond Inside/Outside? Frontex, the Citizen–Detective and the War on Terror." *Space and Polity* 12, no. 1 (2008): 63–79. doi:10.1080/13562570801969457.

Volpp, Leti. "The Citizen and the Terrorist." *Immigration and Nationality Law Review* 23 (2012): 561–86.

Wacquant, Loïc. *Punishing the Poor: The Neoliberal Government of Social Insecurity.* Durham, NC: Duke University Press, 2009.

Wagner, Travis. "Reframing Ecotage as Ecoterrorism: News and the Discourse of Fear." *Environmental Communication* 2, no. 1 (2008): 25–39. doi:10.1080/17524030801945617.

Wakin, Daniel J. "Imams Reject Talk That Islam Radicalizes Inmates." *New York Times,* May 23, 2009, A22.

Webber, Andrew J. *The Doppelgänger: Double Visions in German Literature.* Oxford: Oxford University Press, 1996.

Weinstein, Adam. "The Sikh Temple Shooter's Racist Tattoos, Deciphered." *Mother Jones,* August 6, 2012. www.motherjones.com.

Weiser, Benjamin. "3 Men Get 25 Years in Plot to Bomb Bronx Synagogues." *New York Times,* June 30, 2011, A22.

Western, Bruce. *Punishment and Inequality in America.* New York: Russell Sage Foundation, 2006.

White, Ed. "Luqman Ameen Abdullaj, Leader of Radical Islam Group, Killed in Raid." *Huffington Post,* October 28, 2009. www.huffingtonpost.com.

White House. "Statement by the Press Secretary." April 23, 2015. www.whitehouse.gov.

Whitlock, Craig. "After Yemen Attack, Little Comment." *Washington Post,* October 23, 2011. www.washingtonpost.com.

"Who Won?" *New York Post,* October 16, 1949.

William H. Webster Commission. "Final Report on the Federal Bureau of Investigation, Counterterrorism Intelligence, and the Events at Fort Hood Texas on November 5, 2009." Federal Bureau of Investigation, 2012. www.fbi.gov.

Wilson, Scott. "No Safe Haven Anywhere in the World." *Washington Post,* October 1, 2011. www.washingtonpost.com.

Wines, Michael, and Ian Lovett. "The Dark Side, Carefully Masked." *New York Times,* May 5, 2013, A1.

Yaccino, Steven, Michael Schwirtz, and Marc Santora. "Gunman Kills 6 at Sikh Temple in Wisconsin." *New York Times,* August 6, 2012, A1.

Yang, Wesley. "The Terrorist Search Engine." *New York Magazine,* December 5, 2010. www.nymag.com.

Yardley, William. "Radical Environmentalist Gets 9-Year Term." *New York Times,* May 26, 2007, A9.

"You Are Either with Us or against Us." *CNN,* November 6, 2001. www.cnn.com.

Žižek, Slavoj. "Are We in a War? Do We Have an Enemy?" *London Review of Books,* May 23, 2002.

———. *The Sublime Object of Ideology.* New York: Verso, 1989.

INDEX

Italic page numbers refer to illustrations.

ABOUT THE AUTHOR

Piotr M. Szpunar is Assistant Professor in the Department of Communication at the University at Albany, State University of New York.